Christianity

for Blockheads

Also by Douglas Connelly

Amazing Discoveries That Unlock the Bible

The Bible for Blockheads

The Book of Revelation for Blockheads

Also by Martin Manser

Zondervan Dictionary of Bible Themes (editor)

The Facts on File Dictionary of Proverbs

Good Word Guide

Prayers for Good Times and Grim

A User-Friendly Look at What Christians Believe

Christianity
for Blockheads

**Douglas Connelly
& Martin Manser**

ZONDERVAN®

ZONDERVAN.com/
AUTHORTRACKER
follow your favorite authors

ZONDERVAN

Christianity for Blockheads
Copyright © 2009 by Douglas Connelly and Martin Manser

This title is also available as a Zondervan ebook.
Visit www.zondervan.com/ebooks.

Requests for information should be addressed to:

Zondervan, *Grand Rapids, Michigan 49530*

Library of Congress Cataloging-in-Publication Data

Connelly, Douglas, 1949-
    Christianity for blockheads : a user-friendly look at what Christians believe / Douglas Connelly and Martin Manser.
        p. cm.
    ISBN 978-0-310-25290-0 (softcover)
    1. Theology, Doctrinal—Popular works. I. Manser, Martin H. II. Title.
BT77.C72 2009
230—dc22

2008054096

09 10 11 12 13 14 15 16 17 18 19 20 21 22 23 24 • 25 24 23 22 21 20 19 18 17 16 15 14 13 12 11 10 9 8 7 6 5 4 3 2 1

Contents

Welcome

The Christian faith is really pretty simple. Christians believe that Jesus is their Lord and Savior and they have put their hope for heaven in him alone. That's the Christian faith in twenty words. As you begin to explore those words, however, you are led into a wonderful network of information that grows and expands into ocean-sized truths. This book will help you find your way along those paths.

Each chapter in this book explores one of the big areas of Christian belief. When we come to key foundational truths, I will give you a lot of detail. When Christians disagree on issues, I will try to give you all sides of the debate in fairness and balance. You will find some issues you won't agree with me on and some issues we all agree on. But that's the joy of a journey through the Christian belief system. We all have so much more to learn and understand and live out!

This book was written primarily for Christians who want to explore what they believe in easy-to-understand language — and who want to have a little fun doing it! If you are a new Christian, this book will help you put down spiritual roots in nourishing soil. If you are an experienced Christian, you will find your perspective expanded and your beliefs renewed. Maybe you are not a Christian at all and you just want a reliable source of information on what Christians really believe. You are welcome to explore the faith in a nonintimidating way. No one will harass you in these pages.

What you believe matters. It shapes every decision and determines the path of your life. What you believe about God and Jesus affects eternity as well. Unfortunately most of us carry around a whole stockpile of beliefs and have no idea where most of them came from. We've picked them up from parents, a guest interviewed on *Oprah*, or a comment from a friend. We hold on to those beliefs and act on them but rarely do we actually take the time to examine our beliefs. This book will help us all put our beliefs on the table under a bright light. Some will pass the test and be held more firmly; other beliefs will be changed or discarded. We will emerge from the process, however, strengthened and encouraged and blessed.

Finding Your Way

You can approach this book in several ways. The best way (I think) is to read it straight through. Each chapter (to a degree) builds on the ones before it.

Or for you the best approach may be to dip in where you are interested. You may want to know more about Jesus or the Bible or the future from a Christian perspective. Drop in where you are interested, and connect to other chapters from there.

Whatever approach you take, I hope you will have a Bible handy. As you read what I say, lay it next to what the Bible says. This book is not the final word for Christians; the Bible is that ultimate word. I hope this book will help you understand the Bible's teaching more clearly but, if anything I say departs from the Bible, trust what the Bible says over what I say every time.

Two Guys

Two writers wrote this book. One (Martin) is a British author and editor. He's also a Baptist. The other (Doug) is an American pastor in the Missionary Church and the author of other books in the Blockhead series. We have written the book with one voice. On nearly all issues we have fully agreed with each other; on some issues we've disagreed but we've made sure our views were fairly represented. You will have to guess where we disagreed! Our desire—and our prayer—is that God will be honored by our efforts in this book and that you will be challenged to go deeper in your walk with the Lord than you've ever gone.

A Few Sidelights

The breakout sections in each chapter will help you pursue certain aspects of Christian belief more deeply.

Heads Up: Brief overviews of what lies ahead in the chapter

Help File: Fascinating facts or insights about Christian faith or teaching or about the world around us

Walking the Walk: Suggestions for making what you've read more personal

Bible Networking: Crucial passages from the Bible

In Other Words: Pointed quotations from outside experts

Great Debates: Explanations of some of the bigger controversies
  among Christians
Digging Deeper: Resources to help you investigate further
Points to Remember: Concise summaries of key points from each
  chapter

Don't Be a "Dummy" about Doctrine

The teachings of the Christian faith are sometimes called Christian
doctrines. That word conjures up images in most people's minds of
thick, dusty books and long, dry sermons! The word *doctrine*, however,
just means "teaching." Any belief or teaching of Christianity is a doctrine.

Christians also use the word *theology* a lot. This word means "the
study of God," but we've expanded its reference to mean "the study of
all that relates to God." Christian theology encompasses all that Christians believe as it relates to their faith.

Don't be intimidated by those words! The chapters in this book will
help you get a handle on doctrine and on Christian theology so you
won't have to feel like a Blockhead anymore. You may find in a few
weeks that you actually know more than some of the people around you
about what Christians believe. Be nice with all that knowledge! Hold
it with a big measure of humility. We are all pilgrims on the path to a
fuller understanding of God's truth.

> Welcome with open arms fellow believers who don't see things
> the way you do. And don't jump all over them every time they do
> or say something you don't agree with—even when it seems that
> they are strong on opinions but weak in the faith department.
> Remember, they have their own history to deal with. Treat them
> gently.
>
> Romans 14:1 *The Message*

> Do your best to present yourself to God as one approved, a
> worker who does not need to be ashamed and who correctly
> handles the word of truth.
>
> 2 Timothy 2:15

OK, that's all the introduction you need. The journey begins with
Jesus!

CHAPTER 1

Leader and Lord: Jesus

Leader and Lord: Jesus

- ▶ Learn who Jesus was—and why we care.
- ▶ Watch God step down and meet us face-to-face.
- ▶ Encounter a God who loves you deeply!

For Christians, everything begins and ends with Jesus. He is the center of all we believe. Every biblical teaching is shaped by what we know and believe about Jesus. So he is the place to start. If you take Jesus out of Christianity, you have only a hollow shell of powerless religion.

Jesus' Life among Us

Beginning

Jesus was born in the town of Bethlehem in Roman-occupied Palestine (modern-day Israel). The date of his birth, according to the Roman calendar then in use, was around 750 AUC (*ab urbe condita* = after the founding of the city [of Rome]). According to our modern calendars, Jesus was born about 4 BC (I know this is "before Christ," but the medieval monks who tried to figure it out didn't have all the information we have, and so they missed it by a few years).

Jesus grew up in Nazareth, another small town up north in the territory of Galilee. He was raised in a fairly typical Jewish home and had the same experiences that most boys in first-century Israel had.

- He was circumcised as an infant as a mark of his inclusion in God's covenant promises to Israel (Luke 2:21).
- His parents, in obedience to the words of an angel, named their son *Jesus*—a form of the Hebrew name *Joshua*. It means "The LORD saves."
- Jesus learned a trade, the craft of carpentry, from his adopted father, Joseph. A carpenter in that culture built furniture and homes and even made some farm equipment.

- Jesus attended synagogue school and learned to read the Hebrew of the Bible. In the everyday discourse of Galilee, he probably spoke a related language, Aramaic. He would also have learned to speak Greek, which was the language of commerce in the Roman Empire.

Jesus did have one out-of-the-ordinary experience as a boy. When he was twelve years old, he went with his parents to the city of Jerusalem. He got so engrossed in a theological discussion with the religious scholars in the temple that he missed the family caravan home to Nazareth! Mary and Joseph had to backtrack an entire day's journey to find him, and they weren't happy about it! (Read the whole story in Luke 2:41–50.)

In the Spotlight

When Jesus was around thirty years old, he began his public ministry. Thirty was the age of maturity in Israel. Priests in God's temple did not begin to perform their sacred duties until that age. Jesus waited in humility until he reached the age when his teaching would be respected.

Early in his ministry Jesus chose twelve men from among his followers to be his disciples. These men stayed around Jesus all the time. They were students and learners, but they were also being groomed to be leaders and spokesmen for Jesus. They would eventually stand as eyewitnesses of all that Jesus said and did. They would be his representatives to spread the message about Jesus to the whole world. These men are also called *apostles*—ones who are sent out as official ambassadors and representatives of a person who holds great authority.

Help File

BOYHOOD STORIES

Most of us would like to know a lot more about Jesus' infancy and boyhood, but the Bible is almost totally silent about those years. When Scripture is silent, creative minds try to fill in the blanks. Several "gospels" were written long after Jesus lived (200 to 300 years after), and these accounts claimed to have knowledge of Jesus' early years. In these dubious "gospels," Jesus is pictured as making birds out of clay and then changing them into real birds. He also supposedly turned a neighborhood bully into a goat and refused to reverse the miracle until Joseph rebuked him. None of these stores have any basis in fact, and these "gospels" are universally rejected by Bible scholars as not adding any truth to the story of Jesus.

"The Twelve" recognized Jesus as more than just a rabbi (teacher) or miracle worker. Soon after they started spending time with Jesus, they came to the realization that he was the Messiah, the Christ, the anointed one God had promised to send as Israel's Redeemer and King. Much of what Christians believe about Jesus comes from the written testimony and witness of these apostles preserved in the New Testament. They followed Jesus and watched everything he did. They listened to everything Jesus said. They were empowered by Jesus to speak and to act with his own authority after he left the world. God's own Spirit guided them as they wrote down their remembrances, and Jesus promised that the Spirit would give them profound understanding of the significance of Jesus' actions and words.

The common people listened intently to what Jesus taught and received Jesus' miracles with joyful appreciation. The religious leaders in Israel, however, were not impressed. They dismissed Jesus' teaching as the ramblings of an untrained upstart. They attributed the power of his healing miracles to an evil power, not to God. As Jesus' influence among the people grew, the religious leaders became more and more nervous. They feared that Jesus would spark a political revolution that would jeopardize their positions of influence. They also feared that the Roman army would move quickly to put down any disturbance and might destroy the nation in the process. The leaders of Israel decided that Jesus needed to be eliminated.

Fulfilling His Destiny

The opportunity to take Jesus down came sooner than the religious leaders ever expected. One of Jesus' closest followers offered to hand Jesus over to his enemies in exchange for a sack of silver coins. Jesus was arrested, pushed through a bunch of trials, and finally condemned on trumped-up charges. The Jewish leaders accused Jesus of blasphemy, of speaking against the holy character of God. They had a bigger problem, however. The Jewish Council could condemn all they wanted, but only the Roman authorities could legally execute a criminal. Pontius Pilate, a third-rate Roman bureaucrat in charge of a troublesome province on the farthest edge of the empire, was pressured into doing what the religious leaders wanted. He ordered Jesus to be crucified.

Jesus lived for six hours on the cross. At the end he simply gave up his spirit and died. A few brave followers put his body in a stone tomb and said good-bye. Nervous religious leaders had the Romans position some soldiers near the tomb so the disciples of Jesus wouldn't be tempted to steal their master's body. No chance of that, of course. The disciples were hiding, not planning to rob a grave.

Three days after Jesus' death, some women came to Jesus' tomb and found it empty. Later Jesus himself appeared on several occasions to widely diverse groups of his followers as confirming evidence that he had risen from the dead. Forty days after his resurrection, Jesus ascended back to heaven where he remains to this day.

Help File

THE HISTORICAL JESUS

The four New Testament gospels are the main source of information about Jesus but other ancient writers also provide verification that Jesus lived and sparked a new religious movement:

Tacitus (best guess: AD 55–120) was a Roman historian who lived through the reigns of more than half a dozen emperors. In his massive history called the *Annals*, Tacitus dropped in this passage as he wrote about the great fire in Rome during the reign of Nero:

> Consequently, to get rid of the report [that Nero himself had set the fire], Nero fastened the guilt and inflicted the most exquisite tortures on a class hated for their abominations, called Christians by the populace. Christus, from whom the name had its origin, suffered the extreme penalty during the reign of Tiberius at the hands of one of our procurators, Pontius Pilate.
> *Annals*, 15.44*

Josephus, a Jewish historian who was born a few years after Jesus' death and who died in AD 97, wrote a much-debated passage about Jesus. The surviving version of the *Antiquities* reads as though

Josephus was a true believer in Jesus. Later Christian scribes who copied and distributed the work may have altered his statement to reflect Christian teaching. The tenth-century Arabic version of Josephus's book is probably closer to his original, but it still gives stunning testimony to Jesus' life and ministry:

> At this time there was a wise man who was called Jesus. And his conduct was good, and [he] was known to be virtuous. And many people from among the Jews and other nations became his disciples. Pilate condemned him to be crucified and to die. And those who had become his disciples did not abandon his discipleship. They reported that he had appeared to them three days after his crucifixion and that he was alive; accordingly he was perhaps the Messiah concerning whom the prophets have recounted wonders.
> *Antiquities*, 18.63–64*

*Both quotations are taken from Gary Habermas, *Ancient Evidence for the Life of Jesus* (Nashville: Nelson, 1984), 87–92.

JESUS' ARRIVAL

The Bible makes it clear that Jesus was unique. No one has ever been born as Jesus was born. Well, that's not exactly correct. Jesus was *born* normally, but he was *conceived* miraculously. He was conceived in a virgin woman by a miraculous work of God's power. Your mother may think of you as her "miracle baby," but you and I and every other human being on this planet were conceived the same way. (Just think back to that "birds and bees" lecture in high school health class.) A man and a woman (our parents) both contributed a tiny part of themselves that united to produce a new human being. Jesus, however, was conceived in Mary, his mother, without the contribution of a man. Jesus was conceived by a work of God.

Some people (even some Christians) have a difficult time with "the virgin birth." They think it is too fantastic to believe or it was just a story some early Christians made up to spice up the early years of Jesus' life a little. But there are several solid reasons for accepting Jesus' miraculous conception as an essential part of Christian belief.

- First, the Bible specifically says that this is how it happened. In both the gospel of Luke (1:26–38) and in the gospel of Matthew (1:18–25), Mary is presented as a virgin who has never had sexual intimacy with any man. Joseph, her promised husband, is presented as a man who has not been intimate with Mary. If Jesus was conceived normally from a man and a woman, the Bible, at least at this point, is false.
- Second, the virgin conception is consistent with Jesus' eternal existence. Jesus did not begin to exist in Mary's womb. Jesus had existed from eternity. Jesus did not *begin* in Mary; he *became human* in Mary. You and I had a starting point. I did not exist (except in God's mind) before my conception. Jesus, however, had always existed.
- Third, Jesus' conception by God's miraculous plan is consistent with Jesus' sinlessness. Ever since Adam sinned in the garden of Eden, parents have passed on more than genetic material to their kids. They also pass on a human nature that is bent in one direction—toward evil. From the Bible's perspective, that sinful nature comes from the father (sorry, guys). Jesus, who had no natural human father, was conceived and born without a sinful bent.
- Fourth, while the virgin conception is not taught directly anywhere else in Scripture except in Matthew 1 and Luke 2, the rest of Scripture seems to assume that Jesus was conceived in a supernatural way. The apostle Paul in the New Testament book of Galatians, for example, says that Jesus was "born of a woman" (Galatians 4:4)—not born of a man and a woman, but born of a woman.

Jesus' conception is not just some minor point that we can choose to believe or disregard. It touches the whole issue of who Jesus really was.

Who Was This Man?

I've just given you the historical story of Jesus' birth, life, death, and resurrection. Almost all that information comes from the first four books of the New Testament in the Bible. The books are referred to as "gospels"—the gospel according to Matthew, one by Mark, one by Luke, and the last by John. Two of these writers—Matthew and John—were Jesus' disciples during his ministry. They were eyewitnesses of the things they wrote about. The man named Mark was a close associate of the disciple Peter, and Luke conducted a careful personal investigation into the life and death of Jesus just a few years after all the events took place. These books were written within fifty or sixty years of Jesus' death when many of those who knew Jesus personally would have still been alive to challenge anything that was not true. The four gospels are accurate, trustworthy accounts of the things Jesus said and did.

But Christians believe much more about Jesus than simply that he lived and died. We also have a theological understanding of Jesus based on the gospel records and on the interpretation of what Jesus did provided in the rest of the New Testament. As Christian thinkers and believers contemplated all that the biblical writers said about Jesus, they came to some firm convictions about who Jesus really was. This deeper understanding of the significance and importance of Jesus is also part of Christian belief and teaching.

Jesus Is Fully Human

Christians believe that Jesus was a genuine human being. And your response is—why did *that* require any deep contemplation? Of course he's human! He was born, he lived in human society for thirty-three years, and he died. What's to question?

The questions and affirmations about Jesus' humanity arose because some people wanted to make Jesus so divine, so heavenly, that he became like an angel or like God just appearing on earth as a man. But the Bible makes the point in a number of ways that Jesus was actually and fully human:

- *Jesus had a human body.* He was born; he grew up; he learned how to walk and talk and feed himself. Jesus even referred to himself as "a *man* who has told you the truth" (John 8:40).
- *Jesus shows all the characteristics of being human.* If you had met Jesus, you would have realized immediately that he was a human

being. He got hungry and thirsty and tired. He experienced love and sorrow and compassion. Jesus knew from personal experience what being human was all about.

- *Jesus also possessed human names and human ancestors.* He called himself "the Son of Man" regularly (Luke 19:10). He was referred to as the "Son of David" (Mark 10:47) and the New Testament writer Paul says that Jesus is "the man Christ Jesus" (1 Timothy 2:5 NIV). In Matthew's gospel we have the family tree of

WHY IS JESUS' HUMANITY SO IMPORTANT?

Jesus became human so he could fully identify with us. His purpose from the beginning was to rescue human beings from the curse of evil and the penalty of sin. Our sin before God required a sacrifice. Someone had to bear my penalty for me if I was ever to be set free. Jesus willingly came to die in our place. But to die in our place, he had to become what we are—human beings—and that's exactly what he did. That's the first reason it's so important that Jesus was fully human—so he could be an acceptable sacrifice to God for human sin.

There are other reasons Jesus' humanity means so much:

- Because he was human, Jesus knows what our life is like. He has sensed the disappointments that we experience. He knows what betrayal feels like because he has been there. Jesus is our priest before God, but he is not a cold, condemning priest who tells us how badly we've failed. Jesus is a sympathetic, sensitive priest (Hebrews 5:1–2) who understands our struggles. This doesn't mean he just blows off our failures; but he does come to us with compassion and understanding.

- Jesus as a human being also provides an example of what it means to live a fully God-honoring life. He is a model for us to follow. The WWJD question is a valid one for every Christian to ask—*What would Jesus do*? He wasn't living on resources that we don't have access to. He was showing us how we can live lives that are fully committed to God. We can walk in the same spiritual light that Jesus walked in, be guided by the same words of wisdom, listen to the same loving Father, and be filled with the same living Spirit.

- The only "human" factor that Jesus never shared with us was personal sin. Jesus lived an absolutely obedient, faithful life to God. He never committed moral error of any kind. He was tempted to sin, pressured to act against God's will or God's law, but he never yielded to that temptation. His sinlessness, however, doesn't make Jesus *less* human. Sin is not part of genuine humanity as God designed it. Adam and Eve were created in innocence, but they were fully human. Sin is the invader into humanity's makeup. It was not part of God's original design. So Jesus could be sinless and still be fully what God intended human beings to be.

Bible Networking

2 Corinthians 5:21

God made him who had no sin to be sin for us.

Hebrews 4:15

We have [a high priest] who has been tempted in every way, just as we are — yet he did not sin.

Jesus — in a conversation with some people in his day
John 8:46

"Can any of you prove me guilty of sin?"

Joseph, Jesus' adoptive father (Matthew 1:1 – 17), but the genealogy in Luke's gospel is probably the family tree of Mary, Jesus' biological mother (Luke 3:23 – 38). Jesus had fully human DNA in his body. He was one of us!

Jesus Is Fully God

The amazing claim of Christianity is that Jesus was a man — but more than a man. Christians believe that Jesus was also God. He was the infinite, eternal God who broke into our world of time and space and joined his God-ness with our humanness. We call that act the *incarnation* of Jesus — God became flesh. All other religious leaders were, by their own admission, only human. Only Jesus Christ claimed to be God as well.

The Bible provides several lines of evidence that Jesus is God. Theologians refer to this biblical teaching as the *deity* of Jesus — from the Latin word *deus*, meaning God.

The Bible Declares It

First, and most convincingly, *Jesus is called God* in the Bible. The opening verse of the gospel of John reads, "In the beginning was the Word, and the Word was with God, and the Word was God" (John 1:1). John is obviously referring to Jesus with the title "the Word" because later in John

In Other Words

Jesus painted no pictures, yet some of the finest paintings of Raphael, Michelangelo, and Leonardo da Vinci were created by the inspiration they received from thinking about him. He wrote no poetry, yet Dante, Milton, and thousands of the world's greatest poets were inspired, again, by him. He composed no music or sang a song, yet Haydn, Handel, Beethoven, Bach, and Mendelssohn reached the apex of their profession and perfection while writing hymns, symphonies, and oratorios dedicated to his glory. Every sphere of human achievement has been enriched and inspired by this simple, humble carpenter from an obscure place called Nazareth. Even after all these years where fads, philosophies, governments, and revolutionary regimes have risen only to recede like the tides, Jesus prevails.

David Foster, in *A Renegade's Guide to God*
(New York: Faith Words, 2006), 22–23.

Enemy-occupied territory — that is what this world is. Christianity is the story of how the rightful king has landed.

C. S. Lewis, in *Mere Christianity* (New York:
Macmillan, 1952), 36.

1:14 he writes, "The Word became flesh and made his dwelling among us." In verse 18 of John 1, the writer makes his point again: "No one has ever seen God, but the one and only Son, who is himself God and is in closest relationship with the Father, has made him known." John wants us to understand and believe that Jesus of Nazareth is also the eternal God!

The writer of the New Testament book of Hebrews makes the same point, although not as directly as John. The author of Hebrews is quoting a verse from the Old Testament (from Psalm 45:6–7 to be precise) but he adds an interesting note as he introduces the verse from the Psalms:

> But about the Son he says,
> "Your throne, O God, will last for ever and ever."
> Hebrews 1:8

According to Hebrews, God the Father says this about his Son, Jesus: "Your throne, O God." God the Father calls Jesus God. You can circle the words *Son* and *God* in that verse and draw a line between them. Our discussion of the relationship of God the Father to Jesus will come later in the book, but the point I want you to see now is that Jesus is referred to in the Bible as God.

Jesus himself intimated the same thing on a couple of occasions. Once he told his accusers, "My Father is always at his work to this very day, and I too am working." His enemies understood perfectly what Jesus was saying when he called God "*my* Father." The next verse reads, "For this reason they tried all the more to kill him; ... he was even calling God his own Father, *making himself equal with God*"(John 5:17–18, italics added). On another occasion, Jesus said, "Before Abraham was born, I am!" (John 8:58). It was a clear claim to the eternal existence of God. Abraham had lived 1,800 years before Jesus uttered those words, but now Jesus says that before Abraham was born, Jesus already existed. His opponents picked up stones to kill Jesus for making such an outlandish claim, but Jesus was able to escape (John 8:59).

The New Testament writers and Jesus himself were convinced that Jesus was far more than a humble carpenter from Nazareth. He was nothing less than God in human flesh and in human form. Even the Old Testament prophets knew that God's Messiah would be more than a man. Isaiah referred to him as Immanuel—a name that means "God

For this reason [Jesus] had to be made like his brothers and sisters ...

We do not have a high priest who is unable to empathize with our weaknesses, but we have one who has been tempted in every way, just as we are—yet he did not sin.
Hebrews 2:17; 4:15

I was walking down the road feeling sorry for myself. Did God really know what I was going through? That I was sad, alone, and misunderstood; that I had no one to turn to; that I was facing an uncertain future, wondering what life was really all about? Friends had tried to help, but I was rather fed up with their pious attempts.

Then the thought hit me, and I can show you the exact spot on the sidewalk where it happened! I suddenly realized afresh that God became a human being in Jesus, and he faced the same things. That was the whole point. He knows what it is like to be rejected, abandoned by his closest companions, sorrowful to the point of extreme anguish. He knows!

In Other Words

A man who was merely a man and said the sort of things Jesus said would not be a great moral teacher. He would either be a lunatic — on a level with a man who says he is a poached egg — or else he would be the Devil of Hell. You must make your choice. Either this man was, and is, the Son of God: or else a madman or something worse.

C. S. Lewis, in *Mere Christianity* (New York: Macmillan, 1952), 45.

Every attribute related to Deity and ascribed to the Father or the Holy Spirit can also be attributed to Christ.

John Walvoord, in *Jesus Christ Our Lord* (Chicago: Moody, 1969), 27.

with us" (Isaiah 7:14; Matthew 1:23). The prophet also called the promised Messiah "Mighty God" (Isaiah 9:6).

Jesus' Works Demonstrate It

A second line of biblical evidence for the deity of Jesus is that *Jesus does things that only God can do.* Here's a list of works that the Bible says Jesus has done or will do. See if you want to sign up for any of these responsibilities:

- *Jesus is the Creator.* Through him everything was made. When God spoke the earth and the stars and the animals into existence in Genesis 1, that was Jesus who spoke. When God formed Adam from the dust of the ground and breathed life into him, that was Jesus, the Creator, who did this. The Bible declares, "For in him [Jesus] all things were created ... all things have been created through him and for him" (Colossians 1:16).
- *Jesus forgives sins.* When a paralyzed man was brought to Jesus one day, he said, "Son, your sins are forgiven." Then, to prove that he had full authority to forgive sins, Jesus instantly healed the man! (The whole story is in Mark 2:1 – 12).
- *Jesus will raise the dead at the final resurrection.* Here's what Jesus said: "Just as the Father raises the dead and gives them life, even so the Son gives life to whom he is pleased to give it" (John 5:21).

- *Jesus gives eternal life to those who believe in him.* Another startling claim from Jesus: "I give them eternal life, and they shall never perish" (John 10:28).
- *Jesus will be the final judge of all mankind.* "For [God] has set a day when he will judge the world with justice by the man he has appointed. He has given proof of this to everyone by raising him [Jesus] from the dead" (Acts 17:31).

Worshiped as God

A third line of evidence for the deity of Jesus is that *he receives the worship that belongs only to God.* Angels worship Jesus (Hebrews 1:6); demons tremble before him (Mark 5:6–8). His own followers saw his miracles and fell before him in adoration (Matthew 14:32–33). Thomas, one of Jesus' closest followers, who doubted the resurrection of Jesus from the dead, when he saw the risen Lord, said, "My Lord and my God!" (John 20:28).

Jesus accepted the worship that rightly belongs only to God. Contrast that with the shock in the apostle Paul's voice when some people tried to worship him as some kind of god. He tore his clothes and said, "We too are only human, like you" (Acts 14:15). When the apostle John was overcome by the majesty of heaven and fell down in worship before a

Bible Networking

Colossians 2:9

For in Christ all the fullness of the Deity lives in bodily form.

Hebrews 1:3

The Son is the radiance of God's glory and the exact representation of his being, sustaining all things by his powerful word.

John 1:3

Through [Christ] all things were made; without him nothing was made that has been made.

magnificent angel, the angel's words were even more direct. "Don't do that!" he said. "I am a fellow servant [of God] with you .... Worship God!" (Revelation 22:9).

But Jesus never rebuked those who worshiped him. He never told them to stop or to get up. He received their worship and blessed them for it.

"I Am"

If all these lines of evidence weren't enough to convince us that Jesus is God, we also know that *Jesus himself claimed to be God*. He made that assertion in several ways:

- Jesus claimed authority over institutions that God had established. In Matthew 12:8, he said he was "Lord of the Sabbath." Jesus claimed authority over the seventh day of worship and rest marked out in the fifth of the Ten Commandments (Exodus 20:8 – 11). When Jesus drove the money changers and marketers out of the temple of God in Jerusalem, he said, "My house will be called a house of prayer (Matthew 21:13). Jesus saw himself as the one in charge of God's things.
- Jesus made a clear claim that he was eternal—that he had been in existence in Abraham's day (who lived centuries before Jesus was born). "Before Abraham was born, I am!" (John 8:58).
- Jesus placed himself on the same level as God the Father as the object of saving faith. In a discussion with his disciples, Jesus said, "You believe in God, believe also in Me" (John 14:1 NKJV).

Bible Networking

Philippians 2:9 – 11

> Therefore God exalted him to the highest place
>   and gave him the name that is above every name,
> that at the name of Jesus every knee should bow,
>   in heaven and on earth and under the earth,
> and every tongue acknowledge that Jesus Christ is Lord,
>   to the glory of God the Father.

- Finally when asked directly if he was the Messiah, the Son of God, Jesus responded, "I am" (Mark 14:61–62; see also Matthew 26:63–64).

The Bible's testimony is unanimous and clear. Jesus is more than a man. He is also fully God, the unique Son of God.

TITLES AND NAMES GIVEN TO JESUS

The Lord Jesus Christ
(Acts 11:17)

Lord
(Acts 9:5–6; Romans 10:9)

Jesus
(Matthew 1:20)

Messiah [the Christ, NIV]
(Matthew 16:16, 20)

Son of David
(Matthew 1:1)

Son of Abraham
(Matthew 1:1)

Joseph's son
(Luke 4:22)

Mary's son
(Mark 6:3)

Son of God
(Luke 1:35; John 1:49)

My Son [by God the Father]
(Mark 1:11)

Son of Man
(Matthew 8:20)

The bread of life
(John 6:35)

Living bread
(John 6:51)

The light of the world
(John 8:12)

The good shepherd
(John 10:11, 14)

The resurrection and the life
(John 11:25)

The way and the truth and the life
(John 14:6)

The true vine
(John 15:1)

Master
(Matthew 23:8)

Teacher
(Mark 14:14)

Great priest
(Hebrews 10:21)

Savior
(1 John 4:14)

The Lamb of God
(John 1:29)

The firstborn from among the dead
(Colossians 1:18)

The Word
(John 1:1)

The Lion of the tribe of Judah
(Revelation 5:5)

Head over everything for the church
(Ephesians 1:22)

The living Stone
(1 Peter 2:4)

King of the nations [ages, NIV]
(Revelation 15:3)

KING OF KINGS AND LORD OF LORDS
(Revelation 19:16)

Human Being and Divine Being

Jesus was one of a kind! He was the God-man—fully God and fully human. That union of humanity and deity in one person is one of the holy mysteries of the Christian faith. We can say the words and believe that it is true, but we have a difficult time explaining how it works.

Early Christian leaders struggled with understanding and describing how Jesus could be both human and divine. What they boiled it down to was this: Jesus possessed two natures (human and divine), and those two natures resided in one person (Jesus). Jesus always acted as a unified person. He did not walk around saying, "Today I have to act like a human—until I heal someone, and then I will act like God." He was both God and man, but he acted and reacted and felt emotion and spoke as one fully integrated person.

The closest the Bible comes to explaining the incarnation (the coming in the flesh of God the Son) is found in Philippians 2:5–9:

> In your relationships with one another, have the same attitude of mind Christ Jesus had:
>
> Who, being in very nature God,
> > did not consider equality with God something to be used
> > > to his own advantage;
> > rather, he made himself nothing

SON OF GOD

Some people have gotten the wrong idea from the title "Son of God." Mormons and Muslims, for example, see some hint about Jesus' origin in that title. Muslims react against it by saying that the true God (Allah) did not have any offspring. Mormons have embraced the idea, saying that Jesus was a literal spirit-child conceived by the god over our world, Jehovah, and one of his covenant wives. Other groups have taken the term *Son of God* to mean that Jesus was something less than God—a lesser god or simply a man who lived close to God.

The term *Son of God*, however, has nothing to do with Jesus' origin. He was not somehow conceived in Mary by a sexual or physical union between God and a human woman. The term refers instead to Jesus' position. Jesus stands in the position of a son to God the Father. He willingly submitted himself as a son to the will of God the Father, but Jesus is equal in his deity to the Father. Jesus is not just the Son of God; he is also God the Son—fully God but carrying out a different role in the plan of redemption from that of God the Father or God the Holy Spirit.

by taking the very nature of a servant,
being made in human likeness.
And being found in appearance as a human being,
he humbled himself
by becoming obedient to death—
even death on a cross!

Therefore God exalted him to the highest place
and gave him the name that is above every name.

Several truths about Jesus stand out in these verses:

- Jesus was God and remained God throughout this process—
"being in very nature God." Jesus' inward form, the reality of his
being, was deity.
- Jesus did not insist on holding on to what was his—he "did not
consider equality with God something to be used to his own
advantage." Because he was God, Jesus could have said, "I don't
want to enter the human world of pain and suffering. I deserve
better than that." But he was willing to let go of his own rights and
privileges to rescue those who were far from God.
- Jesus emptied himself—"he made himself nothing ... he humbled
himself." Did he empty himself of God-ness? No way! That would
have been impossible. Jesus could not become less than what

Help File

HOW CAN GOD GET TIRED?

The gospel writers (and Jesus himself) never saw any contradiction between Jesus' humanity and Jesus' deity. They were very candid about some of the limitations Jesus lived under voluntarily while he was here on earth. The self-emptying of Jesus meant that he relied on the Father, not on his own personal power, and so Jesus experienced some of the same limitations we face.

- Jesus became tired (John 4:6).
- Jesus admitted that he didn't know certain things (Matthew 24:36), and

he had to ask questions to get certain information (Mark 9:21).
- Jesus was limited in his presence to one place at a time. His friend Martha wished that he had been at the town of Bethany before her brother, Lazarus, had died (John 11:21).
- On the cross, Jesus was thirsty (John 19:28).
- In the end, Jesus, the eternal God in human flesh, died (Matthew 27:50).

he was. But to his divine nature he added a human nature. That required him to lay aside certain privileges and power. For example, Jesus emptied himself of his outward glory. Contrary to most religious pictures, Jesus did not have a halo above his head or an eerie glow. Jesus looked like a man. Jesus also emptied himself of the use of his own power. Everything Jesus did during his ministry came from the Father, not from his own power as God the Son. Jesus said it himself: "The Son is able to do nothing out of his own power; he is only able to do what he sees the Father doing" (John 5:19, my paraphrase).

THE ERROR OF THEIR WAYS

Over the years since the New Testament was written, several errors or false teachings have arisen about the union of God and man in Jesus. This is just a brief summary:

- *Nestorianism* (named after Nestorius, who died around AD 451) taught that Jesus had two personalities, not just two natures. Sometimes he acted as God and sometimes as a man.
- *Docetism* (derived from the Greek verb *dokeō* which means "to seem") taught that Jesus was fully God but he only *seemed* to be a man. His body was only an apparition.
- The *Ebionites* said that Jesus was just a man and that the "divine Christ" came on him at his baptism and left him on the cross.
- *Modalists* believe that one God revealed himself in different forms at different times—God the Father in the Old Testament, Jesus in the Gospels, the Holy Spirit today. In other words, no Trinity. You can still find this view in what is called the "Jesus Only" movement.
- *Arianism* (named for its founder, Arius) denied the deity and eternality of Jesus. Arius believed that Jesus was created by the Father and then Jesus created everything else. Jehovah's Witnesses hold this view today. Jesus was near God and like God but not God.

The Christian church (no denominations in those early days) met at Chalcedon (AD 451) and Constantinople (AD 680) and hammered out the orthodox position:

> We confess one and the same Son, our Lord Jesus Christ, the same perfect in Godhead and also perfect in manhood; truly God and truly man, of a reasonable soul and body; consubstantial with the Father according to the Godhead, and consubstantial with us according to the Manhood.
>
> The Confession of Chalcedon (AD 451)

Bible Networking

John 8:28

So Jesus said, "When you have lifted up the Son of Man, then you will know that I am he and that I do nothing on my own but speak just what the Father has taught me."

Jesus — to his disciples
John 14:10

"Don't you believe that I am in the Father, and that the Father is in me? The words I say to you I do not speak on my own authority. Rather, it is the Father, living in me, who is doing his work."

- Jesus came for a single great purpose — "becoming obedient to death — even death on a cross." Jesus stepped down from heaven's glory and from the place of majesty and power to die as the sacrifice for human sin. He set his feet on a path that ended at the cross.
- Jesus' time of emptying came to an end — "God exalted him to the highest place." When Jesus rose from the dead and then ascended back into heaven, he returned to the glory he had before he came. He took back the use of his power and the aura of majesty. Jesus resides in heaven today in splendor as God the Son.

In Other Words

He was weary; yet he called the weary to himself for rest. He was hungry; yet he was "the bread of life." He was thirsty; yet he was "the water of life." He was in agony; yet he healed all manner of sickness and soothed every pain.... He prayed, which is always human; yet he himself answered prayer.... He wept at the tomb [of Lazarus]; yet he called the dead to arise.... He dies; yet he is eternal life.

Lewis Sperry Chafer, in *Systematic Theology* (1947; repr.,
Grand Rapids: Kregel, 1993), 1:369.

Points to Remember

☑ For Christians, everything we believe begins and ends with Jesus.

☑ We have the historical record of Jesus' life in the four gospels; we have the theological interpretation of Jesus' significance in the rest of the New Testament.

☑ The Bible teaches that Jesus was conceived in a virgin woman by a miraculous work of God.

☑ Jesus is fully human and fully God. He possesses all the attributes of both.

☑ Jesus became human so he could fully identify with us.

☑ Jesus' incarnation (his coming in human form and human flesh) is one of the central mysteries of the Christian faith.

☑ Jesus has identified with us forever by choosing to live in a human body even in heaven.

☑ We can know Jesus personally.

Only one thing about Jesus remains the same as when he was on earth. He has limited himself to a human body forever. Jesus did not stop being God when he came to earth and he has not stopped being human since returning to heaven. He is "the man Christ Jesus" (1 Timothy 2:5 NIV).

Why We Care

The Christian faith centers on Jesus. That's why I started with him. To his followers Jesus is much more than a religious teacher or miracle worker or spiritual guide. Jesus is God himself who saw our desperate condition and who laid aside heaven's glory to do something about that condition. He stepped down into human history as a tiny baby, unnoticed and poor. As a man he spent three years teaching his followers and healing the sick. Jesus then willingly laid down his own life as a sacrifice for our failures and wrongs. Death took Jesus, but it couldn't hold him for very long. He burst out of the grave alive! He's alive today and stands in heaven as our Savior and Lord.

If you don't have a relationship with Jesus, now is the perfect time to start down that path. Be open to him as you read this book because he is fully aware of who you are. He loves you with an amazing love that has been seeking you out. As you open your mind and heart to Jesus, as you seek to know him, he has promised to let you find him.

✗ John A Witmer, *Immanuel: Experiencing Jesus as Man and God*. Nashville: Word, 1998.

An excellent study of who Jesus is and his significance in our lives today.

CHAPTER 2

A Book We Can Trust: The Bible

A Book We Can Trust: The Bible

- ▶ Listen to God speaking!
- ▶ Find out how God has communicated in the natural world, in Jesus, and in a book!
- ▶ Discover why Christians believe the Bible is true.
- ▶ Have we left out any books that should be in the Bible?

The God Who Speaks

Christians believe that God wants us to know him and that he has taken the initiative to reveal himself to us. God has not hidden himself away in heaven and laid the task of finding him on us. He is the one who came seeking us—not because he was lonely and needed the company, but because he loved us and desired friendship with us. We are limited, fairly weak creatures; God is the infinite, supreme being in existence. We could discover very little reliable information about him on our own. God has overcome that obstacle by revealing the truth about himself to us.

God has spoken in several ways:

- *God has revealed his existence and his power in the created universe.* Anyone looking at the beauty of the earth or the vast expanse of the stars can see God's presence. The universe could not have just appeared by accident; God was the great designer. "Since the creation of the world God's invisible qualities—his eternal power and divine nature—have been clearly seen, being understood from what has been made" (Romans 1:20).
- *God has revealed his goodness through rain and sunshine, through the seasons and ripening crops, through the joys and blessings of life.* "[God] has not left himself without testimony: He has shown

kindness by giving you rain from heaven and crops in their seasons; he provides you with plenty of food and fills your hearts with joy" (Acts 14:17).

- *God has also spoken through specially chosen individuals called prophets.* Over and over again, God's prophets would say, "This is what the LORD says."
- *God has spoken completely and finally in his Son, Jesus.* We learn what God is like by looking at Jesus. He is the visible image of the invisible God! "In the past God spoke to our ancestors through the prophets ..., but in these last days he has spoken to us by his Son" (Hebrews 1:1–2).

God has spoken in one more way—*through his written Word, the Bible.* This chapter will explore how the Bible was written and why Christians value its truth so highly.

Stage One: God Prepares the Writers

The Bible is a unique book. It claims to be the direct product of God. But the Bible did not drop out of heaven as a completed book! It was

Bible Networking

Psalm 19:1 – 4

The heavens declare the glory of God;
   the skies proclaim the work of his hands.
Day after day they pour forth speech;
   night after night they display knowledge.
They have no speech, they use no words;
   no sound is heard from them.
Yet their voice goes out into all the earth,
   their words to the ends of the world.

1 Corinthians 1:21 NASB

The world through its wisdom did not come to know God.

written over a period of almost 2,000 years by at least forty different authors. The Bible was written in ancient languages that are no longer spoken. God did not deliver his message through an angel or as a print-out from a heavenly computer. God delivered his message through men and women—*prepared* men and women. God used some very carefully chosen individuals to be the channels of his truth.

God's preparation of the biblical writers began long before high school or college: it began at conception. The apostle Paul, for example, said that God "set me apart, even from my mother's womb" (Galatians 1:15 NASB). God controlled even the biological process of conception to produce in Paul exactly the temperament and character that God wanted to use to bring his message to the world.

The Old Testament prophet Jeremiah gives an even more detailed explanation of God's work in his life. His testimony is that God prepared him in four ways:

- First, God formed Jeremiah in the womb. God controlled that event.
- Second, even before Jeremiah was formed, God knew him. To "know" someone in Jeremiah's language meant to set your love and approval on that person.
- Then God tells this prophet that he had set him apart before Jeremiah was born.
- Finally, God appointed Jeremiah as a prophet—a spokesman for the Lord.

Here's the word of the Lord spoken to Jeremiah:

> "Before I formed you in the womb I knew you,
>   before you were born I set you apart;
>   I appointed you as a prophet to the nations."
>   Jeremiah 1:5

God actively directed the birth, development, temperament, and experiences of those he had chosen to be the writers of his message. A brilliant, well-trained scholar like Isaiah wrote in classical Hebrew style with an immense vocabulary of words. A fisherman like John wrote in a simple, straightforward style that even young children can appreciate.

One of the attacks on the Bible has come at precisely this point. Some people have read the Bible and said, "This is just a collection of writings from people who were searching for God. They all write in different styles. They lived in different periods of history. How can this book be God's message to us?"

The answer is that God did use different authors with different styles and backgrounds to write the Bible, but they were all prepared in such a way that what they wrote in their own style and historical setting was precisely what God wanted written.

Stage Two: God Reveals His Message

Once God prepared the writers to receive his message at the right time and in the right situation, God began to communicate with them. God revealed himself and his message to those uniquely chosen and prepared men and women who would in turn communicate God's message to his people. Remember that God's activity of revealing himself comes from his side, not ours. The Bible is not a record of our search for God but an unfolding of God's search for us. God shows us who he is. He talks to us in person.

God communicated to his chosen representatives in several ways:

- The Ten Commandments were written on stone tablets directly by God (Exodus 31:18).
- Most of the time, God spoke directly to his prophets. "The LORD would speak to Moses face to face" (Exodus 33:11). Was it an audible voice? If we had been standing next to Moses would we have heard it? God may have used an audible voice at times, but I think he usually spoke to the prophet's spirit and mind.
- A few times God used dreams or gave his spokesman the interpretation of a dream to communicate the message (Genesis 40–41; Daniel 2).

Help File

LEARNING TO BE A KING

The writer of Psalm 78 had this to say about God's preparation of a shepherd boy to be the "shepherd" king of his people Israel:

[God] chose David his servant
   and took him from the sheep pens;
from tending the sheep he brought him
to be the shepherd of his people Jacob,
   of Israel his inheritance.
And David shepherded them with
   integrity of heart;
with skillful hands he led them.
                    Psalm 78:70–72

- Some prophets received visions of what God was doing or was going to do in the future. The book of Revelation is a series of visions that God gave to the apostle John. Ezekiel in the Old Testament saw visions of God himself (Ezekiel 1; 10).
- Sometimes miracles or works of God's power conveyed God's message. Jesus healed a man in order to prove that he also had the authority to forgive the man's sins (Mark 2:10–12). God delivered his people Israel from slavery in Egypt to show the Egyptians that he was the only true God (Exodus 14:4).
- Certain rituals and sacrifices in the Old Testament were designed to picture Jesus and his sacrifice on the cross. The outward ritual pictured a deeper reality.

God has used different methods and channels to get his message to us but the main point is that God has spoken. He is not a silent God sitting far away from the arena of our lives. He has told us what he wants us to know.

God's message to humanity is marked by three characteristics:

- God's message, first of all, is *propositional* — God has spoken in clear, understandable, informative statements. Yes, the Bible uses figurative language sometimes or parables or weird visions, but God's basic message of salvation and grace can be summarized in statements that we can all grasp and understand. Christians may disagree on some issues, but at the core of the Christian faith is a set of truths that we all believe.
- Second, God's message has been revealed *progressively*. Abraham and Moses knew God but not in the fullness that we can know him. Later truth was given not to correct the earlier message but to add to it and to unfold the depths of its meaning.
- Finally, God's message is *personal.* He wants you and me to get it, to understand it. God still speaks through what he has spoken in the past. The best way to hear God's voice in our lives is to listen to what he said centuries ago.

God's friendship with us begins and grows through communication. In the Bible, God talks to me. I talk to him in prayer or in my expressions of adoration and worship or in my cries for his help. God loves to communicate with his people, and he is always ready to hear from his children.

Stage Three: God Guards the Writing of His Message

God has spoken—and I'm glad he did! But revealing his message to chosen, prepared messengers was not enough. God spoke to Moses and Paul and Ezekiel, but they lived a long time ago. God did come to earth as a man to explain God to us, but he's not here in the flesh anymore. How did God's message get passed on to us?

The Bible explains that God did another work. He prepared his messengers (step 1); he revealed his message to them (step 2); then (step 3) God saw to it that the message he had revealed was written down accurately. God's message is recorded for us in the Bible. God didn't write it directly, but he guided those who did so that they wrote God's truth exactly as he wanted it written.

Theologians call that work *inspiration*—a word that comes from the English translation of 2 Timothy 3:16. The King James Version (also called the Authorized Version) reads like this:

> All scripture is given by inspiration of God, and is profitable for doctrine, for reproof, for correction, for instruction in righteousness.

Bible Networking

Deuteronomy 5:24

"The LORD our God has shown us his glory and his majesty, and we have heard his voice from the fire. Today we have seen that people can live even if God speaks with them."

John 1:14, 18

The Word became flesh and made his dwelling among us....

No one has ever seen God, but the one and only Son, who is himself God and is in closest relationship with the Father, has made him known.

Psalm 119:89

Your word, LORD, is eternal;
   it stands firm in the heavens.

The modern version (TNIV) we are using says essentially the same thing:

> All Scripture is God-breathed and is useful for teaching, rebuking, correcting and training in righteousness.

The key phrase for our discussion is *given by inspiration of God* or *God-breathed*. What Paul is teaching is that the Bible is the direct product of God. God "breathed out" his message through the writers of Scripture. The Bible then is inspired—God's accurate message written down.

No other book or piece of writing can truthfully make that claim. Commentaries on the Bible are not inspired; sermons are not inspired. They may correctly teach what the Bible says, but only the Bible is God-breathed. God's work of revealing his message is the *inflow* of truth from God to the human mind of the prophet or apostle. God's work of inspiration is the *outflow* of that truth to others through a written record. We know the message that God revealed to the apostle Paul, for example, because we have the inspired written record in the New Testament.

God Moved

It's important to notice that Paul does not say that the writers were inspired. That's how we hear this truth presented sometimes—that God "inspired" Paul to write the book of Romans, for example. But 2 Timothy 3:16 says it is the *writing* that is inspired, not the writer.

Help File

INCREDIBLE VARIETY

The Bible came from God through the writers to us, but that doesn't mean it is just one long, dry sermon! The writers include visions, poems, historical records, wars, stories, songs, crying, laughing, arguing—showing the whole range of human emotion and literary techniques. Most of the Bible is narrative, the accurate record of events that happened between God and his people—and most of the Bible can be understood by just about any reader. The difficult parts are difficult for everyone. If you ever come upon someone who says they can explain every verse in the book of Revelation or every prophecy in the book of Daniel, back away or change the channel.

The Bible even contains a few lies—but they are accurately recorded and are always clearly identified as lies! God breathed out the entire book, carrying the authors along in various ways so that we have his full message in the words of the Bible.

Bible Networking

David's testimony about the sections of Scripture he wrote
2 Samuel 23:2

"The Spirit of the Lord spoke through me;
his word was on my tongue."

Ezekiel's testimony of how God spoke to him
Ezekiel 3:4

He then said to me: "Son of man, go now to the house of Israel and speak my words to them."

Paul's testimony of the authority of his message
1 Corinthians 2:13

This is what we speak, not in words taught us by human wisdom but in words taught by the Spirit, explaining spiritual realities with Spirit-taught words.

Peter's testimony of how God speaks in his Word
2 Peter 1:3

[God] has given us everything we need for a godly life through our knowledge of him.

So what part did the writers play in this? Were they just taking dictation from God? Actually the writers were very much involved. But God was guarding the process. Here's how 2 Peter 1:20–21 explains it:

> Above all, you must understand that no prophecy of Scripture came about by the prophets' own interpretation of things. For prophecy never had its origin in the human will, but prophets, though human, spoke from God as they were carried along by the Holy Spirit.

The phrase *carried along* is a boating term. It refers to a sailboat caught in a high wind with no steering device. The boat is carried along by the wind. That is a picture of how God worked through human writers to produce the Bible. The Holy Spirit used the personalities and styles

In Other Words

What Scripture says, God says.

Often attributed to Saint Augustine

Holy Scripture should be thought of as God preaching — God preaching to me every time I read or hear any part of it.

J. I. Packer, in God Has Spoken (Grand Rapids:
Baker, 1993), 97.

These books [of the Bible], therefore, ought to be much in our hands, in our eyes, in our ears, in our mouths, and most of all in our hearts.

Thomas Cranmer, in "A Fruitful Exhortation to the Reading
and Knowledge of Holy Scripture,"
Anglican Homilies (1547).

and vocabularies of the writers but so directed their writings that what they wrote was exactly what God wanted written. The writers were not "inspired" to write; what they wrote was the inspired message of God.

Jesus said that the authority of Scripture extended not just to the thoughts expressed or even the words that were used but to every letter and part of a letter (Matthew 5:18). Jesus also said this: "Heaven and earth will pass away, but my words will never pass away" (Matthew 24:35). The Bible is the reliable record of God's message. You can count on it, rest on its promises, believe it as God's truth. It will never fail you.

Stage Four: God Preserves His Message So We Can Hear It

God has spoken. Chosen, prepared messengers received the message and wrote it down exactly as God wanted it written. The problem for me is that God's message was originally written in ancient, difficult languages that take years of study to read accurately. How can I hear God's message if it's sealed in a language I can't understand? If your pastor reads the Scripture next Sunday in Hebrew or Greek, you probably won't leave the service with much of a message. So how do we hear God's message today?

WHY WE BELIEVE THE BIBLE IS TRUE

It's one thing to say that the Bible claims to be God's message, God's Word. The problem is the Bible is not the only book to make that claim. The Qur'an, the holy book of Islam, claims to be the direct word of Allah, the final message of God to humanity. The Book of Mormon also claims to be God's written word—a "third testament" to lay alongside the Bible's Old Testament and New Testament. Christians believe that the Bible *alone* is God's Word.

Defenders of the Bible usually appeal to one of two lines of defense for their belief in the Bible. Some will appeal to the inner witness of the Holy Spirit. They will say, "When I read the Bible, the Holy Spirit confirms to me that this is God's truth." The inner confirmation by the Holy Spirit is a wonderful experience, but it doesn't really defend the authority of Scripture. I talked to a Mormon not long ago who said that when he read the Book of Mormon, it had "the ring of truth" to it.

Other Christians will point to Christian evidence—fulfilled prophecy, confirmation from archaeology, the unity of the Bible's message, and so on. These evidences are excellent tools, but they only confirm the accuracy of specific statements in the Bible. Furthermore, it's impossible to prove the central truths of the Christian faith. You can prove historically that Jesus died, but only the Scriptures can prove that Jesus died *for our sins*.

I think the key reason to believe that the Bible is true is because Jesus Christ put his stamp of approval on the Bible as the genuine Word of God. Here's a summary of Jesus' testimony:

Jesus' Attitude toward the Old Testament

- Jesus displayed complete familiarity with the entire scope of Old Testament Scripture. His mind and teachings were saturated with the Hebrew Bible.
- Jesus always regarded the Old Testament as God's Word. An appeal to Scripture settled any argument as far as Jesus was concerned.
- Jesus confirmed that the events in the Old Testament actually took place and that the people mentioned there were genuine human beings.
    A few examples:
      Adam and Eve (Matthew 19:3–6)
      Noah and the great flood (Matthew 24:37–39)
      Abraham (John 8:56)
      Sodom's destruction (Luke 10:12; 17:28–29)
      Moses and the burning bush (Luke 20:37)
      Jonah and the great fish (Matthew 12:40)
- Jesus believed that an important aspect of his ministry was to fulfill Old Testament prophecy.
- Jesus relied on the truth of Scripture in times of great personal crisis (such as his temptation by Satan in Matthew 4:1–10).

Our conclusion has to be that Jesus accepted the Old Testament as the written Word of God, final in its authority and completely true.

Jesus' Attitude toward His Own Teaching

- Jesus put his own words on the same level as he put the written Scriptures. "Heaven and earth will pass away, but my words will never pass away" (Matthew 24:35).
- Jesus believed that a person's eternal destiny hinged on that person's response to Jesus' own words (Matthew 7:24–26; Luke 6:46–49).
- Jesus equated his own words with God's words and with absolute truth (John 8:28, 40; 18:37).
- Jesus claimed to speak without error (John 8:43–46).
- Jesus called his followers to put absolute trust in every word he spoke (John 14:10–11; 15:7).

Jesus' Attitude toward the New Testament

Jesus not only accepted the Old Testament and his own words as God's truth; he also put his stamp of approval ahead of time on what his authorized representatives would write.

- Jesus told his disciples before his death that he had more to reveal to them (John 16:12) and that they would receive it in the future (John 16:13).
- Jesus outlined in advance the content of the New Testament.
  Everything Jesus had said to them = *the Gospels* (John 14:26).
  The correct interpretation of all that Jesus did on the cross and through his resurrection = *the New Testament letters* (John 16:14–15).
  Prophecy about the future = *the book of Revelation* (John 16:13).
- Jesus gave the future written witness of his apostles the same authority as his own words (John 17:17–20). Christians today have come to believe in Jesus "through their [the apostles'] message."

Our Attitude toward the Bible

Why do Christians believe the Bible is God's true word?

- The Bible claims to be the Word of God.
- Jesus taught and believed that the Old Testament, his own teaching, and the yet-to-be-written New Testament were true.
- Jesus is God, and he cannot lie or deceive.
- Jesus is our Lord, and he sets the standard for what we believe.

Conclusion: We believe about the Bible what Jesus believed about it—that what the Bible claims for itself is correct. The Bible is the unfailing, absolutely trustworthy Word of God.

Once again, God has been at work to protect and preserve his truth. He has seen to it that the books of the Bible were copied, collected, hidden when necessary, and translated into hundreds of languages. Almost anyone in the world can pick up a Bible or part of a Bible in their own language and read God's message. But the story of how that happened centers around four types of biblical material.

1. The Original Documents: The "Autographs"

The actual letters the apostle Paul wrote (or dictated to a secretary) are all missing. None of the original writings of the Bible have survived—and for very good reasons. If we had Paul's original letter to the Ephesian Christians, for example, someone would have it in a gilded shrine and worshipers would be lining up to venerate such a holy object. God wanted the words of the message to endure, not the physical parchment (smooth leather) on which it was first written.

2. Manuscripts: Copies of the Originals

The ancient Jews and the early Christians spread God's message by making copies of the original writings—and copies of copies. No one had a Xerox machine, of course, or a laser printer, so copies were made slowly and meticulously by devout scribes. These copyists were obsessed

Help File

COMPARING THE VERSIONS

Read Mark 10:14 in these different English translations and see which one helps you get God's message the best.

Authorized (King James) Version

When Jesus saw it, he was much displeased, and said unto them, Suffer the little children to come unto me, and forbid them not; for of such is the kingdom of God.

English Standard Version

But when Jesus saw it, he was indignant and said to them, "Let the children come to me; do not hinder them, for to such belongs the kingdom of God."

Today's New International Version

When Jesus saw this, he was indignant. He said to them, "Let the little children come to me, and do not hinder them, for the kingdom of God belongs to such as these."

Contemporary English Version

When Jesus saw this, he became angry and said, "Let the children come to me! Don't try to stop them. People who are like these little children belong to the kingdom of God."

with accuracy. Every letter was carefully copied, every line checked and rechecked. Old Testament scribes counted every letter of every biblical book, and each new copy had to come out exactly right or they started over from scratch.

God in his watchfulness has allowed hundreds of these ancient copies to survive. We have fragments of copies made just a few years after the originals were written. But even with meticulous care, occasionally a word would be dropped or two letters mixed up. By comparing the manuscripts, however, we can easily determine the correct reading. Less than 1 percent of the text of the New Testament is even questioned—that's one word in 4,000! Furthermore, no major teaching of the Christian faith rests on a disputed or doubtful reading.

How can we make God's Word come alive today? Here are a few ways I have found helpful.

- Saturate yourself in a biblical book by reading through it each day for a month. Start with Ephesians or Philippians or 1 Peter.
- Learn Scripture by heart. Memorize a verse or a section every week—for example, Psalm 23 or Isaiah 9:6–7 or Matthew 6:9–13 or John 14:1–6 or 1 Corinthians 13. Meditate on these verses when you wake up in the morning or as you go to sleep at night.
- Put yourself in the setting of some of Jesus' teaching—for example, in the crowd as a paralyzed man is let down through the roof (Mark 2:1–12). Imagine what you can see, hear, and smell.
- Use a Bible study guide to help you dig into the biblical text. Suggestions: LifeGuide Bible Studies (InterVarsity), Lifebuilder Bible Studies (Scripture Union), the Bringing the Bible to Life series (Zondervan), and the New Community series (Zondervan).
- Read a commentary as you study a section of the Bible. Your pastor can give you some direction, or check out the suggestions in the companion volume, *The Bible for Blockheads* (Zondervan, 2007).
- Read a chapter of Proverbs each day. Proverbs has thirty-one chapters so, if today is the 15th day of the month, read chapter 15.
- Follow a plan for reading through the Bible in a year—for example, find a plan at *www.oneyearbibleonline.com*. But be realistic. If life's demands slow you down, do it in two years—or three!

Bible Networking

Jesus' words to his followers
John 16:12 – 15

"I have much more to say to you, more than you can now bear. But when he, the Spirit of truth, comes, he will guide you into all the truth. He will not speak on his own; he will speak only what he hears, and he will tell you what is yet to come. He will glorify me because it is from me that he will receive what he will make known to you. All that belongs to the Father is mine. That is why I said the Spirit will receive from me what he will make known to you."

1 John 2:26 – 27

I am writing these things to you about those who are trying to lead you astray. As for you, the anointing you received from him remains in you, and you do not need anyone to teach you. But as his anointing teaches you about all things and as that anointing is real, not counterfeit—just as it has taught you, remain in him.

3. Versions: Translations of the Original Writings into a New Language

As the ancient manuscripts are compared and compiled, a complete text of the Old Testament (originally written in Hebrew) and the New Testament (originally written in Greek) emerges. But most of us don't know these languages and don't have the time to learn them. That's when faithful, believing biblical scholars come to our aid. These men and women accurately and carefully translate the Bible into our language—English, French, Swahili, Hindi, Mandarin, and hundreds more! These translations are *versions* of the Bible. In this book we use *Today's New International Version*—a contemporary but accurate translation of the Greek and Hebrew texts in American English. Dozens of other English versions are also available. Each version expresses God's original message and carries God's authority to the extent that it communicates accurately the meaning of the original text. You can read and learn and obey your Bible with confidence that God is speaking to you through its words.

4. Paraphrases and Commentaries: Interpretations of the Bible's Meaning

Throughout the history of the church, men and women, scholars and preachers and poets, have tried to explain and apply the Bible to life in the modern world. Some have produced paraphrases of Scripture—loose translations that include modern expressions. One example is Eugene Peterson's paraphrase, *The Message*. Here's how Matthew 6:28–29 reads in his expressive style:

> Instead of looking at the fashions, walk out into the fields and look at the wildflowers. They never primp or shop, but have you ever seen color or design quite like it? The ten best-dressed men and women in the country look shabby alongside them.

Is this a literal translation of what Jesus said? No—but it conveys Jesus' meaning in contemporary language. Paraphrases make Scripture easier to read and to comprehend.

Help File

ARE WE MISSING ANY BIBLICAL BOOKS?

Occasionally a bestselling book or a scholar looking for attention will suggest that one or more other books should be included in our Bibles. *The Gospel of Thomas* is one that gets a lot of attention—and other suggestions make it seem like there are dozens of "lost" biblical books.

It's true that many books and letters were written (most of them long after the writing of the New Testament) that claimed to come from the closest followers of Jesus. The early Christians, however, unanimously rejected these books as part of the New Testament. The "new" books came from groups that held false doctrines or from authors who lived long after the first followers of Jesus had died.

Church leaders eventually included only the twenty-seven books in our present New Testament. You will sometimes hear people say that "the church chose what books to include," but that's not really correct. It was the Holy Spirit who made clear what books to include. The early Christians simply recognized that these books were inspired by God. The rest of the so-called biblical books were not.

The collection of books in our Bibles (39 books in the Old Testament; 27 books in the New) are referred to as the *canon* (pronounced just like the big gun). The word *canon* means "a measuring stick." These particular books are the measuring stick of the Christian faith. Everything we believe comes from their teachings, and they are used to measure the teachings of others. We do not bend the Scriptures to accommodate our beliefs; we bring what we believe into line with what the Bible declares.

In Other Words

Defend the Bible? I would just as soon defend a lion. Just turn the Bible loose. It will defend itself.

Charles Spurgeon

Throughout the history of the church the greatest preachers have been those who have recognized that they have no authority in themselves, and have seen their task as being to explain the words of Scripture and apply them clearly to the lives of their hearers. Their preaching has drawn its power not from the proclamation of their own Christian experiences or the experiences of others, nor from their own opinions, creative ideas, or rhetorical skills, but from God's powerful words. Essentially, they stood in the pulpit, pointed to the biblical text, and said in effect to the congregation, "This is what this verse means. Do you see the meaning here as well? Then you must believe it and obey it with all your heart, for God himself, your Creator and your Lord, is saying this to you today!"

Wayne Grudem, in *Bible Doctrine* (Grand Rapids: Zondervan, 1999), 40.

Commentaries do the same thing. They help us understand what the Bible means by pointing out the historical or cultural setting or by explaining the original words more clearly or by drawing our attention to other relevant passages of Scripture. A sermon from your pastor or a Bible study on a certain passage is focused on the same goal—to help us understand and live out God's message.

God has expended a lot of effort to get his message to us—preparing the writers, revealing his truth, guiding the writing, preserving the text, and prompting scholars to provide translations we can read and understand. The question I have to ask myself is this: How serious am I about listening to God's message? Or do I take it for granted that I will always have access to God's written truth?

Stage Five: God Helps Us Understand His Message

God is so committed to getting his truth into our hearts and minds and lives that he takes one more step in communicating with us. As we read or hear the Bible, God the Holy Spirit works to help us understand what God has said. The Spirit illumines our hearts and minds. He turns on the light so we can better grasp the meaning and significance of what God has said.

The apostle Paul describes the Spirit's work like this:

> The Spirit searches all things, even the deep things of God. For who knows a person's thoughts except that person's own spirit within? In the same way no one knows the thoughts of God except the Spirit of God. We have not received the spirit of the world but the Spirit who is from God, that we may understand what God has freely given us.
>
> 1 Corinthians 2:10–12

Through reading, study, prayerful thought and through the ministry of teachers and pastors and wise friends, God helps us understand what the Bible is saying and how it applies to our lives and jobs and marriages. The end result of the Spirit's work is to exalt Jesus through us. His goal is not just to fill our minds with facts about the Bible; the Spirit's goal is to make the Bible's truth come alive in us.

Great Debates!

THE APOCRYPHA

In some Bibles you will find a few additional books in the Old Testament or tucked between the Old Testament and the New Testament. These are the books of the Apocrypha—fourteen or fifteen books that some Christians want to include in the Bible and others fiercely exclude.

The books of the Apocrypha are historical or wisdom or visionary books that were written late in the Old Testament era or in the period between the end of the Old Testament and the opening of the New Testament. Many Jews revere these books as part of their spiritual heritage but reject them as part of the Bible. Most Protestants do not regard the Apocrypha as part of the Bible. The Roman Catholic Church, however, declared at the Council of Trent in 1546 that the books of the Apocrypha are *canonical* (belonging to the canon, the officially recognized collection of biblical books). In Roman Catholic Bibles the books of the Apocrypha are scattered through the Old Testament. In Bibles used in the Anglican or Eastern Orthodox churches, the Apocrypha is in a separate section. In most Protestant Bibles, the Apocrypha does not appear. The major argument against including the Apocrypha as a part of the canon of Scripture is that while the New Testament writers quote often from the whole range of Old Testament Scripture, they never quote from an apocryphal book as the inspired Word of God.

Points to Remember

☑ God has spoken! He has taken the initiative to reveal himself to us.

☑ God carefully prepared chosen individuals to be the channels of his truth.

☑ In God's time and in a wide variety of ways, God began to reveal his message to those he had prepared.

☑ God the Holy Spirit guarded and guided the writing of the message so that the writers recorded God's truth exactly the way God wanted it.

☑ The Bible is the only *inspired* writing—the direct product of God through the styles and personalities of the writers.

☑ Christians believe the Bible is true because Jesus put his stamp of approval on the Bible alone.

☑ God has watched over the transmission of his message so we can have complete confidence in our translations of the original writings.

☑ The Bible is the measuring stick for what Christians believe and how we live.

The Bible in Your Hand

So what about that Bible of yours? Do you open it any time other than when you are in church? Maybe you feel intimidated by the Bible—nervous about reading it on your own. The one fact that this chapter has hammered home is that God *wants* to communicate with you. God is more committed to the process of getting his truth to us than we ever are of discovering what that truth is. So plunge in!

There's another Blockheads book that will help you—*The Bible for Blockheads*. It's an easy-to-follow guide to the books and themes that make up our Bible, but you don't need a guidebook to get started. Carve out five minutes most days to open God's Word. Read one of the gospels or some of the psalms. Think of this as God's message to you for your day. Listen to what God might be saying to your heart.

For more on the origin and transmission of the Bible, check out:

✗ Norman Geisler and William Nix, *From God to Us: How We Got Our Bible*. Chicago: Moody, 1980.

For a stunning visual tour of Bible manuscripts, look at:

✗ Clinton Arnold, *How We Got the Bible: A Visual Journey*. Grand Rapids: Zondervan, 2008.

If you need some direction on how to interpret and understand the Bible, one of the best guides is:

✗ Gordon Fee and Douglas Stuart, *How to Read the Bible for All Its Worth*. 3rd edition. Grand Rapids: Zondervan, 2003.

If you want to explore the Apocrypha, try:

✗ Daniel Harrington, *Invitation to the Apocrypha*. Grand Rapids: Eerdmans, 1999.

CHAPTER 3

More Than the Man Upstairs: God

More Than the Man Upstairs: God

▶ Discover that God exists—and that he is like nothing else!

▶ Some big words about a big God—impress your friends!

▶ Find out a few things God cannot do.

▶ Is God angry or loving—or both?

MR. BLOCKHEAD

HEADS UP

Creating God in Our Image

It seems like everyone has an opinion about God. Just bring up the subject at the next party you attend, and you will hear people say things like this: "Well, I think God is like this," or "I believe in a God like this." We have a tendency to look at God the way we *want* him to be.

In this chapter we will explore what the Bible teaches about God—and the question to ask is not, What do I think God is like? The question to ask is, How does my view of God compare with what the Bible teaches? One of the things we will learn about God is that he is a God who reveals himself. If all we had to rely on to learn about God were our own resources and powers of investigation, we would know very little about God. But the good news is that God has chosen to reveal himself to us. The primary source of reliable information about God is in the Bible. God tells us what he is like in the pages of Scripture.

One thing needs to be made clear right at the beginning: the Bible never tries to *prove* the existence of God. The Bible just assumes that God exists. The first words of the first book proceed on the basis that God is and that he is active in his world: "In the beginning God created the heavens and the earth" (Genesis 1:1). Theologians and philosophers have tried over the centuries to come up with proof that God exists, but the Bible simply states it as fact. If you have trouble with God's existence, it's OK. Just keep reading. God doesn't need me to defend him.

He will make himself real to you if you will come to the Bible with an open mind.

Getting Personal with the Unexplainable

One of the best summaries of who God is that I've come across is this short sentence:

God is the highest being in existence — a living, personal, eternal Spirit.

God is the greatest, highest being there is. He is far above everything and everyone we know. He reigns over all in majesty and power and supreme authority. Theologians refer to God's greatness as the *transcendence* of God. He is above every other being. He is different from anything — and everything — else.

But Christians believe that this awesome, transcendent God has come near to us. God has revealed himself to us, even though no one could force him to reveal anything about himself if he didn't want to do it. God has spoken to us in his creation and in his Word. God has even stepped down into human history and lived here with us when Jesus, God the Son, came to earth. God's willingness to come close to us is described as the *immanence* of God. The eternal, transcendent God has reached all the way down to us.

Christians believe we can know God in a personal way — not because we can somehow reach up to him, but because in love God has reached all the way down to us. God is infinitely greater than any human being, but he wants to know us personally in a relationship of love. Keep that in mind as we explore the character of God together. The more we learn *about* God, the more we come to *know* God. We can never comprehend all that God is, but what we can comprehend should draw our hearts closer to him. God's purpose for creating us, God's purpose for revealing himself to us, is that we should know him.

Help File

ALTERNATE FAITH STYLES

More than 70,000 Australians (.37 percent of the population) identify themselves as followers of the Jedi faith. They draw their beliefs from the *Star Wars* movies. Adherents say they believe in the Force, the spiritual energy that empowers the Jedi warriors like Yoda and Luke Sky-walker. An e-mail campaign has been launched to get the faith recognized as an official religious movement in Australia.

USA Today, August 28, 2002, 1D.

Bible Networking

Psalm 19:1

The heavens declare the glory of God.

Hebrews 3:4

Every house is built by someone, but God is the builder of everything.

Romans 2:15

[The people who do not have God's written law] show that the requirements of the law are written on their hearts, their consciences also bearing witness, and their thoughts now accusing, now even defending them.

What God Is Like

If God is revealed to us in the Bible, the big question we have to ask is, What is God like? The best answer is that God is not like anyone or anything. God is unique, one of a kind, in a class by himself.

That's why God has such condemnation in the Bible for making or worshiping idols. Human beings down through history have tried to picture God by making carvings or setting up holy objects or images or sacred animals as embodiments of a god. But nothing created can

In Other Words

What were we made for? To know God. What aim should we set ourselves in life? To know God. What is the "eternal life" that Jesus gives? Knowledge of God. "This is life eternal, that they might know thee, the only true God, and Jesus Christ, whom thou hast sent" (John 17:3). What is the best thing in life, bringing more joy, delight, and contentment than anything else? Knowledge of God.

J. I. Packer, in *Knowing God* (Downer's Grove, Ill.:
InterVarsity, 1973), 29.

adequately picture the Creator. So God tells his people over and over that we are not to make any graven images or worship any object. God consistently ridicules idols and false gods. They have no power at all!

In fact, the only image of God that correctly and fully reflects the character of the invisible God is Jesus, God the Son. Paul says this in Colossians:

> The Son is the image of the invisible God .... For God was pleased to have all his fullness dwell in him.
>
> Colossians 1:15, 19

Help File

MAKING A CASE FOR THE EXISTENCE OF GOD

Down through the centuries, men and women have thought deeply about God and about the rational evidence for God's existence. Four main arguments have emerged that have been used to try to prove that God exists.

1. *The Ontological Argument.* The very fact that human beings have an idea of God points to the reality of his existence. Every human culture has some desire for and belief in a supreme being.

2. *The Cosmological Argument.* Every effect has a cause. The existence of our universe points back to a beginning. Even totally secular scientists agree that the universe has not always existed. So where did it come from? There must have been a powerful "first cause" for all that exists.

3. *The Teleological Argument.* The order and complexity of nature and the universe point to the existence of a great designer. If you travel to a major world city and come upon a magnificent skyscraper, you have to conclude that someone had designed that building.

In the same way, the complexity of the human body, the beauty of the ocean, and the harmony of our solar system all point toward an intelligent designer.

4. *The Moral Argument.* Human beings have a built-in sense of right and wrong, a moral compass or moral code. Every culture observes a higher law. The sense of right and wrong is evidence of a moral Creator.

Those four arguments make a case for God's existence, but no one is ever argued into becoming a Christian! In the end, belief in God requires just that—belief. God can't be proven in a science laboratory or in a debate session. The arguments for God's existence may help to lower some of the barriers to belief, but, in the end, God calls us to an act of faith.

> Without faith it is impossible to please God, because anyone who comes to him must believe that he exists and that he rewards those who earnestly seek him.
>
> Hebrews 11:6

A STEP OF FAITH

When the Russian cosmonaut Yuri Gagarin returned from orbiting the earth, he declared, "I didn't see any God out there."

The American broadcaster Paul Harvey made this suggestion: "If he had just stepped outside his spacecraft, he would have met God."

If you want to see what God is like look at Jesus. All that God is was made visible in him.

One of the simplest truths about who God is and what God is like is that God is a person. God is not just an impersonal force (like "the Force" in the *Star Wars* movies or like electricity). God is a person. He has all the characteristics of a personal being—he knows, speaks, expresses emotions. Because God is a person and I am a person, we can have a personal relationship. We can communicate. We can grow in our understanding of each other. I can hurt God or grieve God or please God. All the dynamics of human personal relationships enter into my relationship with God.

But beyond the fact that God is a person, God has also revealed aspects of his character to us. In theology books you will see these described as "God's attributes"—the qualities that can correctly be attributed to God. We can't look at every biblical statement about God's character, but I want to focus on a few of the most significant.

The qualities of God's character can be grouped in three categories drawn from three biblical declarations about God:

1. "God is spirit" (John 4:24): *God's unique qualities.* These are the aspects of God's character that make God—well, God! They are qualities you and I will never possess.

2. "God is light" (1 John 1:5): *God's qualities of moral perfection.* These are the aspects of God's character that point to his purity and moral uprightness—qualities that we are called to reproduce in our lives as God's people.

3. "God is love" (1 John 4:8, 16): *God's qualities of goodness.* These are also character traits that can be cultivated in our lives—aspects of God's character that show his love and goodness.

Under each category I will describe some of the prominent qualities and simply list others. Remember, however, that each aspect of

"Are not two sparrows sold for a penny? Yet not one of them will fall to the ground outside your Father's care."

Matthew 10:29

Jesus said to her, "I am the resurrection and the life. Anyone who believes in me will live, even though they die; and whoever lives by believing in me will never die. Do you believe this?"

John 11:25–26

The critical time for our faith isn't at the end of a sermon in church; it's when we've come to the end of our own resources in life. Several times in my life I have sensed God gently—and sometimes not so gently!—nudging me and asking, "Do you really believe this?" Times when the money was running out, when I had no work and could see no prospects. Nine days after the 9/11 attacks when my mother died suddenly on the other side of the world, and to board a flight to go there posed a great risk.

It's not so much believing with my mind, but do I really trust that God is who he says he is? Do I really believe that God is in charge of my life—both the big matters and the tiny details? Is he genuinely concerned with me? Will he take care of me? Do I believe that God is ultimately in control of everything, that not even a sparrow falls to the ground outside the Father's care?

God's character is like a single facet of a magnificent diamond. All of the character traits we find in God are perfections, and they all blend together flawlessly in God's matchless character. Exploring each aspect draws us closer to God in love and adoration and trust. He is an awesome God!

"God Is Spirit": His Unique Qualities

I will never share in these traits. Theologians call them the *incommunicable* aspects of God's character. They can't be passed on to someone. They are true only of God.

- *God is a spirit.* God has no body. He is not limited by space. God is invisible and pure spirit.

    "God is spirit, and his worshipers must worship in the Spirit and in truth."

    John 4:24

In Other Words

Because God knows all things perfectly, he knows no thing better than any other thing, but all things equally well. He never discovers anything, he is never surprised, never amazed. He never wonders about anything.

A. W. Tozer, in *The Knowledge of the Holy* (New York: Harper and Row, 1961), 62.

- *God is eternal.* God has no beginning and no end; he is not limited by time. The answer to the old question Who created God? is that no one created him. He has always been.

  > Now to the King eternal, immortal, invisible, the only God,
  > be honor and glory for ever and ever.
  > > 1 Timothy 1:17

  Other passages to check out: Deuteronomy 33:27; Psalms 41:13; 90:2; Lamentations 5:19; Colossians 1:17; Hebrews 1:10–11.
- *God is all-powerful.* The big-time theological word is *omnipotent* (from two Latin words meaning "all" and "powerful"). God never gets tired; he never needs rest. He is greater than Satan or any angel or *all* the angels!

  > "Hallelujah!
  > For our Lord God Almighty reigns."
  > > Revelation 19:6

  Other verses: Psalm 115:3; Amos 4:13; Matthew 19:26; Philippians 3:21.
- *God is all knowing.* Big word = *omniscient*; God has infinite knowledge of all things. Nothing is hidden from him. He is never

Help File

"ALMIGHTY"

The word *Almighty* is used more than 300 times in the Bible—only and always to describe God. God has revealed himself as the Almighty to Abraham (Genesis 17:1), to Moses (Exodus 6:3), to Christian believers (2 Corinthians 6:18), and to the universe in Revelation (1:8; 19:6).

stumped; he never learns; nothing is outside the realm of his understanding (even college-level algebra).

> Great is our Lord and mighty in power;
>> his understanding has no limits.
>>>> Psalm 147:5

Some more: Job 34:21; Psalm 139:1–6; 1 Corinthians 2:11–12; Hebrews 4:13; 1 John 3:20.

- *God is present everywhere.* Or, everything is in God's presence, including the past and the future, including every person and every angel. Big word: *omnipresence.*

> Where can I go from your Spirit?
>> Where can I flee from your presence?
> If I go up to the heavens, you are there;
>> If I make my bed in the depths, you are there.
>>>> Psalm 139:7–8

Check out: Deuteronomy 4:39; Joshua 1:9; 2 Chronicles 16:9; Isaiah 66:1; Jeremiah 23:24; Acts 17:27; Hebrews 13:5.

- *God is unchanging.* Another big word = *immutable*, which means "not changeable." That doesn't mean God is old-fashioned or out-of-date. It means that his character is always the same. God is never in a bad mood. His love, for example, is the same today as it will be in a million years and on into eternity.

> "I the LORD do not change."
>>>> Malachi 3:6

And also: Numbers 23:19; Psalms 33:11; 102:27; Hebrews 1:12; James 1:17.

- *God is sovereign.* The word *sovereign* means "to be in control," "to have total authority and power." No one and nothing is outside God's knowledge and power.

> "The Most High is sovereign over the kingdoms on earth
> and gives them to anyone he wishes."
>>>> Daniel 4:25

In addition: Exodus 15:18; Psalm 9:7; Isaiah 45:9–12; Daniel 4:35; Acts 17:24; Romans 9:20–21; Ephesians 1:14.

Other distinctive attributes of God are:

- *God is transcendent.* He created all things but he is greater than his creation and exists apart from it (1 Kings 8:27; Acts 17:24–28).
- *God is free,* uncoerced by any outside force (Isaiah 40:13–14).
- *God is incomprehensible.* We will never reach the depth of God's character or knowledge or goodness (Romans 11:34; 1 Corinthians 2:11).
- *God is self-sufficient.* He doesn't rely on air or food or water for his existence. (Psalm 50:12–13: John 5:26)

"God Is Light": His Moral Perfection

When the apostle John declared that "God is light" in 1 John 1:5, he went on to write, "In him there is no darkness at all." God is absolutely transparent. He has nothing to hide—no skeletons in his closet, no past failures to keep under wraps, nothing going on that he hopes you will not discover. Every corner of God's character is illuminated with brilliant light. That doesn't mean God is easy to understand. He's not! He's the infinite God. What it means is that no matter how deeply we explore God's character, we will never find something in God that is wrong or twisted or evil.

- *God is holy.* God is set apart from everything that is evil or wrong. He is morally perfect in every way—and God desires holiness in his people. That doesn't mean we walk around in white robes with

SOME THINGS GOD CANNOT DO

When we think about God's all-powerfulness, we sometimes say, "God can do anything." But the Bible makes it clear that there are some things God *cannot* do.

- God cannot act in a way that contradicts his nature. God is holy; so he cannot act in an unholy way. Habakkuk 1:13 says that God cannot look at sin and wrong and call it good. James 1:13 says that God cannot sin. He cannot act against his character as God.
- God cannot act contrary to his Word. God cannot lie (Titus 1:2). Whatever God has promised he will do.
- God also chooses not to do certain

things. He could have spared Jesus from the agonizing death of the cross, but he chose not to spare his own Son (Romans 8:32). God has the power to deliver us from any difficulty or trial, but he may allow us to endure that trial for his own good purposes.

You've probably wrestled with the old question, "Can God make a rock so large that he can't lift it?" It's really a nonsense question. God can do anything! He is the God who works wonders. But God's actions are always in line with his character, his Word, and his will.

a ten-pound Bible. It means our lives are pure. We are set apart from wrong and are reserved for God.

> "Be holy, because I am holy."
>
> Leviticus 11:44; 1 Peter 1:16

In addition read: Exodus 15:11; Psalm 99:5, 9; Isaiah 6:3–4; John 17:11; Hebrews 7:26; 1 Peter 1:15; Revelation 4:8.

- *God is just and right.* The Bible's word is *righteous.* God does what is right and he is the one who determines what is right. He pursues justice and honor. Nothing is swept under the rug with God. Eventually every wrong will be made right; every injustice will receive justice. God doesn't ignore evil; he judges it.

> Righteousness and justice are the foundations of your throne;
>   love and faithfulness go before you.
>
> Psalm 89:14

> He is the Rock, his works are perfect,
>   and all his ways are just.
> A faithful God who does no wrong,
>   upright and just is he.
>
> Deuteronomy 32:4

Help File

HE OR SHE? FATHER OR MOTHER?

The Bible consistently refers to God with masculine pronouns. God is called "he," not "she" or "it." But the reality is that God has no gender. God has no body. The Bible talks about God's eyes and ears and mighty right arm, but God the Father is pure spirit and therefore has none of those body parts. The Bible uses the language of God's eyes and arm only to help us understand how God works.

Some people don't like all the masculine names and images for God so they try to be more inclusive in how they describe God. They will call God "our Father *and Mother* in heaven."

Most Christians reject this terminology not because we think God is literally a male but because the Bible refers to him as "our Father." It's a matter of faithfulness to what the Bible says.

It is interesting, however, that occasionally the Bible uses distinctly feminine images to picture God. Jesus told a story about a woman who had lost one of her ten coins. Her diligent search for the lost coin is a picture of God's commitment to search for those who are lost and separated from him (Luke 15:8–10). Jesus also pictured himself as a mother hen who would have gathered the people of Jerusalem under her sheltering wings (Matthew 23:37). The Old Testament prophet Isaiah uses the picture of a gentle mother to give us insight into the nurturing love of God:

> "As a mother comforts her child,
>   so will I comfort you."
>
> Isaiah 66:13

Check also: Ezra 9:15; Psalms 11:7; 145:17; Isaiah 11:5; 30:18; Romans 3:26; 1 Corinthians 1:30; 1 John 2:29.

- *God is faithful.* God can be trusted to do what he has promised to do. If God promises in his Word to forgive us when we confess our sins to him (which he does promise in 1 John 1:9), then we can count on his faithfulness to do it.

> Because of the LORD's great love we are not consumed,
>> for his compassions never fail.
> They are new every morning;
>> great is your faithfulness.
>>>> Lamentations 3:22–23

And also: Deuteronomy 7:9; Psalms 36:5; 89:8; Isaiah 11:5; 1 Corinthians 10:13; 1 Thessalonians 5:24; 2 Timothy 2:13; Hebrews 10:23.

- *God is wise and true.* God in his wisdom always chooses what is best—the best goals and the best way to reach those goals. God's plans and desires are perfect. He always speaks the truth. He never acts in a deceptive manner. God can be trusted. The Bible refers to him as "the only wise God" (Romans 16:27).

> How many are your works, LORD!
>> In wisdom you made them all;
>> the earth is full of your creatures.
>>>> Psalm 104:24

Read: Isaiah 40:28; 55:8; Jeremiah 10:10–11; John 17:3, 17; 1 John 5:6.

In Other Words

It should be a cause for thanksgiving and gratitude when we realize that righteousness and omnipotence are both possessed by God. If he were a God of perfect righteousness without power to carry out that righteousness, he would not be worthy of worship and we would have no guarantee that justice will ultimately prevail in the universe. But if he were a God of unlimited power, yet without righteousness in his character, how unthinkably horrible the universe would be!

Wayne Grudem, in *Bible Doctrine* (Grand Rapids: Zondervan, 1999), 93–94.

- *God displays his wrath against evil.* We tend to look at anger or hatred as a negative. I've even heard God's wrath referred to as "God's dark side." But remember that every aspect of God's character is a perfection. God has no dark side. If God is pure and holy, we would expect him to have a hatred for what is impure and wrong and perverted. That doesn't mean that God is sitting up in heaven with a scowl on his face, looking for someone to zap with a bolt of lightning! It means that whenever God is confronted with wrong or evil or injustice, he always displays one consistent attitude — hatred of anything that is opposed to his holy character.

> The wrath of God is being revealed from heaven against all the godlessness and wickedness of human beings.
>
> Romans 1:18

More: Psalms 2:4–5; 95:10–11; Isaiah 13:6–22; Amos 4:6–13; Colossians 3:5–6; Hebrews 10:30–31; Revelation 10:9–15.

- *God is patient.* When we think of God's wrath and his anger against what is evil, we should at the same time be thankful for his patience. God purposefully delays his judgment on those who do wrong to give them a chance to repent and to turn to God for forgiveness. God's wrath is tempered by his compassion.

> The LORD is compassionate and gracious,
> slow to anger . . .
>
> Psalm 103:8

And then: Psalm 103:8–13; Jonah 4:2; Micah 7:18–19; Romans 2:4; 2 Peter 3:9–10.

Other moral perfections in God are:

- *his jealousy,* his zealous protection of his name and his people (Exodus 20:5; Isaiah 48:11; 2 Corinthians 11:2).
- *his goodness* (Psalm 100:5; Matthew 7:11; James 1:17; Hebrews 12:10).

"God Is Love": His Capacity to Care

The most astonishing information the Bible gives us about this great, transcendent, holy God is that he is a God of love. He doesn't simply look down on us as his creatures and demand our worship or else. He comes near us in compassion and love. God offers us mercy and grace and forgiveness. If you think of God as an austere, distant, grumpy Ruler with a club in his hand, you have missed some wonderful aspects of his character.

- *God is loving.* The fundamental fact revealed about God in the Bible is summarized in what is probably the best-known verse in the Bible—John 3:16: "For God so loved the world that he gave his one and only Son, that whoever believes in him shall not perish but have eternal life." God's love is the aspect of God's character that most people know about. It's also the aspect of God's character that most people misunderstand. They think that God's love is a warm, fuzzy feeling God gets. In fact, in many people's minds, God is so overcome by the feeling of love that he overlooks almost everything bad we do. In their thinking, God is a doting, somewhat forgetful grandfather who is easily persuaded to give us what we want if we just pay a little attention to him once in a while. But we've already seen that God is holy and all-knowing and pure, so the "senile old grandfather" picture just won't work.

"If your enemy is hungry, feed him;
    if he is thirsty, give him something to drink.
In doing this, you will heap burning coals on his head."

Do not be overcome by evil, but overcome evil with good.
Romans 12:20–21

I don't have great enemies. I try to lead my life according to this biblical directive: "If it is possible, as far as it depends on you, live at peace with everyone" (Romans 12:18).

I do have one enemy when I'm trying to work and that is *noise*—loud music, children playing football, workers repairing the road. It was during this last kind of interruption that God spoke to me.

"Go and make them a cup of tea."

"What—me?" I thought.

"Yes!"

So after arguing with the Lord for a few minutes, I cautiously went out. They saw this guy coming and clearly thought, "Here's another one who's come to complain." You should have seen their faces when I offered them a cup of tea or coffee! They were so grateful! I've even done it a couple more times since.

In Other Words

When we looked at God's wisdom, we saw something of his mind; when we thought of his power, we saw something of his hand and his arm; when we considered his word, we learned about his mouth; but now, contemplating his love, we are to look in his heart. We shall stand on holy ground.

J. I. Packer, in *Knowing God* (Downers Grove, Ill.: InterVarsity, 1973), 108.

God's love is a love of action, a love of choice. God chooses to act toward us in the best possible way by giving his Son, Jesus, to provide the opportunity for unholy people to have a relationship with a holy God. God's love does have an emotional aspect to it. He does genuinely care for us. But his love emerges primarily from his decision to act in love toward us.

This truth gives us insight into our love for others too. When Jesus told his followers to "love their enemies," he wasn't asking us to try and whip up warm, cuddly feelings about people who dislike us. Jesus was telling us to love them with a Godlike love, to choose to act properly and for their good, regardless of their response to us. We find it easiest to love the lovable and the lovely; God's love reaches to the rebellious and unlovely.

> God demonstrates his own love for us in this: While we were still sinners, Christ died for us.
>
> Romans 5:8

Some other passages to read: Psalm 57:10; Jeremiah 31:3; John 16:27; Ephesians 2:4; 1 John 3:1; 3:16; 4:8–9, 16; Revelation 1:5.

- *God is merciful and gracious.* Grace and mercy go together. *Mercy* is when God does not give us what we justly deserve. Every one of us has done things and said things and fantasized about things that are against the pure and holy character of God. We deserve judgment. But God in his mercy has not brought that judgment on us.

Grace is God's determination to do good to those who deserve the opposite of his goodness. We deserve punishment or judgment; God in grace makes us his own children. We are rescued from our lost condition not because we are inherently good or because we have earned that reward by our virtuous deeds; we are rescued by God's grace alone.

So mercy spares us from wrath; grace gives us an abundance of good gifts. Mercy saves us from hell; grace takes us to heaven. The apostle Peter calls God "the God of all grace" (1 Peter 5:10). The classic Old Testament expression of God's grace comes from Exodus 34:6:

> [The LORD] passed in front of Moses, proclaiming, "The LORD, the LORD, the compassionate and gracious God, slow to anger, abounding in love and faithfulness."

Read these too: Psalms 86:15; 116:5; John 1:14; Romans 3:23–24; Ephesians 2:4, 8–9; Titus 3:5; 1 Peter 1:3.

- *God is forgiving.* God's holy purity demands justice for wrong, but God's gracious heart is willing to forgive. God doesn't *forget* sin. Sin is still judged, but someone else pays the penalty. Because someone else willingly paid the penalty of our wrong, God is free and eager to forgive those who receive his forgiveness.

> You, Lord, are forgiving and good.
>> Psalm 86:5

Additional info: Numbers 14:19; Psalms 32:1–2; 78:38; 85:2; 86:5; Isaiah 43:25; Daniel 9:9; Acts 10:43; 13:38; Ephesians 1:7; 4:32.

- *God is generous.* God loves to give. He doesn't give expecting to get a gift in return. He doesn't give a stone when we ask for bread. He gives good gifts simply because it is his nature to give. God gives generously and freely and joyfully. Do you think God is tightfisted and sour-faced and that every blessing has to be pried out of his hand? The God of the Bible is generous. He loves to bless us.

> You [the LORD] open your hand
>   and satisfy the desires of every living thing.
>> Psalm 145:16

And also: Psalms 84:11; 107:8–9; 145:9; Matthew 7:11; Luke 11:11–13; James 1:5, 17.

Other qualities of our loving God:

- *comforting* (Isaiah 66:13; John 14:1; 2 Corinthians 1:3–4)
- *understanding* (Hebrews 10:15)

Points to Remember

- ☑ The primary source of reliable information about God is the Bible.

- ☑ God is the highest being in existence.

- ☑ Because God is a personal being, you and I can know God in a personal way.

- ☑ God is not like anyone or anything. He is unique, one of a kind.

- ☑ Every aspect of God's character is a perfection.

- ☑ God is holy, absolutely pure.

- ☑ God loves us not with warm sentiment but with practical action for our good.

- ☑ We will never reach the end of God—his character, his mercy, or his love.

Whom Have I in Heaven but You?

Asaph wrote several of the Old Testament psalms. He seemed to struggle at times with the character of God, and he wasn't afraid to ask hard questions: Where is God when bad things happen? Why do the godly people suffer but evil people seem to have easy lives? Why am I always broke but my unbelieving neighbor has plenty of money? After one long, difficult debate with God, Asaph was drawn back to what he knew about the perfect character of God, and he ended his struggle with this question: "Whom have I in heaven but you?" (Psalm 73:25).

Asaph's answer reveals that his restless heart had found rest in the holy, loving, compassionate character of God:

My flesh and my heart may fail,
    but God is the strength of my heart
    and my portion forever.
                              Psalm 73:26

Learning about God is not just an exercise in the depths of theology. The point is not just to memorize big, important-sounding words so you can impress your pastor. The point of knowing more about God is to grow in your relationship with him and to grasp personally how deeply you can trust and rely on him. The knowledge of God also prompts us to love him more deeply and worship him more fervently.

You and I will never reach the end of God. We'll never know all there is to know about him. We won't even exhaust *one* of his character traits, much less the fullness of who he is. But every small step we take in our understanding, every insight we grasp as we read the Bible, secures our

Digging Deeper

hearts more firmly to him. The God revealed in the Bible is the only true God—a God majestic in power and wisdom, a God who loves us deeply, and a God who cares about the smallest details of our lives.

Two classic books on the character of God that are worth reading and rereading!

✗ J. I. Packer, *Knowing God*. Downers Grove, Ill.: InterVarsity, 1973. A wonderful exploration of who God is. Not light reading, but it's not a light subject!

✗ A. W. Tozer, *The Knowledge of the Holy*. New York: Harper and Row, 1961. Your heart and mind will be stirred to worship and to new levels of trust in God.

CHAPTER 4

Untangling the Trinity

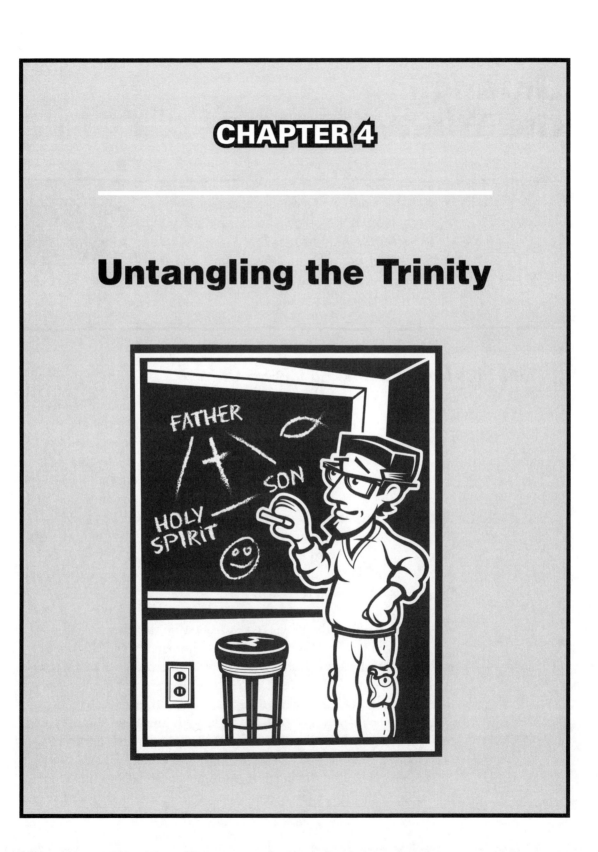

Untangling the Trinity

- ▶ Try to get your brain around a puzzling reality.
- ▶ Three persons are called God in the Bible. Do you know who they are?
- ▶ Can an agnostic and an atheist get along?
- ▶ Find out why we believe in the Trinity and why it matters.

One Plus One Plus One Equals — One!

The God of the Bible is an awesome God. But in our exploration of God's character in the last chapter we left out one important point. Christians believe that God is a trinity. He is three-in-one (which is what *trinity*, or *tri-unity*, means). I'll tell you right at the beginning that the biblical teaching on the Trinity will stretch your brain. There's an element of mystery in this belief that challenges our minds, but isn't that what we expect when we try to figure out what God is like? He is the infinite God and we are limited human beings. In the end, we just have to take God's word for some things. We accept by faith what he has revealed about himself. Do we fully understand? No. Will we ever reach the depths of who God is? Never.

What brings Christians to believe in God's tri-unity are two clear biblical statements. First, the Bible is consistently firm that there is only one true God. You will find that declaration all through the Old Testament, most clearly in Israel's confession of faith in Deuteronomy 6:4: "Hear, O Israel: The LORD our God, the LORD is one." The prophet Isaiah records the same truth as God speaks, "I am the LORD, and there is no other; apart from me there is no God" (Isaiah 45:5). In the New Testament we find the same truth. The apostle Paul, for instance, writes, "For there is one God" (1 Timothy 2:5), and, "There is only one God" (Romans 3:30).

The second biblical statement that prompts us to believe that God is a trinity is that three separate persons are referred to as God. The essence of the Trinity is that one God exists in three persons—God the Father, God the Son, and God the Holy Spirit. Each member of the Trinity is distinct and each is fully God, and yet they all make up the single entity called God. We do *not* have three Gods. We worship three persons in one God. God does not have three forms—in the past as God the Father, then as Jesus, and third as the Holy Spirit. The three persons exist and function together. God is one; three persons are called God. See, I told you this would stretch your mind!

God in Three Persons

Maybe some more biblical information will help. I want you to see that this is not just some difficult doctrine cooked up by theologians with too much time on their hands. The teaching about the Trinity comes directly from Scripture.

The Bible clearly distinguishes between the three persons of the Trinity. The Father is not the Son. Jesus, God the Son, is not the Holy Spirit. John 1:1–2 says this:

> In the beginning was the Word [a name for Jesus], and the Word was with God [Jesus is distinct from God the Father], and the Word was God [Jesus was as much God as God the Father is]. He was with God [distinct] in the beginning.

TECHNO-SPEAK

You will hear these words bandied about in our culture, and you should really know what they mean:

- *Monotheism* is the belief that there is only one God. Jews, Christians, and Muslims are monotheists.
- An *agnostic* is a person who can't say with certainty that God exists. They have no basis for belief or denial.
- An *atheist* is a person who is convinced that there is no God.

- *Polytheism* is belief in many gods. The ancient Greeks were polytheists because they acknowledged and worshiped several gods and goddesses.
- *Pantheism* sees God in everything. God is one with the universe, not separate from it. Hindus are pantheists.
- *Dualism* is the belief that a good god and an evil god battle it out for supremacy. The religion of Zoroastrianism is a dualistic religion.

In Other Words

[The idea of the Trinity] is so obscured from a human standpoint that no one would have invented it. We do not hold the doctrine of the Trinity because it is self-evident or logically cogent. We hold it because God has revealed this is what he is like.

Millard Erickson, in *Introducing Christian Doctrine* (2nd ed.; Grand Rapids: Baker, 2001), 115.

That's pretty clear! Both God the Father and Jesus the Word are called God, and yet they are marked out as distinctly different persons. Jesus is always set apart from God the Father as a person. In 1 John 2:1, John writes, "If anybody does sin, we have an advocate with the Father—Jesus Christ, the Righteous One." The only way this verse makes sense is if there are two distinct persons.

The Holy Spirit is also distinguished from God the Father and God the Son. Jesus told his disciples in John 14:26—"The Advocate, the Holy Spirit [person #1], whom the Father [person #2] will send in my name [person #3], will teach you all things."

All three members of the Trinity are mentioned together several times in Scripture. Here are the key references. I've emphasized the names in each verse:

- When Jesus was baptized, all three members of the Trinity were present—"When all the people were being baptized, *Jesus* was baptized too. And as he was praying, heaven was opened and the *Holy Spirit* descended on him in bodily form like a dove. And a *voice* came from heaven: "You are my Son, whom I love; with you I am well pleased" (Luke 3:21–22; read also Matthew 3:16–17).
- In Matthew 28:19–20, Jesus spoke these words to his followers just before he ascended into heaven: "Therefore go and make disciples of all nations, baptizing them in the name of the *Father* and of the *Son* and of the *Holy Spirit*, and teaching them to obey

everything I have commanded you." There is only one name but three persons.

- As the apostle Paul closes his second letter to the Corinthians, he writes, "May the grace of the *Lord Jesus Christ*, and the love of *God*, and the fellowship of the *Holy Spirit* be with you all."

Other passages to check out: 1 Corinthians 12:4–6; Ephesians 4:4–6; 1 Peter 1:2; Jude 20–21.

The mention of these three names together implies that they are on an equal plane. They are all divine beings. Imagine what it would sound like to read in Matthew 28:19—"baptizing them in the name of the Father and of the Son and of Pastor Jones." We would immediately realize that a created being (Pastor Jones) had been placed inappropriately on an equal level with God.

Three Persons as God

The final biblical support for our belief in the Trinity is that each person—the Father, the Son, and the Spirit—is called God in the Bible.

Help File

HINTS OF THE TRINITY IN THE OLD TESTAMENT

The truth of God's tri-unity is revealed clearly in the New Testament, but even in the Old Testament we find some hints of a plurality of persons in one God.

- **God sometimes uses plural pronouns to refer to himself**.

   "Let *us* make human beings in *our* image, in *our* likeness" (Genesis 1:26, italics added).

   "Then I heard the voice of the Lord saying, 'Whom shall I send? And who will go for *us*?'" (Isaiah 6:8, italics added).

   Some interpreters refer to these plural pronouns as the "we" of majesty, but such use was unknown in the ancient world.

- **God addresses another being like himself**.

   In Psalm 110:1 (NIV), David writes,
   "The LORD says to my Lord:
      'Sit at my right hand.'"

   In the New Testament Jesus used this passage to prove that the Messiah would be more than a man and more than David's son. The Messiah would also be David's Lord. (See Matthew 22:41–46; Acts 2:33–36.)

- **Isaiah 48:16 seems to refer to three persons who are revered as divine beings**.

   "Now the *Sovereign LORD* has
      sent *me*,
      endowed with his *Spirit*"
   (italics added).

In Other Words

I have a confession to make. Ever since I began to believe in God (which has taken place only in my adult life), I have pictured God as ... alone. Sovereign, powerful, all that. But by himself. Perhaps the notion sprang from the fact that I felt myself to be alone in the universe. Or perhaps it came from religious images of God seated on a great throne way up there ... somewhere. How wonderful to discover that God has never been alone. He has always been Trinity — Father, Son, and Holy Spirit. God has always been a fellowship. This whole story began with something relational.

John Eldredge, in *Epic* (Nashville: Nelson, 2004), 20.

- *God the Father is clearly called God.* Jesus refers to the "heavenly Father" as "God" (Matthew 6:30, 32). In John 6:27, Jesus refers to the Father as "God the Father."
- *Jesus is also called God.* We've already looked at John 1:1 — "the Word was God." In John 20:28, the apostle Thomas falls down before Jesus after Jesus had risen from the dead and exclaimed, "My Lord and my God!" Jesus didn't rebuke Thomas or correct him. Instead, Jesus accepted Thomas's acknowledgment of his deity. (There is a longer discussion of the biblical evidence for Jesus' "God-ness" in chapter 2.)
- *The Holy Spirit is called God too.* In Acts 5:3–4, the apostle Peter confronted a man who was lying about money from a property sale with these words: "How is it that Satan has so filled your heart that you have lied to the Holy Spirit ...? You have not lied just to human beings but to God." (You will find a full exploration of the deity of the Holy Spirit in chapter 5.)

The point is this: three persons who are distinct from each other are called God — but there is only one God. The biblical teaching of the Trinity takes all that the Bible teaches into account and comes to the conclusion that the one God exists as a tri-unity — God the Father,

PROBLEMS WITH THE TRINITY

Down through the centuries of Christian belief, certain people or groups have had a difficult time with the idea of the Trinity. They end up denying one (or more) of the biblical statements about God, which leads them into error (or, in church-speak, into heresy). Here are a few erroneous teachings to watch out for:

- Some people have denied that there are three distinct persons in the Trinity. They believe that only one person exists who appears to us in different "modes" at different times. (The teaching is called "modalism.") For example, in the Old Testament God revealed himself to human beings as "the Father." In the Gospels, the same divine person appeared as "the Son" in Jesus. Today, this one God reveals himself as "the Spirit." Here's the problem with this view: What about when Jesus prays to the Father? Was he praying to himself? Or how about Jesus' statement that the Father would send the Holy Spirit? It doesn't make sense if they were all the same person.

- Another misdirected approach has been to claim that God the Father was the one true God and that Jesus and the Holy Spirit were not God. A man named Arius came up with this approach in the early centuries of the church. The view is still referred to as Arianism. Arius taught that the Son of God was created by God the Father. The Son is therefore a heavenly being who is greater than the rest of creation but who is not equal to the Father. The Holy Spirit in the Arian view is just the power or energy of God, not a person. The Arian view is held today by Jehovah's Witnesses. Their own translation of the Bible in John 1:1 reads, "In the beginning was the Word, and the Word was with God, and the Word was a god" (New World Translation). The Arian view was condemned at the Council of Nicea in AD 325. The Nicene Creed went on to claim the full deity of Jesus and say that he was "of the same substance as the Father."

- Another (less popular) explanation of the Trinity is the belief in three gods. The Church of Jesus Christ of Latter-day Saints (Mormons) holds to the belief that there are many gods. Jehovah, the god of our world, was the father of Jesus in a literal sense, and Jesus eventually reached the level of godhood himself. The Jesus of Mormon theology is not the Jesus revealed in the New Testament whom Christians worship as the eternal God.

God the Son, and God the Spirit. All are equally God, and we can come to God through any of the three. Does it all make perfect sense to our minds? No. Does it agree with all that God has revealed about himself in the Bible? Yes.

May the grace of the Lord Jesus Christ, and the love of God, and the fellowship of the Holy Spirit be with you all.
2 Corinthians 13:14

I've wanted to preach a sermon on this verse for some years but have never gotten around to it. There are a few things about it that puzzle me, and since we're discussing the complex matter of the Trinity, it doesn't seem out of place to add slightly to that complexity.

Why does Paul begin with the Lord Jesus Christ? If I were writing it, I'd begin with the Father. Maybe it's because we can all associate most closely with the perfect God-man Jesus Christ: he is one of us. We need his love day by day. We don't deserve it any day.

Where does the grace of Christ come from? The love of God the Father—his eternal, generous commitment to, affection for, and delight in all people. His love is seen especially in the sacrifice of his Son on the cross (John 3:16).

I can almost hear you saying, "So what?" That's where the fellowship of the Spirit comes in. The Spirit of God wants to lead us on, to partner with us in spiritual growth. I'm a lousy swimmer, and a couple of years ago some friends took us to Mexico. One day the deal was I'd teach my Mexican friends English, and they would teach me to swim. As I put my head below water in that swimming pool just south of Cancun, I realized I hadn't moved on in my swimming skills in forty years!

That's not how we're to be! We are to grow in grace (2 Peter 3:18), to keep in step with the Spirit (Galatians 5:25), to keep up with where the Spirit wants to lead us.

Equal in God-ness, Different in Function

God the Father, God the Son, and God the Holy Spirit are equal in their deity. The Father is not "more God" than the Son. All are equally worthy of our adoration and worship and obedience. But in the out-working of God's eternal plan, the three members of the Trinity took on different roles. The Son submitted himself to the Father. God the Son willingly agreed to be the one who would come to earth and who would pay the penalty for sin. He placed himself under the Father's authority.

That's why Jesus would say, "I do nothing on my own but speak just what the Father has taught me" (John 8:28). He went on to say, "I always do what pleases [the Father]" (John 8:29). Jesus willingly, voluntarily, joyfully submitted to the Father.

The Holy Spirit submitted to both the Father and the Son. Jesus was sent by the Father, but the Spirit was sent by the Father and the Son (John 14:26; 16:7). The three persons of the Trinity are equal in nature

In Other Words

An ordinary simple Christian kneels down to say his prayers. He is trying to get in touch with God. But if he is a Christian he knows that what is prompting him to pray is also God: God, so to speak, inside him. But he also knows that all his real knowledge of God comes through Christ, the Man who was God — that Christ is standing beside him, helping him to pray, praying for him. You see what is happening. God is the thing to which he is praying — the goal he is trying to reach. God is also the thing inside him which is pushing him on — the motive power. God is also the road or bridge along which he is being pushed to that goal. So that the whole threefold life of the three-personal Being is actually going on in that ordinary little bedroom where an ordinary man is saying his prayers.

C. S. Lewis, in *Mere Christianity* (New York: HarperCollins, 2001), 163.

Bible Networking

1 Thessalonians 1:3 – 5

We remember before our God and Father your work produced by faith, your labor prompted by love, and your endurance inspired by hope in our Lord Jesus Christ.

For we know, brothers and sisters loved by God, that he has chosen you, because our gospel came to you not simply with words but also with power, with the Holy Spirit and deep conviction.

1 Corinthians 2:2 – 5

For I resolved to know nothing while I was with you except Jesus Christ and him crucified. I came to you in weakness with great fear and trembling. My message and my preaching were not with wise and persuasive words, but with a demonstration of the Spirit's power, so that your faith might not rest on human wisdom, but on God's power.

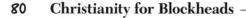

In Other Words

Praise ye the Father! for his loving kindness . . .
Praise ye the Savior! great is his compassion . . .
Praise ye the Spirit! Comforter of Israel . . .
Praise ye the Triune God!

> Hymn: "Praise Ye the Triune God"; words by Elizabeth R. Charles

and glory and power, but in their function in God's plan, the Father is first, the Son is second, and the Spirit is third.

The Trinity at Work

In every great activity of God we see the Trinity involved. In *creation*, for example, God the Father was the prime mover in initiating the act of creation (Genesis 1:1). Jesus, God the Son, was the agent of creation—"through him all things were made" (John 1:3). The Holy Spirit was also at work in creation as he hovered over the earth, bringing life and order and beauty to the Son's creation (Genesis 1:2; Job 33:4).

Help File

BANISHMENT

First John 5:7 in the King James Version of the Bible seems to be the perfect verse to defend belief in the Trinity.

> For there are three that bear record in heaven, the Father, the Word, and the Holy Ghost [Spirit]: and these three are one.

What the verse says is a true reflection of what Christians believe, but the overwhelming evidence is that this verse was not an original part of 1 John. Most likely a scribe or pastor wrote these words in the margin of a manuscript, and a later copyist then inserted them as part of the text. The verse appears in only a few very late manuscripts and in none of our earliest copies of 1 John. All modern versions of the Bible remove these lines from John's letter. So—as tempting as it may be to appeal to this "verse"—we are adding words to the Bible if we do, words that did not originally appear there.

☑ Christians believe that God exists as a fellowship—a tri-unity, or trinity.

☑ The Bible clearly says that there is only one God, but three distinct persons are referred to as God—God the Father, God the Son, and God the Holy Spirit.

☑ If we deny any one aspect of the biblical teaching on the Trinity, we will end up on a false path.

☑ All three persons in the Trinity are equally God and are worthy of our adoration and worship.

☑ The members of the Trinity have different functions in the plan of God—the Son submits to the Father; the Spirit submits to the Father and the Son.

☑ In every great work of God, all three persons of the Trinity are involved.

The Trinity is active in the *salvation* of human beings too. The plan of redemption was the Father's, but God the Son came as the one who would die on the cross. Today it is God the Spirit who draws us to believe and indwells those who follow Jesus.

Jesus' *resurrection* was certainly a mighty work of God, and the Trinity was also involved in that powerful event. It was God who raised Jesus to life (Acts 2:32), and yet Jesus himself said, "I have authority to lay [my life] down and authority to take it up again" (John 10:18). At the same time it was "through the Spirit of holiness" that Jesus "was appointed the Son of God in power by his resurrection from the dead" (Romans 1:4).

God's *providence*—his care for us and his provision for the world—is another work of God that includes each person in the Trinity. God the Father maintains and sustains the world. He knows when a tiny sparrow swoops to the ground (Matthew 10:29), and he knows every need in your life. God is able to work in all things for the good of those who love him (Romans 8:28). God can take life's worst tragedies and bring glory to himself and good to us. Luck or fate or our astrological signs are not the controlling factors of our lives. God is the one in control. Nothing just happens.

God the Son has a role to play in God's providential care too. Jesus actively sustains all things by his power (Hebrews 1:3)—"in him all things hold together" (Colossians 1:17). The universe is sustained by the power of God the Son.

ESSENTIALS: THE NICENE CREED

Primarily because of the false teaching of Arius and his denial of the Trinity, the leaders of the early church met in council in the city of Nicea in AD 325. They stated the orthodox, biblical view of the Trinity in a written summary or a creed. The Nicene Creed was later expanded at the Council of Constantinople in 381. It is one of the great statements of the Christian faith. In some churches the Nicene Creed is read (or spoken from memory) as part of their worship service.

I believe in one God the Father Almighty,
Maker of heaven and earth,
And of all things visible and invisible.

And in one Lord Jesus Christ, the only-begotten Son of God,
Begotten of the Father before all worlds,
God of God, Light of Light,
Very God of very God,
Begotten, not made,
Being of one substance with the Father,
By whom all things were made:
Who for us men, and for our salvation, came down from heaven,
And was incarnate by the Holy Ghost of the virgin Mary,
And was made man,
And was crucified also for us under Pontius Pilate.
He suffered and was buried,
And the third day he rose again according to the Scriptures,
And ascended into heaven,
And sitteth on the right hand of the Father.
And he shall come again with glory to judge both the quick and the dead:
Whose kingdom shall have no end.

And I believe in the Holy Ghost,
The Lord and giver of life,
Who proceedeth from the Father and the Son,
Who with the Father and the Son together is worshiped and glorified,
Who spake by the prophets.
And I believe one Catholick and Apostolick Church.
I acknowledge one Baptism for the remission of sins.
And I look for the Resurrection of the dead,
And the life of the world to come.
Amen.

Book of Common Prayer (1662)

The Spirit is active in directing and guarding our hearts and minds. Paul, in Galatians 5:25, tells Christians that we "live by the Spirit" and urges us to "keep in step with the Spirit" as he guides us day after day.

The fellowship of the Trinity extends to all of God's works—and the reality of the Trinity should affect our lives in very practical ways. It's easy to focus on one member of the Trinity to the exclusion of the others. Some Christians find it easier to hold closely to God the Father as our Creator and Master. Other Christians prefer to focus on Jesus as Savior and Friend. Still other Christians seem to look exclusively to the Spirit to sustain their spiritual life. We certainly aren't "wrong" to focus on one member of the Trinity. Each one is fully God. But the writers of the New Testament preferred to draw all three persons of the Trinity into their worship and prayer and spiritual walk. The Father is the source of all things, and we love and adore him; Jesus is the Lord of our lives, and we love and follow him; the Spirit is God living in us, and we love and listen to him. Our worship should include all three!

In Other Words

The doctrine of the Trinity arose out of reflection on the nature of God as revealed in the text of Scripture in an attempt to explain how the one God could also be three.

James Sawyer, in *The Survivor's Guide to Theology*
(Grand Rapids: Zondervan, 2006), 153.

God, in his very being, has always existed as more than one person. In fact, God exists as three persons, yet he is one God.

Wayne Grudem, in *Systematic Theology* (Grand Rapids:
Zondervan, 1994), 226.

CHAPTER 5

Extreme Transformation: The Holy Spirit

Extreme Transformation: The Holy Spirit

▶ Meet the least-known member of the Trinity—God the Holy Spirit.

▶ Learn what Jesus said about the Spirit's coming.

▶ Find out what it really means to be "born again."

▶ Discover what happens when the Spirit is offended.

A Personal God

If we were to sit down together at the local Starbucks and I were to ask you, "Is Jesus a person and do you sense a personal connection with him?" you would probably say, "Yes, Jesus is a very real person to me."

Then if I asked, "Is God the Father a person and do you sense the same personal connection with him?" you might say, "Yes, I know God the Father is a person, and even though I feel closer to Jesus, I recognize a personal bond with the Father."

Then a third question comes to mind. (You can see where this is going, right?) I would ask, "Is the Holy Spirit a person and are you aware of a personal relationship with him?" Most of us would say, "I've heard of the Holy Spirit, but to be honest, I don't have much of a connection with him."

In this chapter we are going to explore what the Bible teaches about the Holy Spirit. My goal is to introduce you to a wonderful helper and friend who is ready to stand with you and strengthen you in every experience of life.

Who Is the Spirit?

Three biblical facts summarize what Christians believe about who the Spirit is.

Fact #1: The Holy Spirit Is — He Exists

Jesus believed that the Holy Spirit actually existed. In fact, Jesus talked about the Spirit repeatedly during his ministry. Every New Testament writer refers to the Holy Spirit, and many Old Testament writers talk about him as well. The Spirit is given a variety of names and titles in Scripture—all of which point to his real existence.

Fact #2: The Holy Spirit Is a Person — He Possesses Personality

About 300 years after Jesus went back to heaven, a false teaching arose in the Christian community—a teaching called Arianism after its leader Arius. His primary error was that he denied the deity (God-ness) of Jesus, but Arius also denied the personality of the Holy Spirit. To him, the Holy Spirit was simply a force, an influence, the energy of God. Arius's error is still around. Unitarians and Jehovah's Witnesses hold the same view. In the Jehovah's Witness translation of the Bible, the words *holy spirit* are written just that way, not capitalized as in other translations.

The claim that the Holy Spirit is not a person is based on an argument from the Greek language (the language in which the New Testament was originally written). The Greek word used in the New Testament for *spirit* is neuter—not masculine ("he") or feminine ("she"), but neuter ("it"). So, as the argument goes, the Holy Spirit must be a force (an "it"), not a person.

The challenge to that argument comes from Jesus himself. Jesus breaks the rules of Greek grammar and refers to the Spirit as "he"—a person.

> "Unless I go away, the Advocate [a name for the Holy Spirit] will not come to you; but if I go, I will send *him* to you....
>
> But when *he*, the Spirit of truth, comes, *he* will guide you into all the truth. *He* will not speak on his own; *he* will speak only what he hears, and *he* will tell you what is yet to come."
>
> John 16:7, 13, italics added

Jesus deliberately and intentionally calls the Holy Spirit a person, not a force or a manifestation of energy. So the proof of the Spirit's personality is that the Bible consistently refers to the Spirit as a person.

Here are other evidences of the Spirit's personhood:

- The Spirit has all the qualities of personality.
  Intellect (Romans 8:27; 1 Corinthians 2:10–11)
  Emotion: He can feel; he can be grieved (Ephesians 4:30; Romans 15:30).

He has a will—the capacity to decide and to act (1 Corinthians 12:11).

- The Spirit displays the actions of a person.
  He teaches (John 14:26).
  He testifies (Romans 8:16).
  He prays (Romans 8:26).
  He speaks (Acts 8:29).
- The Spirit is linked with other persons.
  "Go and make disciples of all nations, baptizing them in the name of the Father and of the Son and of the Holy Spirit" (Matthew 28:19).
  "It seemed good to the Holy Spirit and to us" (Acts 15:28).

I am spending time on this not just to hammer a theological point but to show that because *you* are a person and the *Spirit* is a person, you can have a personal relationship with each other. He already knows us. We need to grow in our knowledge of him.

Fact #3: The Holy Spirit Is a Divine Person — He Is God

Several lines of biblical evidence convince us of the deity of the Holy Spirit:

- *The Spirit is given names of God.* Sixteen times in the New Testament the Holy Spirit is related to God the Father and God the Son. In 1 Corinthians 6:11, the Spirit is called "the Spirit of our God"; in Acts 16:7, he is called "the Spirit of Jesus." The Holy Spirit is associated with the other two members of the Trinity on a level of equality.
- *Jesus places the Holy Spirit on a level equal to himself as God.* Jesus spoke to his disciples just before his arrest and crucifixion and told them that when he left, another source of help would arrive: "And I will ask the Father, and he will give you another advocate to help you and be with you forever—the Spirit of truth" (John 14:16–17). Jesus called the Holy Spirit, "another advocate." Jesus had been their advocate or helper during his years of ministry, but now he was leaving. In his place would come another advocate—not a different kind of advocate but the same kind as Jesus was. The word translated *another* means "one of the same kind"—just as strong, just as wise, just as much God as Jesus.
- *The Spirit possesses the character qualities of God.* Remember all those big words I used earlier to describe God—*omnipotent, omniscient, immutable*? (Check chapter 3 if you need a refresher

course.) All those character traits are used in the Bible to describe the Holy Spirit. Here's a list:

Eternal (Hebrews 9:14)

Source of life (Romans 8:2)

All-powerful (Job 33:4; Luke 1:35)

All-knowing (1 Corinthians 2:10–12)

Present everywhere (Psalm 139:7–10)

Holy (the Spirit is called the *Holy* Spirit 89 times in the New Testament)

Does that sound like a description of anyone less than God?

- *The Spirit is said in Scripture to do things that only God can do.* Here are a few things the Spirit has been involved in. See if any of them sound like things you could do:

  He was active in creation (Genesis 1:2; Job 26:13; 33:4).

  He was instrumental in the writing of the Bible (2 Peter 1:21).

  He was the agent in the miraculous conception of Jesus in Mary (Luke 1:35).

  He participated in the resurrection of Jesus from the dead (Romans 1:4).

- *The Holy Spirit is called God in Acts 5.* A man named Ananias lied to the leaders of the early church about the sale of some property (not a wise thing to do!). The apostle Peter exposed the lie and said, "How is it that Satan has so filled your heart that you have lied to the Holy Spirit ...? You have not lied just to human beings but to God" (Acts 5:3–4).

Does your view of the Holy Spirit conform to what the Bible teaches? I hope you have been impressed with the Spirit's character and his equality with the Father and with Jesus as God. I hope you sense yourself drawn a little closer to the Spirit because he has done and is doing some fantastic things in your life. You may not realize it, but almost every aspect of your spiritual life and growth emerges from the ministry of the Holy Spirit to you, in you, and through you. That's what I want to explore with you next — the Spirit's work. You may find your life totally transformed by what you learn.

How the Spirit Works

The Holy Spirit began to work in your life before you ever knew about him or believed in Jesus. If you have never believed but are just curious

Bible Networking

Jesus in John 16:8 – 11

"When he [the Holy Spirit] comes, he will prove the world to be in the wrong about sin and righteousness and judgment: about sin, because people do not believe in me [Jesus]; about righteousness, because I am going to the Father, where you can see me no longer; and about judgment, because the prince of this world now stands condemned."

Jesus in John 14:6

"I am the way and the truth and the life. No one comes to the Father except through me."

about Christianity, your curiosity arose because the Spirit of God stirred that curiosity in you. Before any of us ever search for God, God is searching for us. One of the Spirit's great works is to draw men and women and children to Jesus. When we hear the message about Jesus' death and resurrection and his desire that we accept his gift of eternal life, it is the Spirit who convinces us that the gospel message is true (John 16:8 – 11). A person may reject the message and refuse to believe in Jesus, but in his or her heart they know that the message is true.

Theologians (who seem to like long, difficult words) call this drawing, convincing work of the Spirit *prevenient* grace. It means grace that "comes before" we believe. You may think that *you* made the decision to believe in Jesus or to be a Christian — and in a sense you did make that decision. But you and I only came to that point of understanding and faith because all along the Holy Spirit was drawing us in and opening our minds and hearts to hear and to receive the message. Left to ourselves, we would all have chosen to reject Jesus and to keep on running away from him. The gospel message would have sounded like foolishness to us (1 Corinthians 1:21 – 25), but God's love and grace conquered even our initial unwillingness.

Born of the Spirit

The Holy Spirit's work doesn't end once we hear the message of the gospel and believe in Jesus as Savior and Lord. We are "born" in a new way by the power of God the Holy Spirit. Our first birth from our mothers gave us human life, but something was terribly wrong. We had an unbreakable bent inside to do wrong, to sin before God. The remedy for our condition is not trying harder or keeping religious rules; the only remedy is a transformation of our hearts—and that's exactly what happens when we believe in Jesus. We are born a second time. It is not a physical birth but a spiritual birth, and it comes from the Holy Spirit.

Jesus made this very clear in a conversation he had with a religious scholar named Nicodemus (John 3:1–8). Nicodemus came to Jesus with some very flattering words. He said that obviously Jesus had come from God because of the stunning miracles that Jesus was performing. But Jesus saw the real need in Nicodemus's life. Nicodemus was religious but not reborn. Here's what Jesus said: "No one can see the kingdom of God without being born again" (John 3:3).

Three times in that conversation Jesus mentions the Holy Spirit. The Spirit is the one who brings spiritual life to the believing person. Jesus would say later in John's gospel, "The Spirit gives life" (John 6:63). Those who believe in Jesus receive life—eternal life—from the Holy Spirit. We are born in a new way, born from above, born of the Spirit.

God Inside

The new birth is only the first step of the Spirit's work in a new believer. He also comes to live in us when we believe in Jesus. God lives inside every genuine Christian. We may not know it. We may quench the Spirit's fire in us or grieve him by some action or attitude that is not pleasing to God. But the fact remains that the Spirit resides in each believer. Our body becomes the temple, the sacred home, of the Spirit (1 Corinthians 6:19–20).

WHO'S AFRAID OF THE HOLY GHOST?

Older translations of the Bible refer to the Holy Spirit as "the Holy Ghost." You will hear that phrase in some of the older hymns of the church too. The word *ghost* in "King James" English could refer to any spirit being. Originally the word did not have the creepy connotation it has today. Most Bible translations and songs and preachers today refer to the third member of the Trinity as "God the Holy Spirit."

Bible Networking

1 Corinthians 6:19 – 20

Do you not know that your bodies are temples of the Holy Spirit, who is in you, whom you have received from God? You are not your own; you were bought at a price. Therefore honor God with your bodies.

Romans 8:9b

If anyone does not have the Spirit of Christ, they do not belong to Christ.

Just before his death on the cross Jesus explained to his closest friends just how this would work: "I will ask the Father, and he will give you another advocate to help you and be with you forever — the Spirit of truth.... He lives with you and will be in you" (John 14:16 – 17). Several facts about the Spirit's indwelling are made clear in Jesus' statement.

At the time Jesus spoke, the Holy Spirit was dwelling "with" the apostles, Jesus' followers. The Greek word Jesus uses means "beside you." The Holy Spirit was their companion. He was beside them but not yet in them.

The time would come in the future when the Spirit would relate to the followers of Jesus in a different way — the Spirit would begin to dwell "in" them.

The Holy Spirit would be with the believer forever. The Spirit of God links himself to the Christian for eternity. The Spirit indwells us the moment we believe, and the Spirit never leaves the believing heart.

In Other Words

May we, therefore, learn to believe that the Spirit is in us, children of God, simply because the Bible tells us so. Then, when we have believed (and not before), we shall see this Spirit bring forth in our hearts that love, joy, and peace which we had hitherto sought in vain.

René Pache, in *The Person and Work of the Holy Spirit*
(Chicago: Moody Press, 1954), 104.

Jesus also made it clear that people who do not believe in Jesus do not possess the Holy Spirit: "The world cannot accept him, because it neither sees him nor knows him" (John 14:17). There are only two kinds of people — those who possess the Spirit and those who don't, those who have a personal relationship with Jesus and those who don't.

In his teaching about the Holy Spirit, Jesus outlined quite a few ministries of the Spirit in the believer's life:

- *The Spirit will teach.* Jesus had not been able in three years of ministry to teach his followers all that he wanted them to know. But Jesus was not in a panic about it. He knew that the Holy Spirit would continue to teach them the truth of God. "The Advocate, the Holy Spirit, whom the Father will send in my name, will teach you all things" (John 14:26).
- *The Spirit would reveal the truth recorded in the New Testament.* Jesus also assured the disciples that the Holy Spirit would oversee the recording of truth in the Scriptures of the New Testament. The Spirit would "remind you of everything I have said to you" (John 14:26 — referring to the gospels that tell us about Jesus). The Spirit would "testify about [Jesus]" (John 15:26 — referring to the explanation of Jesus' death and resurrection contained in the New Testament letters). The Holy Spirit would even explain "what is yet to come" (John 16:13 — referring to the prophetic sections of the New Testament such as the book of Revelation).
- *The Spirit will glorify Jesus.* According to Jesus, the Spirit's work would be to exalt Jesus: "He will glorify me because it is from me that he will receive what he will make known to you" (John 16:14). The evidence of the Spirit's presence in a worship service is not that the Holy Spirit is exalted but that Jesus is exalted. The Spirit stays in the background. His goal is to see Jesus honored. That's why the apostle Paul boasted in the cross of Christ (Galatians 6:14) and had such a passion for Jesus (Philippians 1:21) and yet was filled with the Holy Spirit.
- *The Spirit will convict the world.* Jesus also taught that the Spirit would convince the world of the truth of the message about Jesus (John 16:9–11). But even in the face of what they know in their hearts to be true, many people reject Jesus and choose to go their own way. One of the works of the Spirit is to convict people of their moral accountability before God.

THE HOLY SPIRIT IN THE OLD TESTAMENT

Even though the Holy Spirit came on the Christians with power on the day of Pentecost that was not the Spirit's first appearance. Actually the Holy Spirit was present and active on earth from the very beginning. From creation until the birth of Jesus, the Holy Spirit played three important roles.

THE INVADING SPIRIT

The Holy Spirit is the breath of God, the wind of God, who comes into the world with mysterious power. At the time of creation, God the Spirit was forming and finishing and making beautiful the creative work of God the Son (Genesis 1:2; Job 26:13 NASB; Psalm 33:6). The Spirit also came on human beings to empower them for great works of art or strength.

- The artists who constructed the tabernacle, Israel's worship center, were guided in their work by the Spirit (Exodus 31:3–5).
- Gideon and Samson and other deliverers of God's people were given wisdom or strength by the Holy Spirit (Judges 6:34–36; 14:6, 19; 15:14; 16:20).
- A pagan sorcerer named Balaam was overpowered by the Spirit when he tried to curse Israel (Numbers 24:2).
- Saul and David were empowered by the Spirit to rule over Israel (1 Samuel 11:6; 16:13).

THE INSPIRING SPIRIT

The Holy Spirit was active in revealing God's truth to the Old Testament prophets and in guiding them as they wrote the Word of God (2 Samuel 23:2; Ezekiel 8:3; 11:1; Amos 7:14–16; Micah 3:8; Zechariah 17:12).

THE SAVING SPIRIT

Men and women believed in the true God because of the enabling power of the Holy Spirit. Jesus was surprised that a religious scholar in Israel did not understand the necessity of being "born of the Spirit" (John 3:8). Several times in the Old Testament the Holy Spirit works in believers to keep them true to God (Joseph, Genesis 41:38; Moses, Isaiah 63:11; the prophets, 1 Peter 1:11).

The Spirit was present in the world and active in human hearts all throughout Old Testament times, but Old Testament believers did not enjoy or experience the full, personal ministry of the Holy Spirit like we do in the New Testament age. In fact, the Spirit's work was so limited that Jesus could say the Spirit "had not been given" yet (John 7:38–39). The Spirit came on believers in his fullness on the day of Pentecost in Acts 2.

Baptized in the Spirit

One of the more controversial works of the Holy Spirit is the baptism in the Spirit (or "with" the Spirit or "of" the Spirit or "by" the Spirit). Some Christians believe that the baptism is a work of the Spirit that comes sometime after our new birth. (Those Christians will refer to the Spirit's baptism as a "second work of grace.") Other Christians believe that the baptism in the Spirit occurs when we believe in Jesus, not sometime later. Some Christians teach that the evidence of the Spirit's baptism is speaking in tongues (uttering an unknown prayer language). Other Christians say that the baptism in the Spirit is a work that God does, and we don't "experience" or feel anything.

Hot debates have been voiced and long books have been written about the matter. I will present one biblical view, but I want to warn you that it won't satisfy everyone. As is true for all debatable issues, committed Christians hold to several different viewpoints. My suggestion is to listen carefully, search out the biblical information, and let the Holy Spirit be your final guide and teacher.

The baptism of the Holy Spirit is mentioned eleven times in the New Testament. If we look at the key references in order, I think it will help us come to a better understanding of what this work of the Spirit is all about.

All four gospel writers attribute the first mention of the Spirit baptism to John the Baptizer. He predicted that the coming Messiah would baptize those who had a repentant heart "with the Holy Spirit and fire" (Matthew 3:11; Mark 1:8; Luke 3:16; John 1:33). The baptism (whatever it was) was a future event for John. Jesus would be the baptizer and would baptize people into the realm of the Holy Spirit. Just as John plunged people into water, Jesus would plunge people into the Spirit.

The problem is that Jesus never baptized anyone in the Holy Spirit during his ministry on earth. He never even mentioned the baptism in all his teaching about the Holy Spirit. It was only on his last day on earth after his resurrection that Jesus finally brought it up: "John baptized with water, but in a few days you will be baptized with the Holy Spirit" (Acts 1:5). Then Jesus left and ascended to heaven.

The fulfillment of Jesus' promise came ten days later when the Holy Spirit "came to rest on" the followers of Jesus on the Jewish feast day of Pentecost (Acts 2:1–17). We've already seen that the Holy Spirit was present and active on earth from the time of creation and all throughout the Old Testament era. So the Spirit didn't come from heaven for the first time in Acts 2. Instead the Spirit came on believers in a new way. Never before had God's people been baptized in or with the Holy Spirit. No one in the Old Testament had been plunged into the Spirit's presence and power like these early Christians were on that amazing day. The phrase *baptism in the Spirit* does not appear in Acts 2, but based on Jesus' promise and other passages of Scripture, we may conclude that the Christians experienced the promised baptism by or in or with the Spirit.

Several years later, God directed the apostle Peter to preach the message about Jesus to a non-Jewish (Gentile) family. When that family believed in Jesus, the Holy Spirit came on them, and they gave evidence of the Spirit's presence by speaking in tongues (Acts 10:44–46). Peter

Bible Networking

Acts 2:1 – 4

When the day of Pentecost came, they were all together in one place. Suddenly a sound like the blowing of a violent wind came from heaven and filled the whole house where they were sitting. They saw what seemed to be tongues of fire that separated and came to rest on each of them. All of them were filled with the Holy Spirit and began to speak in other tongues as the Spirit enabled them.

Acts 2:14 – 18

Then Peter stood up with the Eleven, raised his voice and addressed the crowd: "Fellow Jews and all of you who live in Jerusalem, let me explain this to you; listen carefully to what I say. These people are not drunk, as you suppose. It's only nine in the morning! No, this is what was spoken by the prophet Joel:

> " 'In the last days, God says,
>   I will pour out my Spirit on all people.
> Your sons and daughters will prophesy,
>   your young men will see visions,
>   your old men will dream dreams.
> Even on my servants, both men and women,
>   I will pour out my Spirit in those days,
>   and they will prophesy.' "

went before the Christian leaders a few days later to explain what had happened, and he said this:

> "As I began to speak, the Holy Spirit came on them as he had come on us at the beginning. Then I remembered what the Lord had said: 'John baptized with water, but you will be baptized with the Holy Spirit.' So if God gave them the same gift he gave us who believed in the Lord Jesus Christ, who was I to think that I could stand in God's way?"
> Acts 11:15–17

On both the day of Pentecost and the day Peter preached to a non-Jewish audience, the Holy Spirit "came on" those who believed in Jesus. They were baptized in the Spirit—plunged into a new realm, the realm of the Spirit.

The apostle Paul adds another dimension to our knowledge of the Spirit's baptism in 1 Corinthians 12:13: "We were all baptized by one Spirit so as to form one body—whether Jews or Gentiles, slave or free—and we were all given the one Spirit to drink." The Corinthian church had a lot of problems. Many of the Christians were immature in their spiritual walk, and some were continuing to disobey God's Word. But Paul states with certainty that they were *all* baptized by one Spirit. That tells me that a person is baptized by or in the Spirit when they believe. It is not something that comes later as we mature in our Christian life. We are all baptized by the Spirit when we receive Jesus as Savior. Nowhere does the Bible suggest that some believers have been baptized in the Spirit and some believers have not. Furthermore, we are never commanded in the Bible to seek after the baptism by the Spirit or to pray for it. It is simply declared to be true of those who believe in Christ.

So what does the baptism in the Spirit do in our lives? Wonderful blessings and benefits are connected to the Spirit's baptism. First, it plunges us into a new spiritual realm. We now live and operate in the

Digging Deeper

If you want to pursue this subject in greater depth, check out:

✗ Chad Brand, ed., *Perspectives on Spirit Baptism: Five Views*. Nashville: Broadman and Holman, 2004.

Great Debates!

SHOULD I SPEAK IN TONGUES?

The issue of speaking in tongues has sometimes been a source of bitter debate and division in Christian communities. Some churches teach that the evidence of the Spirit's presence or the Spirit's baptism is uttering a new language of prayer and worship to God. They base this on passages in Acts where new believers received the Holy Spirit and began at the same time to speak in other tongues (Acts 2:4; 10:44–46). While I would agree that speaking in tongues in the early chapters of Acts was the evidence of the Spirit's presence, it is not consistently the pattern even in Acts. In Acts 8, when the Samaritans received the Holy Spirit, nothing is said about speaking in tongues (Acts 8:14–17). In the same chapter, an Ethiopian official believes in Jesus and is baptized in water, but no mention is made of tongues (Acts 8:36–39). When Jesus appeared to Paul on the road to Damascus and Paul put his faith in Jesus, he is not said to speak in other tongues as the evidence of the Spirit's work (Acts 9:1–19). Furthermore, in 1 Corinthians Paul says that all of the believers had been baptized in the Spirit but then made a point of saying that they had *not* all spoken in tongues (12:13, 30). My conclusion is that initially tongues was an evidence of the Spirit's presence, but speaking in tongues is not the proof or confirmation of the Spirit's baptism. The baptism in the Spirit is a work of God in all those who believe in Jesus and is accepted by faith as a reality in every believer's life.

realm of the Spirit. Before believing in Jesus we operated in the realm of sin and our own selfish will. Now we swim in a different ocean—the life-giving, liberating realm of God's Spirit.

The baptism also connects us to the spiritual body of Christ, his true church. You may attend a visible church every Sunday, but Christ's invisible church is made up of all genuine believers in every culture and in every denomination. We are one body because of the Spirit's baptism. There exists a unity among believers in Christ that transcends all social, racial, and religious barriers. The apostle Paul writes in Ephesians, "There is one body and one Spirit" (4:4).

Filled with the Spirit

The Holy Spirit's ministry has another dimension—the filling of the Spirit. The filling is commonly confused with the baptism in the Spirit, but it's not the same. The *baptism* in the Spirit occurs once when we believe. We don't seek it or pray for it. We are never commanded in the Bible to ask for it. It just happens as part of the process of being born again. The *filling* of the Spirit, on the other hand, happens many times — and we are commanded as Christians to be filled with God's Spirit. Here's the key verse from Ephesians 5:18:

> Do not get drunk on wine, which leads to debauchery. Instead, be filled with the Spirit.

Paul makes a strong contrast in this verse. We are *not* to be drunk with wine. Instead, we are to be filled with the Spirit. If you've ever been drunk or seen an intoxicated person, you know that the alcohol takes over. The person is controlled by the alcohol so that they don't act normally. Drunkenness changes how you talk, how you act, and how you perceive your world. That's exactly the idea behind the filling of the Spirit. Paul is not suggesting here that I get more of the Holy Spirit — filled up, as it were, with the Spirit. He's suggesting that the Spirit get more of *me* — that I be increasingly controlled by the Holy Spirit. That control, of course, is not manipulative or oppressive. When the Holy Spirit takes

Whether you believe that the baptism of the Holy Spirit is a way of referring to what happens when we become Christians or a way of describing a distinct experience after conversion, do you and I know the fullness of the Spirit at this moment? Are we longing for a deeper experience of God? Is there an arresting quality, something remarkable, about our lives, a quality that can only be explained in terms of God? Or are we happily going along in our own self-confidence rather than trusting in the power of God? How real is Christ to us right now? Are we dissatisfied with where we are on our spiritual journey? Are we desperate to seek God, to be filled with him? Is this the most urgent desire of our hearts?

It may be good to reflect on these words from Martyn Lloyd-Jones, a Spirit-filled British pastor:

> Got it all? I simply ask in the name of God, why then are you as you are? If you have got it all, why are you so unlike the New Testament Christians? Got it all? Got it all at your conversion? Well, where is it, I ask?

Martyn Lloyd-Jones, sermon on
"Baptism in the Spirit" (May 25, 1961)

control, we behave as Jesus would behave! We talk differently, act differently, and perceive our world and our purpose in life differently. We stop acting "normally" (where it's all about me) and start acting in a way that honors Jesus.

Furthermore, we are commanded to do this as Christians. We are to seek and pray for the filling of the Spirit. But how does this work on a practical level? How can I be filled and controlled by the Spirit right now? The Bible doesn't give us "Four Easy Steps to Becoming Filled with the Spirit," but I think we can work out some principles that will make this a reality in our lives. The first step is *a genuine desire to be more like Christ.* The person who is just coasting along in his or her Christian life is not going to have much of a passion to see things

In Other Words

When we are Spirit-filled and therefore rightly related to the Spirit of God,

- we are surrounded by the Spirit's omnipotent shield of protection, continually and routinely.
- we have an inner dynamic to handle life's pressures.
- we are able to be joyful — regardless.
- we have the capacity to grasp the deep things of God that he discloses in his Book.
- we have little difficulty maintaining a positive attitude of unselfishness, servanthood, and humility.
- we have a keen sense of intuition and discernment; we sense evil.
- we are able to love and be loved in return.
- we can be vulnerable and open.
- we can rely on the Spirit to intercede for us when we don't even know how to pray as we should.
- we need never fear evil or demonic and satanic assault.
- we are enabled to stand alone with confidence.
- we experience inner assurance regarding decisions as well as right and wrong.
- we have an "internal filtering system."
- we can actually live worry free.
- we are able to minister to others through our spiritual gift(s).
- we have an intimate, abiding "Abba relationship" with the living God.

Chuck Swindoll, in *Flying Closer to the Flame*
(Dallas: Word, 1993), 246 – 47.

change. But sometimes God will stop us short or bring conviction to our hearts about our lack of spiritual growth. Maybe this prompting comes in response to a sermon or a personal crisis. Sometimes failure will bring us to an awareness of our lack of spiritual commitment. That's when I have *a deep desire to see God do a fresh work in me.* That "crisis" experience will bring a sense of repentance in me, and I will confess my failures and lack of passion to God. Then I will *ask God to fill my life with his Spirit.* I yield myself fully to the Spirit's direction and love and power. At that moment I am filled by the Spirit. I may not have a tingly feeling, but the Spirit has the place of control in my life.

Paul's command to be filled with the Spirit is a continuing command—"keep on being filled with the Spirit." I may be filled many times in my life. I yield to the Spirit's control every day—sometimes several times. My tendency is to pull back the control of my life. When I do, it becomes obvious that my selfish heart is in the driver's seat, not the Holy Spirit of God. So, once again, I consciously give control back to the Spirit and move on in my life.

More Help from the Holy Spirit

The Spirit works in the Christian's life in many other ways too. He is as close to us as our breath and carefully guards our hearts as God's people. Other significant ministries of the Holy Spirit include:

- *The Spirit assures us of our adoption as God's own children.*
  "The Spirit himself testifies with our spirit that we are God's children" (Romans 8:16).
  See also Galatians 4:4–7.
- *The Spirit seals us, marking us out as God's own and guaranteeing our full inheritance of all of God's blessings.*
  "When you believed, you were marked in him with a seal, the promised Holy Spirit, who is a deposit guaranteeing our inheritance until the redemption of those who are God's possession" (Ephesians 1:13b–14).
  You might also read 2 Corinthians 1:21–22 and 5:5.
- *The Holy Spirit prays on our behalf when we don't know what to ask God for.*
  "The Spirit helps us in our weakness. We do not know what we ought to pray for, but the Spirit himself intercedes for us through wordless groans" (Romans 8:26).

- *The Spirit communicates to us the love and wise direction of God the Father.*

  "Those who are led by the Spirit of God are the children of God. The Spirit you received does not make you slaves, so that you live in fear again; rather, the Spirit you received brought about your adoption to sonship. And by him we cry, '*Abba* [an intimate name for a human father in the Aramaic language], Father'" (Romans 8:14–15).

- *The Spirit helps to defend us from Satan and from spiritual attack.*

  When the apostle Paul describes the spiritual armor that God provides the Christian for defense against the enemy's attacks, the only fighting weapon he hands us is "the sword of the Spirit, which is the word of God" (Ephesians 6:17). The Spirit brings to mind those sections of the Bible that we have read or memorized or studied, and we use God's truth as a rebuke and defense against spiritual assault.

- *The Holy Spirit assists us in delivering the message about Jesus.*

  Paul was confident of the faith of some Christians because the good news about Jesus had come to them "not simply with words but also with power, with the Holy Spirit and deep conviction" (1 Thessalonians 1:5).

  You can also see this truth in 1 Corinthians 2:4 and 1 Peter 1:12.

- *The Spirit works in us to gradually transform us to be like Jesus.*

  "Now the Lord is the Spirit, and where the Spirit of the Lord is, there is freedom. And we all, who with unveiled faces contemplate the Lord's glory, are being transformed into his image with ever-increasing glory, which comes from the Lord, who is the Spirit" (2 Corinthians 3:17–18).

Help File

BIBLICAL SYMBOLS OF THE HOLY SPIRIT

The Bible pictures or describes the Holy Spirit with several startling symbols.

- a dove (Matthew 3:16; Mark 1:10; Luke 3:22; John 1:32)
- fire (Acts 2:3)
- oil (Luke 4:18; Acts 10:38; 2 Corinthians 1:21)
- a seal, a mark of ownership (2 Corinthians 1:22; Ephesians 1:13)
- water (John 4:14; 7:38–39)
- wind (John 3:8; Acts 2:1–2)
- a pledge, an engagement ring (2 Corinthians 5:5; Ephesians 1:14)

Points to Remember

- ☑ The Holy Spirit exists. He is a personal being (like you), and he is God.

- ☑ The Spirit is placed on the same level in the Bible as God the Father and God the Son.

- ☑ The Holy Spirit began to work in you before you ever believed in Jesus. He searches for us before we ever search for God.

- ☑ The Spirit lives in each person who has believed in Jesus.

- ☑ Christians are also baptized by the Spirit into one body, the true church.

- ☑ As we seek to become more like Jesus, we seek the filling (control) of the Holy Spirit.

- ☑ The source of power for holy living is not keeping a list of rules but relying on the Spirit.

- ☑ We can grieve the Spirit by our sin and carelessness.

- ☑ The Holy Spirit can be a wonderful, powerful presence in every Christian's life.

If you miss the Holy Spirit in your spiritual life, you are missing a lot—power, freedom, peace, joy, closeness to God, guidance, help. That's why Jesus called the Spirit our *Advocate* (John 14:16). The Greek word Jesus used is *paraklētos*. (Older writers will sometimes refer to the Holy Spirit as the *Paraclete* based on that Greek word.) The Greek word has been translated several ways simply because no single English word can convey the full meaning of the Greek word—Counselor, Helper, Strengthener, Supporter, Adviser, Ally. The word speaks of someone who comes along close beside us as a friend or helper. The Spirit not only comes along beside us; he comes to live within us. Once he takes up his residence in a person's heart, nothing is ever the same again. We have a source of power and comfort that nothing on the outside can ever remove or destroy.

The Sensitive Spirit

The Holy Spirit is a wonderful source of blessing, but he is never to be taken for granted. The Bible makes a point of telling us that it is possible to sin against the Holy Spirit with disastrous results. Men and women who hear the message of Jesus but who refuse to believe in Jesus as Savior and Lord are said to "resist" or oppose the Spirit (Acts 7:51). The Spirit is convincing them

THE UNFORGIVABLE SIN

Jesus had a way of dropping spiritual bombshells on occasion. One that has had Christians scratching their heads for nearly two thousand years is recorded in Matthew chapter 12. It all started with a serious accusation against Jesus from some religious leaders. They said that Jesus' miracles were done by Satan's power, not by God's power. Jesus made it clear that such belief was totally illogical. How can someone drive out demons, who are Satan's minions, by Satan's power? That's like sending a nation's army to fight the same nation's navy—stupid! Jesus insisted that he drove out demons "by the Spirit of God" (Matthew 12:28).

Then Jesus added this:

> "And so I tell you, people will be forgiven every sin and blasphemy. But blasphemy against the Spirit will not be forgiven. Anyone who speaks a word against the Son of Man will be forgiven, but anyone who speaks against the Holy Spirit will not be forgiven, either in this age or in the age to come."
>
> Matthew 12:31–32

Three characteristics mark this unforgivable sin:

- *It was a sin directed against the Holy Spirit.* These accusers might misunderstand or misinterpret Jesus' work, and while that is wrong, it can be forgiven. These leaders had no reason, however, to misunderstand the power of the Spirit.

- *The sin was committed in a special situation.* This was not just a sin of the tongue. The words of Jesus' enemies revealed their hearts. They were rejecting Jesus to his face. They were denying God's power in what they had personally witnessed. Those who deny God's power and reject God's grace show that their hearts are totally hardened against God.

- *The sin leads to eternal unforgiveness.* Such rejection of God's work will never be forgiven—not because God *cannot* forgive, but because the person *will not* believe. Forgiveness for that sin, therefore, will never come in this age or in any age, since our eternal destiny is determined in this life.

The one thing to do to avoid this sin is to get on Jesus' side! Jesus invites even his enemies to change sides. If they go into eternity unforgiven, it's their fault, not the Lord's.

Now if you are wondering (even as a Christian) if you have committed the unpardonable sin, the very fact that you are concerned about it is evidence that you haven't committed it! Those who sin against the Spirit in this way have so hardened their hearts against God that they never hear the Spirit's voice or sense his conviction again.

of God's truth and prompting them to believe, but they refuse. The writer of Hebrews warns that those who seem to embrace God's truth and then turn away from it not only trample Jesus under their feet; they also "have insulted the Spirit of grace" (Hebrews 10:29).

Even Christians who have the Spirit living in them can sin against the Spirit. Paul, for example, warns the Christians in Ephesus not to "grieve the Holy Spirit of God" (Ephesians 4:30). In the surrounding verses Paul challenges them to live lives of holiness and purity. It seems that our deliberate sin causes pain and sorrow to God's Spirit. He doesn't leave us, but our relationship with him is certainly hindered until that sin is confessed and forgiven.

Paul tells the Thessalonian Christians not to quench the Spirit—"Do not put out the Spirit's fire" (1 Thessalonians 5:19). When the Spirit stirs our hearts to praise or worship or do acts of sacrificial service to God, we are not to be guilty of throwing cold water on the Spirit's leading.

The Holy Spirit seems to be the tenderest member of the Trinity. He knows us most closely and helps us with our most personal concerns, but at the same time he can be grieved by any action or attitude that insults him or goes against God's Word. The Spirit has such a passion to see us transformed that any departure from that path causes him to prompt us to repentance and renewed commitment. If we resist his prompting and deliberately pursue the path of disobedience, the Spirit's voice gets quieter and quieter.

Digging Deeper

Any good theology survey will have a chapter on the Holy Spirit. In addition, you may want to read:

✗ Robert Gromacki, *The Holy Spirit*. Nashville: Word, 1999.
✗ Charles Swindoll, *Flying Closer to the Flame*. Dallas: Word, 1993.

If you would like to pursue a personal study of the Holy Spirit, pick up the LifeGuide Bible Study *Meeting the Spirit* written by Douglas Connelly (Downers Grove, Ill.: InterVarsity, 1995).

CHAPTER 6

You, Me, and the Rest of the World: Humanity

You, Me, and the Rest of the World: Humanity

- ▶ Discover a universe, created by the great Designer.
- ▶ Find out why our tiny planet is the focus of God's attention.
- ▶ Meet your original Dad and Mom!
- ▶ Learn what really went wrong that day in the garden of Eden.

Darwin or Design?

The Bible opens with a stunning account of the creation of the universe: "In the beginning God created the heavens and the earth" (Genesis 1:1). Christians disagree on exactly *how* God carried out the work of creation. Some believe in a sudden, seven-day creation; others contend that God supervised a more evolutionary process. All Christians would agree, however, that our world is not just some accident of nature but the product of God's purposeful design.

We also believe that the crowning achievement of God's creative work was the creation of human beings. The universe and our earth were brought into existence as the dwelling place for the human race. At the end of the creative process, God made human beings—male and female—in his own image. "So God created human beings in his own image, in the image of God he created them; male and female he created them" (Genesis 1:27).

Human beings have a material part—a body—and an immaterial part—a spirit or a soul. The human body was originally formed by God from the dust of the ground, from the elements of the earth that God had already created. But then God "breathed into his nostrils the breath of life," and the first human became a "living being" (Genesis 2:7). Adam's body was animated with the life of God.

The image of God in human beings is not a physical resemblance to God. God is a spirit. He has no physical form. The image of God lies in humanity's capacity to have a relationship with God and to be rationally connected to the world around us. Animals may seem intelligent (especially to their owners), but animals operate according to their innate natures and instincts. No animal can read or compose music or laugh at a joke or invest in the stock market. It takes rational thought and creativity to function as a human being.

Only human beings have the capacity to worship and love God. We were created for fellowship and communication with God. That capacity reflects the nature of God himself, who has unending fellowship

Help File

COSMIC PERSPECTIVE

Israel's King David stood one night on a Judean hillside and gazed in wonder at the vastness of the universe. Here's the question that came to David's mind:

What are mere mortals that you are
    mindful of them,
      human beings that you care for them?
                Psalm 8:4

This little experiment might help you see yourself in the light of our universe. Go to a park or empty mall parking lot and put a basketball in the center of a large open area. That basketball represents our sun. Now step off 82 paces of about 2 feet each and put down a mustard seed. The seed (proportionately) represents the first planet, Mercury. After taking 60 more 2-foot steps, put down a copper BB pellet — the representation of Venus.

Mark off 78 more steps and put down a common, garden-variety pea. You are looking at your home planet, Earth. After 108 more steps, put down a pinhead — to represent Mars. If you have room, take 788 more steps and set an orange on the ground to represent Jupiter.

You would have to take 934 additional steps to represent Saturn with a golf ball; 2,086 more steps to come to Uranus, represented by a marble; and another 2,322 steps to get to Neptune, represented by a cherry.

We've come 2½ miles, and we haven't even talked about tiny Pluto (demoted not that long ago from a planet to an asteroid). Our solar system sits on a 5-mile circle, and yet we would have to travel another 6,720 miles (not steps) to get to the nearest star on the same scale.

We are one tiny speck on the garden pea. No wonder David asked God why he cared about creatures so insignificant! But God's answer was even more startling.

You have made them a little lower than
    the heavenly beings
  and crowned them with glory
    and honor.
You made them rulers over the works
    of your hands;
  you put everything under their feet.
                Psalm 8:5–6

Human beings are the crown of God's creation — the focus of his delight and redemption.

In Other Words

Man wonders over the restless sea, the flowing waters and the sight of the sky —
And forgets that of all wonders Man himself is the most wonderful.

> Saint Augustine

Man's chief end is to glorify God, and to enjoy him forever.

> Westminster Shorter Catechism Answer 1

In a universe of blind physical forces and genetic replication, some people are going to get hurt, other people are going to get lucky, and you won't find any rhyme or reason in it, nor any justice. The universe we observe has precisely the properties we should expect if there is, at bottom, no design, no purpose, no evil and no good, nothing but blind, pitiless indifference.

> Richard Dawkins (a secularist thinker), in *River Out of Eden* (New York: HarperCollins, 1995), 133.

within the Trinity. Humans also have the capacity to ignore God and reject his love, but even that rejection demonstrates their original creation in God's image. No animal can hear the message of God's love and choose to ignore it. God is able to connect with any human being personally and powerfully because we were made in God's own likeness.

How It All Went Wrong

Adam and Eve were created with perfect bodies and placed in a beautiful world. They were also created with innocent spirits. They were not scarred or marked by sin from their parents or from their surroundings. Their holiness and purity, however, were untested. Our first parents had never been placed in a situation where they had the opportunity to do anything but obey God. So God devised a simple test — not with the goal that they would fail, but with the desire that Adam and Eve would pass the test and be confirmed and established in their integrity and obedience toward God.

In the beautiful garden God had made for his human creatures, God placed a tree. The Bible calls it "the tree of the knowledge of good and evil" (Genesis 2:17). The tree bore some kind of fruit, but more importantly, it represented a test of Adam and Eve's obedience. God told them not to eat of the fruit of that tree. God made the restriction as painless as possible! They were given permission to eat from every other tree as often and as much as they wanted. God gave them every opportunity to succeed. The restrictions were minimal; the privileges were abundant—and the penalty was clear. If they ate from the restricted tree, they would certainly die.

Satan, God's enemy and a powerful evil angel, took over the body of a beautiful serpent and tempted Eve to disobey the Lord. He implied that God's restriction was keeping her from something good. Satan planted seeds of doubt in Eve's mind. When Eve saw the fruit as attractive and desirable, she ate some and took more to Adam and he ate it too. (You can read the biblical account in Genesis 3:1–7.)

At that moment of rebellion, Adam and Eve became sinful. They now knew good and evil, just as Satan had promised, but they knew it from the side of evil—and they couldn't escape. Human nature was locked in its sinful condition, and no amount of regret or human effort would ever change that condition. Theologians call this event "the *fall* of humanity." From the lofty place of glory and honor to which God had elevated them, Adam and Eve fell to a place of moral disorder and spiritual separation from God.

WAS ADAM FOR REAL?

Most secularists reject the idea that Adam and Eve really existed. The first chapters of Genesis are dismissed as myths—stories created by the early Hebrews to explain how the world came to be and how human beings made their entrance. The biblical writers (in the secularist's view) were prescientific, unable to understand the process that actually brought the earth and life into being.

Christians, however, understand these chapters as historical accounts. The chapters are not written as mythological tales but in the same straightforward fashion as the later accounts of Abraham or Joseph. Jesus put his stamp of approval on the biblical story of creation by appealing to it to settle a theological argument (Matthew 19:4–5). Jesus referred to Adam and Eve as real people and to the words God spoke to them as an accurate record of true events. Other New Testament writers like Luke (3:38) and Jude (14) and Paul (Romans 5:14–15, 21–22; 1 Corinthians 15:45) speak of Adam as a historical person uniquely created by God.

Bible Networking

Genesis 2:21 – 22

So the LORD God caused the man to fall into a deep sleep; and while he was sleeping, he took one of the man's ribs and then closed up the place with flesh. Then the LORD God made a woman from the rib he had taken out of the man, and he brought her to the man.

Matthew 19:4 – 5

"Haven't you read," [Jesus] replied, "that at the beginning the Creator 'made them male and female,' and said, 'For this reason a man will leave his father and mother and be united to his wife, and the two will become one flesh'?"

1 Timothy 2:13

For Adam was formed first, then Eve.

Whatever Happened to Sin?

Sin seems like an old-fashioned word in our sophisticated society. No one likes to be accused of "sin" or called a "sinner." But the Bible uses the word with no apology. Sin is first and foremost an offense against God. It is going against God's nature or God's Word or God's direction. Other people may be hurt, civil laws may be broken, the environment may be damaged, excuses may be offered, but sin is, above all else, defiance toward God.

The Bible uses some interesting words to describe sin:

- *Sin is missing the target.* The goal, the target, is God's perfection—and all of us, every one of us, has fallen short of that goal. The people we revere as the most holy (think Mother Teresa or Billy Graham) are the first ones to admit that they fail. Reaching God's standard of perfection is like jumping the Atlantic Ocean. Some of us might leap a little farther off the end of the dock than others, but in comparison to the goal, we all fall far short.
- *Sin is breaking through a boundary.* God's standard of perfection is spelled out for us in God's law, summarized in the Ten

Great Debates!

WHERE DID I COME FROM?

The Bible is clear that we can all trace our genealogy back to our original set of parents. Adam and Eve began the line that links every nation, every ethnic group, every race, and every person. We are all "in Adam." The bigger question is this: Where does my spirit, my soul, my inner being come from? Three major views have been proposed:

- *Preexistent spirits.* This view holds that we existed in some form before our conception and birth. Plato, the Greek philosopher, believed that we existed as souls before our bodies were formed. Mormons believe that all human beings exist before birth as spirit beings, the offspring of a heavenly father and mother. Reincarnation teaches that souls migrate from one form of life at death to a new form at birth. Most Christians reject this view because it is not taught anywhere in the Bible.
- *Each spirit is created.* Creationism (as it relates to the human spirit) says that God creates each individual spirit at conception, at birth, or sometime in between.

This view seems consistent with passages of Scripture that picture the soul as coming from God. The writer of Ecclesiastes, for example, says that at death "the spirit returns to God who gave it" (12:7; see also Isaiah 57:16; Hebrews 12:9). The problem with this view is that it seems to make God the author of our sinfulness. It also fails to explain why our children not only look like us but also have similar psychological features as their parents.

- *Our spirits are passed on from our parents.* The theological term for this view is *traducianism.* This view says that along with physical DNA from our parents, we get spiritual DNA. Our spirit or soul derives from our parents, just as our body does. This position seems to provide the best explanation for how we inherit a sinful nature. Jesus said, "Flesh gives birth to flesh" (John 3:6). Adam and Eve gave birth to a son Seth, who was born "in [Adam's] own likeness, in his own image" (Genesis 5:3). This also may be one part of the reason that Jesus was born of a virgin woman without a man's participation. Jesus was conceived in Mary by the miraculous work of God and did not receive an inherent bent toward sin from his parents.

Commandments. The purpose of the law was not to provide a way of salvation but to point out how often we break God's law and how much we need God's mercy.

- *Sin is the twisting of what is good.* Any twisting or misuse of God's good gifts is sin. For example, God told Adam and Eve to fill the new earth with offspring. The sexual relationship in marriage was God's good gift. Sinful human beings have twisted God's gift into the perversions and deviations we see in our culture today.

Adam and Eve were innocent before they sinned. Everything changed once they ate of that fruit. There was no going back. Sin infiltrated their very nature. They now possessed not just the ability or desire to sin but an irresistible urge to sin. They passed on that sinful human nature to every one of their descendants. The result is that every human being since Adam and Eve (with the exception of Jesus) was born with an inner bent, an irresistible urge, to sin. I am not a sinner because I commit acts of sin; I commit acts of sin because I am already by nature a sinner.

In Other Words

Human beings are not machines or robots. We are people to whom God has given the very risky capacity for making up our own minds about things and exercising our own choices. That was the power God gave us when he created us, and sadly we abused it right up front. We took power into our own hands by rebelling against God's authority, rejecting his instructions and choosing to decide for ourselves what we will consider good and evil. The result of this tragic exercise of our own power, which is usually called the Fall and is described in Genesis 3, is the terrible mess that we now live in. Every aspect of human life (spiritual, physical, intellectual, emotional, and social) has been corrupted by sin. So all our boasted power is, spiritually speaking, our weakness — the weakness of sinful human nature.

Christopher J. H. Wright, in *Knowing the Holy Spirit through the Old Testament* (Downers Grove Ill.: InterVarsity, 2006), 36–37.

God gives us the freedom to reject him.
He gives each of us a will of our own.
Good grief, why? He knows what free-willed creatures can do. He has already suffered one massive betrayal in the rebellion of the angels. He knows how we will use our freedom, what misery and suffering, what hell will be unleashed on earth because of our choices. Why? Is he out of his mind?
The answer is as simple and staggering as this: if you want a world where love is real, you must allow each person the freedom to choose.

John Eldredge, in *Epic* (Nashville: Nelson, 2004), 50.

The theological term for humanity's condition is *total depravity*. This doesn't mean that human beings are as bad as they could be; it means they are as bad off as they can be. Apart from God's grace, we can do nothing that pleases God. Leave us to ourselves, and we will always go the opposite way from God. The only way any human being is ever rescued from this condition is if God takes the initiative and seeks us out—and that's exactly what we find God doing all throughout history! He looks for sinners in order to save us, in order to rescue us from the place where sin left us.

Why Should I Suffer for Something Adam Did?

The first question that comes to most people's minds after hearing about Adam and Eve's failure is this: Why should I be punished for something they did? I didn't fail the test! I didn't eat the fruit! At first it seems very unfair.

Bible Networking

Isaiah 64:6

All of us have become like one who is unclean,
    and all our righteous acts are like filthy rags;
we all shrivel up like a leaf,
    and like the wind our sins sweep us away.

Ephesians 2:1–3

As for you, you were dead in your transgressions and sins, in which you used to live when you followed the ways of this world and of the ruler of the kingdom of the air, the spirit who is now at work in those who are disobedient. All of us also lived among them at one time, gratifying the cravings of our sinful nature and following its desires and thoughts. Like the rest, we were by nature deserving of wrath.

Romans 6:23

For the wages of sin is death, but the gift of God is eternal life in Christ Jesus our Lord.

But think about this: If you had been placed in the garden instead of Adam or Eve, would you have succeeded where they failed? Not likely. Adam was not only the *natural* "head" of the human race (even Eve came from Adam); Adam was also the *spiritual* "head" of the human race. We all were "in Adam." If he had succeeded and passed God's test, we would all have enjoyed the benefits. Because he failed, we all suffer the consequences. Furthermore, because one representative could stand in our place in the garden of Eden, another representative, Jesus, a second Adam, could take our place on the cross. We can be rescued from sin's curse and Adam's failure because Jesus paid sin's penalty for us.

Death's Icy Grip

This brings us to another dreadful consequence of Adam and Eve's sin. God told Adam that, if he ate from that single tree, he would certainly die—and death came. Adam and Eve immediately died spiritually. The concept of death always involves separation, and after their sin, there was an immediate separation between human beings and God. Before their sin, Adam and Eve walked with God in close fellowship; after the sin, Adam and Eve hid from God when they heard his voice (Genesis 3:8). That separation produced by sin was pictured dramatically by their expulsion from the garden to make their way in the world outside (Genesis 3:23–24).

Adam and Eve also began to die physically that day in the garden. Adam lived for more than 900 years, but the process of decay and deterioration set in at the moment of his sin. Death and decay spread through the entire universe as a result of human sin. Disease, deformity, and disaster are all evidences of sin's presence in our world and in our hearts.

In Other Words

A London Times columnist once posed this question to his readers: "What's wrong with the world?"

G. K. Chesterton, a noted English Christian writer, gave this simple reply: "I am."

Without God's intervention, Adam and Eve (and every other human being) faced a third kind of death—eternal death. Unless God in his mercy and grace could find a way to rescue his creatures from the consequences of their sin, they would face separation from God forever. God cannot look with approval on what is sinful and evil. God, who is holy and pure, cannot welcome what is unholy and impure into his fellowship. It's like trying to mix oil and water! But God's heart was stirred in love for human beings, even for those who had just rebelled against him. So God set in motion a great redemptive plan that would rescue us from sin's penalty and sin's power.

God wasn't surprised or caught off guard by Adam's sin. God knew exactly what would happen in the garden that day. Could he have stopped it? Of course he could have—but he wanted Adam and Eve to obey him and love him because of their own choice, not because God had manipulated them like puppets. What makes the story so remarkable, however, is that even when Adam and Eve disobeyed, God in his love was determined to go after them.

FALLOUT FROM THE FALL

God's judgment for Adam and Eve's sin was clear and irreversible.

For Adam and Eve

- immediate spiritual death (Genesis 3:7)
- eventual physical death (Genesis 5:5)
- expulsion from the garden (Genesis 3:23)

For Eve and all women after her

- pain in childbirth (Genesis 3:16)
- submission to her husband (Genesis 3:16)

For Adam and all human beings after him

- "painful toil" to get food from the earth (Genesis 3:17–19)

For the serpent

- cursed to crawl on its belly and eat dust (Genesis 3:14)

For Satan

- God promised that Satan would injure the heel of the woman's offspring (that is, hurt him physically), but that in the process her offspring would crush Satan's head (destroy Satan's power permanently; Genesis 3:15). This is the first hint in the Bible that Satan would incite evil men and women to crucify Jesus, but through that death Jesus would defeat Satan forever.

The rescue plan for the human race was already in place. Jesus, God the Son, had already submitted himself to become the Redeemer. He would suffer the eternal death we deserved. The apostle Peter says that Jesus was "chosen before the creation of the world" to be the sacrifice for human sin (1 Peter 1:20).

Why Am I Suffering?

The intrusion of sin into God's perfect world brought another consequence—human suffering. How can a God who is good and all-powerful allow people to suffer? Suffering and pain are not limited to drug dealers and terrorists. People of faith get sick and die. We have to face brain tumors and Alzheimer's disease and the tragic deaths of those we love. Why doesn't God rescue us from such pain?

Bible Networking

Jesus in Mark 7:21 – 23

"From within, out of your hearts, come evil thoughts, sexual immorality, theft, murder, adultery, greed, malice, deceit, lewdness, envy, slander, arrogance and folly. All these evils come from inside and defile you."

Romans 3:10 – 12

"There is no one righteous, not even one;
    there is no one who understands;
    there is no one who seeks God.
All have turned away,
    they have together become worthless;
there is not even one who does good,
    not even one."

Romans 5:12

Just as sin entered the world through one man, and death through sin, and in this way death came to all people, because all sinned.

AREN'T THERE GOOD PEOPLE WHO ARE NOT CHRISTIANS?

The young woman was very upset. "How can you say that we are all sinners and under God's judgment unless we believe in Jesus? I have a neighbor who has no faith and yet he is the most honest, moral, upright person I know!" She raised a good question. What about her neighbor? Won't God look on him with favor?

My answer had two parts. First, my statement that all human beings who don't believe in Jesus are lost is not *my* judgment on them but the clear declaration of God's Word. I am simply agreeing with what God says. Second, some unbelievers may do many good and noble deeds that seem to be in obedience to God's law, but they are not doing those deeds for God's glory. They have their own personal reasons—and, I would say, ultimately selfish reasons—for what they do. God is only pleased with deeds that arise from faith and the sincere desire to please him (Romans 14:23).

The Bible doesn't explain (or explain away) the problem of suffering with pat answers or three-point outlines. Suffering came on human beings as one of the consequences of sin. Sometimes we bring the suffering on ourselves; at other times we are caught in the backwash of someone else's sinful behavior. Even the universe itself through earthquakes or tsunamis or floods can add to the weight of human pain. The Bible says the whole creation groans "as in the pains of childbirth" (Romans 8:22).

We realize that God can work through suffering to bring about his own good results.

- *Suffering can lead a person to believe in Jesus.* Sometimes it is an illness or the loss of a loved one or the breakup of a marriage that brings us to the end of our own resources, and so we turn to God for help.
- *Suffering can deepen a Christian's faith.* Difficult days help us trust the Lord more deeply and cling to him more closely. The Bible uses words like *refines* or *prunes* to describe how God uses the problems and sorrows of life to make us more like Jesus.
- *Suffering deepens our love for and trust in God.* God has not promised to explain our suffering or even to let us see its purpose in this life. What he has promised is that we will never pass

through pain or difficulty alone. Jesus is not a bystander or spectator to our suffering. He has been here, feeling what we feel, suffering pain he did not deserve. He doesn't come to us in our suffering with a sermon or a rebuke; he comes to take our hand and walk beside us.

Surviving in a Fallen World

God in his wisdom and power has not allowed human society to degenerate to the lowest level. Sin affected every relationship and every circumstance of human life, but God has also preserved order and protected human life through several divinely ordained institutions.

- *Marriage*, for example, was instituted by God as the foundation of human society before Adam and Eve's fall into sin. The Bible envisions marriage only one way—one man and one woman who commit to a faithful, life-long relationship. God does permit divorce in certain situations, but his desire is that a married couple remains joyfully united until death.

Bible Networking

Psalm 23:4 (KJV)

Yea, though I walk through the valley of the shadow of death, I will fear no evil: for thou art with me; thy rod and thy staff they comfort me.

Job 13:15

Though [God] slay me, yet will I hope in him.

2 Corinthians 1:3 – 4

Praise be to the God and Father of our Lord Jesus Christ, the Father of compassion and the God of all comfort, who comforts us in all our troubles, so that we can comfort those in any trouble with the comfort we ourselves receive from God.

In Other Words

God whispers to us in our pleasures, speaks in our conscience, but shouts in our pains; it is his megaphone to rouse a deaf world.

C. S. Lewis, in *The Problem of Pain* (New York: Macmillan, 1962), 93.

If my beloved daughter had been murdered, and some sanctimonious vicar [pastor] tried to say that senseless tragedies like this are all part of God's mysterious plan, I'd be tempted to tell him what to do with his stupid candle. And his cruel God. Isn't it more consoling to believe that God doesn't exist than that he is a callous monster?

Richard Dawkins (a leading secularist thinker), in *The Guardian*, August 27, 2002.

- *Civil government* is clearly identified in the Bible as a God-given institution. Paul calls those in authority "God's servants, agents of wrath to bring punishment on the wrongdoer" (Romans 13:4). This does not mean, of course, that we are to follow political leaders blindly or to put our loyalty to a nation above our loyalty to God. Political leaders are to be accountable to the civil law and to God's law. But civil government keeps society from degenerating into complete chaos.
- *Work* is one of God's original gifts to humanity. God gave Adam work to do in the garden of Eden. He was to take care of the garden and know the joy of personal fulfillment in his work. One consequence of Adam's sin was that the ground now lies under God's curse, and, to an extent, work becomes difficult and frustrating (Genesis 3:17–19), but work is still part of God's plan for human beings. Work provides us as human beings with a sense of dignity and fulfillment. It also gives us an opportunity to serve other people and to provide for our families. Most importantly, we work as an act of worship and honor to God. "Whatever you do, work at it with all your heart, as working for the Lord, not for

How many talks have you heard at church on the subject of *work*? But working is what most of us spend most of our time doing!

What usually happens is that the whole church prays fervently for our children's church or Sunday school teachers who are with our children forty-five minutes a week, but we tend to neglect to pray for the schoolteachers who are with our children for thirty-five or forty hours a week.

It's not only important where we are gathered together at eleven o'clock on Sunday morning in our cozy churches; it's also important where members of the congregation are scattered at eleven o'clock on a Monday morning.

We've made an unbiblical divide between the secular and the spiritual. The role of Christian leaders is to "equip [God's] people for works of service" (Ephesians 4:12)—not only to equip the congregation to serve in the church but also to release God's people to serve him in the wider community through their work in the world.

Jesus in Matthew 5:13 – 16

"You are the salt of the earth. But if the salt loses its saltiness, how can it be made salty again? It is no longer good for anything, except to be thrown out and trampled underfoot.

"You are the light of the world. A city on a hill cannot be hidden. Neither do people light a lamp and put it under a bowl. Instead they put it on its stand, and it gives light to everyone in the house. In the same way, let your light shine before others, that they may see your good deeds and glorify your Father in heaven."

Hebrews 2:8 – 9

Yet at present we do not see everything subject to [human beings]. But we do see Jesus, who was made lower than the angels for a little while, now crowned with glory and honor.

1 John 3:2

Dear friends, now we are children of God, and what we will be has not yet been made known. But we know that when Christ appears, we shall be like him, for we shall see him as he is.

human masters .... It is the Lord Christ you are serving" (Colossians 3:23–24). The bumper sticker that says, "My Boss is a Jewish Carpenter" really is true for the Christian. Whatever we do is to be offered up as a gift to him.

- *Rest* is another provision of God for human beings. The ability to reflect and the opportunity to spend time in recreation provide us with new perspective and new energy. In the Old Testament, a day of rest was programmed into every week. The Sabbath (the seventh day) was devoted to worship and ministry to those in need and to quiet times of reflection. In the New Testament age, every day is the Lord's to direct and use, but the principle still applies. Our maddening rush in life batters our spiritual health, our families, and our hearts before God.

Christian Living in a Desperate World

It might be easy to conclude that, since human beings are sinful and our world is under sin's curse, all we Christians can do is throw up our hands and wait for Jesus to come back. But the Bible never gives us an escape route from caring for our earth or caring for the people on it. Human beings are called to be stewards and caretakers of God's creation. The world and its resources were placed here for the blessing of humanity, but we are never to use these resources in a reckless way for purely personal gain.

In Other Words

A happy marriage is the union of two good forgivers.

> Robert Quillen, quoted in Martin Manser, ed.,
> *The Westminster Collection of Christian Quotations*
> (Louisville, Ky.: Westminster, 2001), 240.

Work [before humanity's fall into sin] was a gift, a "may" from God. After the Fall work became a demand, a "must." Before, it was a joyful command: "work and eat." Now, it is a bitter necessity: "no work, no eat."

> Ben Patterson, in *Work and Worship* (Downers Grove, Ill.:
> InterVarsity, 1994), 33.

☑ Our universe is not some cosmic accident but the product of God's purposeful design.

☑ Human beings are the crown of God's creation.

☑ Adam and Eve were created in the image of God—with the capacity to have a relationship with their Creator.

☑ God put Adam and Eve to a test in the garden—and they failed the test!

☑ Their disobedience plunged the entire human race into a state of sin.

☑ Sin resulted in death—spiritual death, physical death, and (unless remedied somehow) eternal death.

☑ The Bible doesn't give an easy answer to why we suffer, but it does promise God's presence through the suffering.

☑ Christians are caretakers of God's creation and light bearers of God's truth to those who are still lost.

Jesus said that in the world of humanity his followers were to act as light and salt (Matthew 5:13–16). The sinful world is the realm of darkness; Christian believers are called to carry Jesus' light into that dangerous realm. The fallen world is decaying; followers of Christ act with pungent, preserving power as we call men and women to join us in the life of faith. Evil will seem to dominate our society at times, but Christians are to stand courageously for the truth of God, even in the face of threats and imprisonment and death. The story of Christians for the last nearly 2,000 years is filled with examples of individuals and small clusters of committed people who faced down the worst kinds of tyranny and evil and who sometimes paid dearly for their devotion to what was just and right.

A man once eagerly told me that he was "surrounded by Christians" where he worked. I told him that was too bad! How could he ever make an impact on a lost and wandering culture if he functioned only in the context of other believers?

In the past, Christians have been at the forefront of the fight for social justice against slavery and for universal education and in support of civil rights. Who will speak in our generation for the oppressed, the poor, the unborn, and the elderly? Christians are called to defend and help the most vulnerable and powerless among us. Your contribution may never be mentioned in the history books, but you may change a life with your love or your financial help or your outspoken defense.

The Majesty of Humanity

Human beings were created as the crown of God's universe. Humanity then crashed to the depths of moral sin. The future, however, promises a wonderful restoration. In our resurrection bodies, we will once again display the glory and honor that God originally intended for human beings. We are a little lower than the angels today in terms of personal glory, but the day will come when we will be given glory greater than angels. We don't see that yet. Human beings still bear the image of God, but it's marred and shadowed by sin's intrusion. We do, however, see Jesus—a human being, risen in majesty—and in Jesus we get a glimpse of our future glory.

Digging Deeper

✗ Robert A. Pyne, *Humanity and Sin: The Creation, Fall, and Redemption of Humanity*. Nashville: Word, 1999.

An excellent, readable examination of the human condition and what God has done about it.

CHAPTER 7

Jesus to the Rescue: The Cross

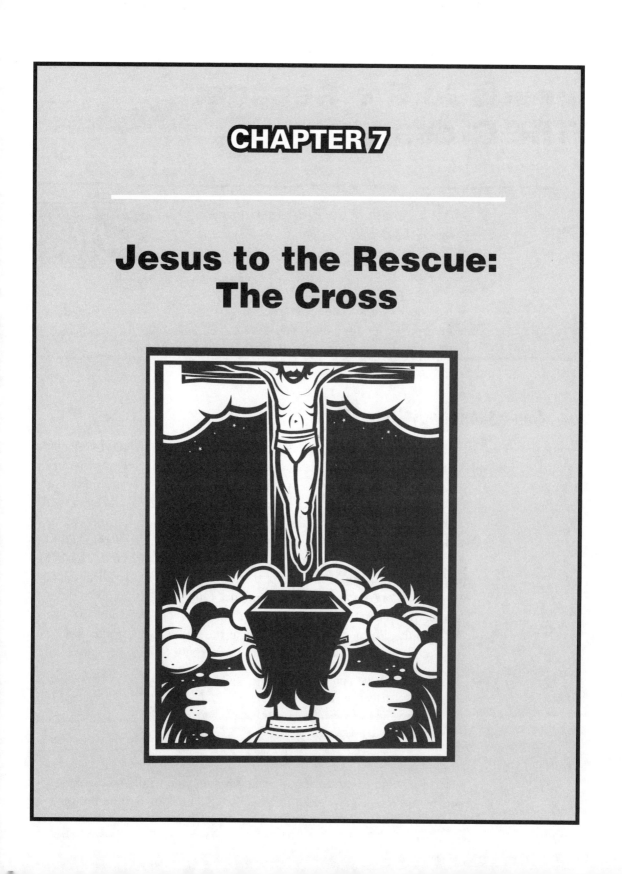

Jesus to the Rescue: The Cross

- ▶ Get a glimpse of God's desire to rescue rebellious people.
- ▶ Stand at the cross as Jesus dies in your place for your sin.
- ▶ God's not angry anymore!
- ▶ No pilgrimages to Jesus' tomb.
- ▶ Find out what Jesus is doing today.

Can't Somebody Help Me?

If the Bible ended with the last verse of Genesis 3, we would be in a lot of trouble. Our first parents had it all—a wonderful place to live, every need supplied, close fellowship with God—and they blew it! Suddenly, the gate to the garden was closed, life became a struggle, and even God seemed far away. The worst part of it was that there was nothing Adam and Eve could do about it. They were now sinners, and someone had to pay the debt that sin had incurred against a holy and just God. That's the problem all throughout the rest of the human story. We are all sinners; we all fall short of God's perfect standard. Our feeble attempts to do "good" things can't begin to recover or restore what Adam and Eve lost.

The only glimmer of hope we have at the end of Genesis chapter 3 is the veiled promise that God made to the serpent (Satan) in verse 15:

> I will put enmity
> > between you and the woman,
> > and between your offspring and hers;
> he will crush your head,
> > and you will strike his heel.

God seemed to promise that someday someone would come along who would begin to reverse the effects of Adam's sin. Satan's power

Bible Networking

John 3:16

For God so loved the world that he gave his one and only Son, that whoever believes in him shall not perish but have eternal life.

1 John 4:9-10

This is how God showed his love among us: He sent his one and only Son into the world that we might live through him. This is love: not that we loved God, but that he loved us and sent his Son as an atoning sacrifice for our sins.

Romans 5:8

God demonstrates his own love for us in this: While we were still sinners, Christ died for us.

would be crushed. Adam and Eve may have hoped one of their sons would be the restorer—a hope quickly shattered when the oldest boy, Cain, murdered his brother Abel (Genesis 4:1–11). Humankind quickly slipped from the place of honor over God's creation to a place of rebellion against their Creator. In the Bible's words, we "exchanged the glory of the immortal God" for idols of our own making (Romans 1:22–23).

But over it all stood a God whose heart burned with love for his creatures. This God had long before determined that he would take the initiative to seek and to restore human beings to a place of friendship. God didn't do this because we were lovely or even lovable. We were rebellious sinners who loved darkness and not God's light. God chose

In Other Words

God never ceases to be loving, but he also never ceases to be holy, and his holiness demands payment for sin.

Robert Pyne, in *Humanity and Sin: The Creation, Fall, and Redemption of Humanity* (Nashville: Word, 1999), 262.

to rescue us from sin's power purely out of his grace, purely from his choice to bless those who deserved the opposite of his blessing.

Promises and Pictures

God began to make promises about the coming Restorer early in human history. He began to picture in the rituals of the Old Testament how the Restorer would act. God began to set apart one family through whom the Promised One would come — the descendants of Abraham through his son Isaac and his grandson Jacob. In time, the whole family of Jacob, renamed Israel, received God's law and a wonderful plan for the worship of God. The law was holy and good, but the law could not change the human heart. The problem was not the law; the problem was our sinful nature. The law made people aware of their sin but had no power to make them righteous.

God recognized that human beings would fall short of the law's demands, so he made provision in the law for forgiveness and grace. An animal was offered as a sacrifice in the sinner's place. The sinner deserved death, but God accepted the animal as a substitute and thus the sinner was allowed to go free. The picture of the Restorer's work became clearer. He would reclaim all that Adam lost by somehow paying the penalty that sin deserved.

The prophets in the Old Testament began to reveal more and more details of the Restorer's work: he would be betrayed by a friend; he would suffer intensely; his bones would not be broken, but he would be pierced through. The most powerful prediction of the Restorer's suffering came from the pen of Isaiah:

> He was despised and rejected by others,
>   a man of suffering, and familiar with pain.
> Like one from whom people hide their faces
>   he was despised, and we held him in low esteem.
> Surely he took up our pain
>   and bore our suffering,
> yet we considered him punished by God,
>   stricken by him, and afflicted.
> But he was pierced for our transgressions,
>   he was crushed for our iniquities;
> the punishment that brought us peace was on him,
>   and by his wounds we are healed.
> We all, like sheep, have gone astray,

> each of us has turned to our own way;
> and the LORD has laid on him
>   the iniquity of us all.
>
> Isaiah 53:3–6

The prophets pictured the glory that would emerge from the Restorer's work too. This promised One, this Messiah, would forgive our sins and change our hearts and lead us into a kingdom of peace and truth where we will enjoy his presence forever. According to the Bible, all the promises and pictures were fulfilled in one person—Jesus Christ, the Son of Abraham, the Son of David, the Son of Man, and the Son of God. He is all the Old Testament prophets hoped for; he is all our stricken hearts long for. Finally someone has come who will change everything.

Death on a Cross

Most of the people in Jesus' day expected a Messiah on a white horse who would destroy all their enemies and give them whatever they wanted. They looked for someone to drive out the oppressive Romans and someone to miraculously provide lunch each day. When Jesus came along making *spiritual* demands, most people tuned him out. A few people, like his disciples, believed he was God's promised Messiah, but most of Jesus' compatriots either ignored him or hated him.

It wasn't that Jesus wouldn't some day set up a kingdom of peace on earth. That's still one of his future attractions. Jesus came to earth first, however, to do something far more significant. He came to deal with the sin issue once and for all. He came to reopen the door into the place of friendship with God. He did all that not by wearing a crown and leading a victorious army. Jesus dealt with our sin problem by going all alone to the place of death. He died a horrible death nailed to a Roman cross. *Crucifixion*, they called it—and it was the worst way to die. But the Bible points to Jesus' death as the most significant event in all of human history.

We refer to the results of Jesus' death as the *atonement*. The cross bridged the gap between a holy God and sinful humanity. Jesus' death opened the door to a spirit of "at-one-ment" between God and his rebellious creation. The blood of animals in the Old Testament provided only a temporary restoration between God and sinners. The blood of Christ opens the way for restoration forever.

Atonement encompasses four key ideas:

Great Debates!

DID CHRIST DIE FOR ALL OR ONLY FOR THE ELECT?

Christians have had long discussions about the extent of atonement. Some Christians believe that Christ died only for those who would ultimately be saved—a position referred to as the "limited atonement" position. They base their views on biblical passages that refer to Jesus dying for *us*, that is, for believers, for those who have been saved by faith. Jesus even said, "The good shepherd lays down his life *for the sheep*" (John 10:11, italics added). Other Christians hold to an "unlimited atonement" view based on passages that describe Jesus' death as sufficient to save the world. The writer of Hebrews says that Jesus "might taste death for everyone" (2:9). The apostle John writes, "[Jesus] is the atoning sacrifice for our sins, and not only for ours but also for the sins of the whole world" (1 John 2:2). John seems to draw a distinction between believers ("*our* sins") and the rest of humanity ("the whole world") but includes the sins of both groups under the death of Jesus. Jesus' death was sufficiently powerful to cover the sins of every human being, but this forgiveness is only applied to those who believe.

A third position regarding the extent of the atonement is a "universal atonement" view. Those who hold this view believe that Jesus' death did, in fact, cover the sins of every person and that God in grace will take everyone to heaven. Proponents of this view base it on verses of Scripture that talk about the atonement in universal terms. Colossians 1:20, for example, says that God in Christ has reconciled "all things" to himself. Those who believe God will save everyone, however, do not take into account the many passages of Scripture that say it is only through faith in Christ alone that we are saved (John 14:6; Acts 4:12; Romans 10:9–10).

1. Substitution

The fundamental meaning of Jesus' death is summarized in one word—*substitution*. On the cross, Jesus died in my place. The penalty I deserved, he paid; the condemnation that was rightly pronounced against me, Jesus accepted. He took our sins on himself and suffered the punishment for them.

Here are some key biblical passages:

- "God made [Christ] who had no sin to be sin for us, so that in him we might become the righteousness of God" (2 Corinthians 5:21).
- "God put the wrong on [Christ] who never did anything wrong, so we could be put right with God" (2 Corinthians 5:21 *The Message*).

- "While we were still sinners, Christ died for us" (Romans 5:8).
- "[Christ] has appeared once for all at the culmination of the ages to do away with sin by the sacrifice of himself" (Hebrews 9:26).

2. Removal of God's Anger

When we sin, we provoke God's holy anger. Sin incurs a *debt* against God that must be paid, a *penalty* that must be carried out. God's justice must be satisfied, his judgment poured out. That's exactly what happened on the cross. My penalty was paid, but not by me! My penalty was paid by Jesus. God's just anger against my sin was poured out on someone else — on God's own sinless Son. All the punishment, all the abandonment I deserved by my own sinful choice, Jesus took. If you think God is still angry with you, you are wrong. He is now free to forgive.

Here are a few key biblical passages:

- "This is love: not that we loved God, but that he loved us and sent his Son as an atoning sacrifice for our sins" (1 John 4:10).

    Some Bible translations use the word *propitiation* in place of the phrase *atoning sacrifice* in this verse. It means to remove God's wrath, or to satisfy God's anger against sin.
- "God made you alive with Christ. He forgave us all our sins, having canceled the charge of our legal indebtedness, which stood against us and condemned us; he has taken it away, nailing it to the cross" (Colossians 2:13–14).

3. Redemption from Slavery

Jesus' death also set us free from the slavery of sin. Before we believed in Jesus, we were powerless to do what was pleasing to God. The Bible describes us as slaves to sin and hostages of Satan — dead, lost, blind to God. Jesus' death paid the ransom to set us free. God himself had set the penalty — "the one who sins is the one who will die" (Ezekiel 18:4). Now it was God himself who paid the price. Jesus died — not just the physical death of a sacrifice but the spiritual death of being made sin and being abandoned by the Father. Because Jesus was a sinless man he could take my place; because he was God he could pay an infinite price and carry the sin of the whole world. God cannot forgive sin simply by wishing it. A price had to be paid — and that price was nothing less than Jesus' life willingly offered up as a sacrifice for us.

In Other Words

Some of the most loved hymns of the church center on the cross and Jesus' sacrifice for our sins.

On a hill far away stood an old rugged cross,
The emblem of suffering and shame;
And I love that old cross where the dearest and best
For a world of lost sinners was slain.
So I'll cherish the old rugged cross,
Till my trophies at last I lay down;
I will cling to the old rugged cross,
And exchange it some day for a crown.

"The Old Rugged Cross"; words and music by George Bennard

Up Calvary's mountain, one dreadful morn,
Walked Christ my Savior, weary and worn;
Facing for sinners death on the cross,
That He might save them from endless loss.

"Blessed Redeemer"; words by Avis Christiansen

Upon that cross of Jesus mine eyes at times can see
The very dying form of One who suffered there for me;
And from my stricken heart with tears two wonders I confess:
The wonders of redeeming love and my unworthiness.

"Beneath the Cross of Jesus"; words by Elizabeth Clephane

He left His Father's throne above,
So free, so infinite His grace —
Emptied Himself of all but love,
And bled for Adam's helpless race:
'Tis mercy all, immense and free,
For O my God, it found out me!
Amazing love! How can it be,
That Thou, my God, shouldst die for me?

"And Can It Be That I Should Gain?"; words by Charles Wesley

When I became a Christian, the minister said a few words in prayer—almost like he would in a marriage ceremony. He first asked me a question: "Sinner, will you have this Savior?" This is the key point—will we by faith accept Jesus Christ to be our Savior and Lord throughout our lives? Each of us needs to say at this point, "Yes, I will."

Then the minister asked, "Savior, will you have this sinner?" And the answer always is, "Yes, I will." We commit ourselves to him, and he unreservedly commits himself to us as our Lord and Savior.

In those early days of the Christian life, I was tempted to doubt the reality of my salvation. One verse in the gospel of John helped me enormously: "Whoever comes to me I will never drive away" (John 6:37). If you have truly come to Jesus Christ, he will never turn you away.

Jesus Christ has broken sin's grip on us, and we are now free to serve God.

Here are a few key biblical passages:

- "The Son of Man did not come to be served, but to serve, and to give his life as a ransom for many" (Mark 10:45).
- "He has rescued us from the dominion of darkness and brought us into the kingdom of the Son he loves, in whom we have redemption, the forgiveness of sins" (Colossians 1:13–14).
- "Sin shall no longer be your master, because you are not under the law, but under grace" (Romans 6:14).

4. Restoration to Friendship with God

Our sin and rebellion had made us enemies of God, but Jesus' death opened the door for a friendship to be restored. The cross brought an end to hostility. We have been reconciled to God—and it was Jesus' sacrifice that made it happen. We are now "at-one" with God, in harmony with him, at peace. If you think God sits in heaven with his arms crossed, ready to club you if you step out of line, you are mistaken. Every demand God has ever made was satisfied by Jesus' death. All God asks of us now is that we believe in Jesus and receive his forgiveness.

Here are a few key biblical passages:

- "All this is from God, who reconciled us to himself through Christ . . . .: that God was reconciling the world to himself in Christ, not counting people's sins against them" (2 Corinthians 5:18–19).
- "We implore you on Christ's behalf: Be reconciled to God" (2 Corinthians 5:20).

Just before Jesus died on the cross, he shouted, "It is finished!" (John 19:30). That phrase came from the world of accounting. It meant "paid in full." Jesus' death was sufficient to satisfy every demand of God, every requirement of the law, every penalty of sin, and every accusation of Satan. My account, the record of every wrong I had ever committed or would ever commit, was marked "paid in full" when I believed in Jesus. My debt and penalty were transferred to the cross, and Jesus' right standing with God was transferred to me. That didn't happen because I was worthy of God's favor. I deserved his judgment. It happened because of God's amazing grace toward all who will believe.

Risen from the Dead

The story of Jesus doesn't end with his death on the cross. When he died, the sin bearing was over. Humanity's debt to God had been paid. Nothing more needed to be done. God's divine stamp of approval on Jesus and on everything Jesus had done came three days later — Jesus was raised from the dead.

Bible Networking

Galatians 6:14

May I [Paul] never boast except in the cross of our Lord Jesus Christ, through which the world has been crucified to me, and I to the world.

1 Timothy 1:15

Here is a trustworthy saying that deserves full acceptance: Christ Jesus came into the world to save sinners—of whom I [Paul] am the worst.

GOD'S MESSAGE TO THE WORLD IN 200 WORDS

God created human beings because he loves them and wants a relationship with them. God designed human beings to have a hunger for what God offers. God also gave human beings the capacity to reject his love—and left to ourselves, that's what we all do. We are sinners who act and think and talk in a way that dishonors God and grieves his holy nature. Sin isn't something God can simply sweep under the table. The penalty of sin is death. The problem is, we can't ever pay the debt on our own. We all fall short of God's holy demands. If the gap between God and human beings is ever to be closed, God must take the initiative to do it. That's why Jesus came—to become human and to die on the cross for the sins of the world. Merely acknowledging these facts, however, is not enough to restore us to God's friendship. God calls each of us to believe that Jesus died for our sins and to personally receive Jesus as Savior and King. When we accept God's gift of grace and forgiveness, we become his own dear children, followers of Jesus, vessels of the Spirit.

How do we know that Jesus' sacrifice on the cross really paid the debt of our sin? Because Jesus rose alive from the dead. How do we know that Jesus was the Son of God? Because he came out of the grave alive. Why do Christians have such confidence that after death we will stand before Jesus in heaven? Because of the resurrection of Jesus from the dead. The resurrection is the foundation of the Christian faith. Everything we believe rises or falls on the fact that Jesus who was dead is now alive forever.

If the resurrection is just a myth or make-believe or a clever hoax that the disciples managed to pull off on the world, the Christian faith is nothing more than a waste of time. But if Jesus really did come back from the dead, everything he said or did or claimed to be is verified as true.

Just the Facts

Our belief in the resurrection is not based simply on wishful thinking. We have eyewitness accounts of what happened, and every line of evidence from every source points to one inescapable fact: Jesus rose from the dead! Here are the lines of biblical evidence:

- *Jesus really died.* If you are going to have a resurrection, you have to start with a corpse! Some people have tried to make the claim that Jesus didn't really die on the cross. He fainted or was drugged or fell into a coma and then, later, was revived by his disciples, who claimed he had risen from the dead. The problem with these views is that the evidence denies them all. The testimony of Jesus' enemies, of his executioners, of his friends and followers, all agree that Jesus died. His closest friends took his body from the cross and carefully prepared it for burial. If they had seen one flicker of life, they would never have sealed Jesus in the tomb.

- *Jesus' body was not stolen.* The oldest attempt at explaining away the resurrection is to claim that Jesus' body was taken from the tomb and hidden. The question is, Who took it? The disciples were hiding. They were convinced that the next execution order had their names on it. Jesus' enemies certainly wouldn't have taken his body. The last thing they wanted was an empty grave! Furthermore, the tomb was guarded to prevent anyone from stealing the body (Matthew 27:62–66). "The body was stolen" theory was cooked up only to provide cover for the guards and to give an alternate account for those who wanted to deny the resurrection (Matthew 28:11–15).

- *The same tomb where Jesus' body was buried was empty three days later.* Another popular explanation for the resurrection is

THE RESURRECTION AND WATERGATE

Charles Colson was one of the people who conspired together to keep the break-in at the Watergate complex a secret during the Nixon administration. Colson was eventually found out and sent to prison, where the Lord found him. Colson emerged a changed man. He addresses the theory that the disciples conspired to make up the resurrection:

> With the most powerful office in the world at stake, a small band of hand-picked loyalists, no more than ten of us, could not hold a conspiracy together for more than two weeks....
>
> Even political zealots at the pinnacle of power will save their own necks in the crunch, though it may be at the expense of the one they profess to serve so zealously.
>
> Charles Colson, in *Loving God* (new ed.; Grand Rapids: Zondervan, 2006), 67, 69.

that in the dim light of the early morning, the women went to the wrong tomb. When they saw it was empty, they ran to tell people that Jesus had risen. The written accounts, however, make it clear that the same women who helped with Jesus' burial on the day of his death returned three days later to the exact tomb to finish the embalming process. They weren't mistaken—and the close scrutiny of the tomb by two of Jesus' disciples confirmed the women's testimony: Jesus' body was gone (John 20:1–10).

- *Jesus appeared to his followers on several occasions over the course of six weeks.* During the forty days following the discovery of the empty tomb, Jesus appeared to different people at different times in different locations. He ate with them and talked with them and even encouraged them to handle his body as proof that he was not a hallucination but a real person in a real body who had been dead but was now alive.

- *Jesus' followers were transformed.* Occasionally someone will come along and make the claim that the resurrection of Jesus was just cooked up by his followers as a way to perpetuate Jesus' legacy—or that they wanted so much for Jesus to live on that the disciples convinced themselves he had returned from the dead. Here's the problem with that claim. Before Jesus died, the disciples were not valiant or brave. They ran away. After his death, they were still hiding in fear for their lives. But an amazing transformation took place after Jesus' resurrection and their empowering by the Holy Spirit. The timid disciples became fearless witnesses! They faced imprisonment, threats, beatings, warnings—all with incredible courage. Most of them would die as martyrs for their faith in Jesus. Would they die to defend a hoax? Would you face torture and prison for a lie? The certain assurance of the disciples is another argument for the reality of Jesus' resurrection.

The only logical conclusion that is consistent with all the evidence is that a supernatural event occurred three days after Jesus died. He rose from the dead as proof that all his claims were true. God the Father declared to the world and to every generation that Jesus was in fact his own unique Son and the Savior of all who will believe in him.

Jesus' resurrection has more eyewitness evidence to support it than any other event in ancient times—more evidence than the military victories of Julius Caesar or the first Olympic games or the death of Alexander the Great, enough evidence to convince thousands of skeptics over the centuries and millions of seekers. Jesus died as the result of a brutal execution on the cross, but death could not hold him. He rose alive and stands alive in heaven today—our conquering King.

Resurrection Power

It didn't take long for a controversy to brew up over Jesus' resurrection. In one of the early Christian communities, some false teachers had begun to preach that there was no resurrection. Jesus may have "risen" in his spirit, but not in his body. The soul, these teachers claimed, was eternal but the body was evil. The apostle Paul told the Christians that the false teachers were wrong. The human spirit continues to exist beyond death, but the human body will not be left behind forever. The Christian's body will someday be raised and changed so it will live forever.

The proof of our future resurrection is the resurrection of Jesus. Jesus did not just come alive in his spirit. His body emerged from the tomb in majesty and glory. This is such a foundational truth of the Christian faith that Paul lists the results if a resurrection really had not taken place on that Sunday morning so long ago.

If Christ has not been raised from the dead,

Help File   WHO KILLED JESUS?

For centuries, Jewish people have been persecuted as "Christ killers"—and it's certainly true that the single generation of Jewish leaders and people in the crowd who called for Jesus' death were guilty of his ultimate execution. But Pilate, the Roman governor who pronounced the death sentence, and the Roman soldiers who carried it out were just as guilty of killing Jesus. To my knowledge, no one has ever persecuted Italians for being Christ killers.

In a sense, God the Father shares some responsibility for Jesus' death. Isaiah the prophet wrote that "it was the LORD's will to crush him [God's servant, the Messiah] and cause him to suffer" (53:10). In a larger sense it was all of us who caused Jesus' death because he gave his life as a ransom and sacrifice for our sin. Isaiah wrote, "He was pierced for our transgressions" and "crushed for our iniquities" (53:5). But one more person was involved in putting Jesus on the cross—Jesus himself. He said, "No one takes [my life] from me, but I lay it down of my own accord. I have authority to lay it down and authority to take it up again" (John 10:18). Jesus went to the cross of his own choice to redeem human beings who were lost and hopeless without his help.

Bible Networking

Peter in Acts 2:22 - 24

People of Israel, listen to this: Jesus of Nazareth was a man accredited by God to you by miracles, wonders and signs, which God did among you through him, as you yourselves know. This man was handed over to you by God's deliberate plan and foreknowledge; and you, with the help of wicked men, put him to death by nailing him to the cross. But God raised him from the dead, freeing him from the agony of death, because it was impossible for death to keep its hold on him.

Paul in 1 Corinthians 15:3 - 4

What I received I passed on to you as of first importance: that Christ died for our sins according to the Scriptures, that he was buried, that he was raised on the third day according to the Scriptures.

Paul in 1 Thessalonians 4:14

We believe that Jesus died and rose again.

- Christian preaching about forgiveness for sins and a home in heaven is a lie.
- Christian belief is useless and invalid.
- Paul and the other New Testament writers are liars.
- Christians are not forgiven, but are still lost and dead in sin, separated from God.
- those Christians who have died are not in heaven; they are in hell.
- the confidence we have of eternal life is a delusion, and we are to be pitied, not followed.

Paul lists these disastrous consequences in 1 Corinthians 15:12 – 19. But Paul doesn't end his discussion in defeat or despair. His declaration is that "Christ has indeed been raised from the dead" (1 Corinthians 15:20). For Paul, there was no doubt — Jesus had been raised. Therefore, you can reverse every consequence listed earlier. We are forgiven! Our faith is in the genuine Savior. Christians who have died are with the Lord. We have not been deceived or deluded.

THE BONES OF BUDDHA

J. Sidlow Baxter, a Christian writer of a generation past, describes a scene in India as the reputed bones of Buddha were paraded through the streets. A Christian missionary watched thousands of people kneel to the ground in homage to the bones and then said to a friend, "If one bone of Jesus were found, Christianity would fall to pieces."

For Christians, the resurrection isn't just a dead doctrine in a book. The resurrection power of Jesus can be experienced in our lives. When we believed in Jesus, we were made new by his power. The Bible says we were raised up with Christ to a new life (Romans 6:4, 11). In the challenges and struggles of life, Jesus offers us his resurrection power to bring new life to situations we thought were beyond hope. Christians are people who "want to know Christ—yes, to know the power of his resurrection" (Philippians 3:10). The fact that Jesus is alive forever changes our entire perspective of life and our purpose and our future.

> Since, then, you have been raised with Christ, set your heart on things above, where Christ is seated at the right hand of God.
> Colossians 3:1

Bible Networking

John 11:25 – 26

Jesus said to [Martha], "I am the resurrection and the life. Anyone who believes in me will live, even though they die; and whoever lives by believing in me will never die. Do you believe this?"

Romans 8:11

If the Spirit of him who raised Jesus from the dead is living in you, he who raised Christ from the dead will also give life to your mortal bodies because of his Spirit who lives in you.

Back to Heaven

After his resurrection, Jesus was on earth for forty days. He appeared several times to his disciples and other followers but then led his closest friends to an area near the town of Bethany, where Jesus was taken back to heaven. "He was taken up before their very eyes, and a cloud hid him from their sight" (Acts 1:9). Jesus today is in heaven, seated in the place of authority at the Father's right hand (Hebrews 10:12).

Jesus' ascension into heaven was a further step in his restoration to the place of power and majesty as God the Son. He was raised from the dead and then exalted in majesty as Lord over the entire creation.

> Therefore God exalted [Jesus] to the highest place
>   and gave him the name that is above every name,
> that at the name of Jesus every knee should bow,
>   in heaven and on earth and under the earth,
> and every tongue acknowledge that Jesus Christ is Lord,
>   to the glory of God the Father.
>
> Philippians 2:9–11

The only limitation that Jesus carried with him into heaven was that he was a glorified human being. He has chosen to identify with us forever by remaining in his human body. He pioneered the way into heaven as the first resurrected human, as "the man Christ Jesus" (1 Timothy 2:5 NIV). When the apostle John saw Jesus sixty years after Jesus' ascension into heaven, he saw a majestic, powerful, sovereign Lord. John did not walk up and slap Jesus on the back and say, "How are you, my friend?" John instead fell at Jesus' feet in adoration and worship. (You can read the account yourself in Revelation 1:12–18.)

Jesus' final words to his disciples before he returned to heaven were a challenge, a call to a global mission: "You will be my witnesses in

In Other Words

Now, today, this moment, is our chance to choose the right side. God is holding back to give us that chance. It will not last forever. We must take it or leave it.

C. S. Lewis, in Mere Christianity (New York:
Macmillan, 1952), 56.

Bible Networking

Hebrews 9:26 – 28

[Christ] has appeared once for all at the culmination of the ages to do away with sin by the sacrifice of himself. Just as people are destined to die once, and after that to face judgment, so Christ was sacrificed once to take away the sins of many; and he will appear a second time, not to bear sin, but to bring salvation to those who are waiting for him.

Hebrews 10:21 – 22

Since we have a great priest over the house of God, let us draw near to God with a sincere heart in full assurance of faith.

Jerusalem, and in all Judea and Samaria, and to the ends of the earth" (Acts 1:8). Jesus wanted the world to know about his restoring love and saving grace. Jesus also promised a new source of power: "You will receive power when the Holy Spirit comes on you." For nearly 2,000 years, Christians have been empowered by the Holy Spirit to live lives of obedience and purity and sacrifice. Jesus did leave to go back to heaven, but he did not abandon us as orphans. He sent the Helper, the Spirit, to take his place in leading and comforting and invigorating the people of God.

Gone a Long Time

Jesus didn't return to heaven just to relax. He is busy caring for his followers. The *past* work was on the cross; the *present* work of Jesus is as our Advocate, our Defender, at the Father's side. Jesus' ministry to his people falls into three categories:

- *Jesus our Advocate.* Jesus defends his people from the accusations and attacks of our spiritual enemy, Satan. Satan accuses us "before our God day and night" (Revelation 12:10). He likes nothing better than to deceive or discourage a believer. But at God's right hand is a defense lawyer, an advocate, "Jesus Christ, the Righteous One" (1 John 2:1). When we sin or when Satan accuses, Jesus appeals to his sacrifice on the cross, and the debate ends.

- *Jesus our Priest.* We confess our sins to our heavenly Priest who, on the basis of his final and complete sacrifice on the cross, is faithful and just in forgiving our sins and cleansing us from sin's guilt (1 John 1:9).
- *Jesus our Coming King.* Jesus also reigns in heaven as our sovereign King. We sometimes make the mistake of saying that we should make Jesus the Lord of our lives. The reality is that Jesus is Lord. We either live like he is or we live like we are. Jesus reigns over his church and over our lives, and one day soon he will reign over all creation in power and majesty. Someday every knee will bow to Jesus' authority and every tongue will confess that he is Lord. The question is this: Will you bow willingly to him today or will you bow unwillingly in the future when you have no choice? The difference is life and death—an eternity in Jesus' presence or an eternity separated from him.

This whole chapter has described all that Jesus has done for us to restore us to the place of friendship with God. We haven't contributed one thing except our lostness and our sin. God offers us grace and forgiveness without cost—at least without cost *to us*, but it cost Jesus everything. All we must do to possess God's gift of life is receive it. When we believe, when we accept Jesus as our very own, we pass from death to life.

Help File

JESUS AND HIS PEOPLE

The Bible uses seven images to describe Jesus' ministry to us during this age:

- He is the last Adam and we are God's new creation (1 Corinthians 15:45; 2 Corinthians 5:17).
- He is the Head and we are his body (Ephesians 5:30; Colossians 2:19).
- He is the great Shepherd and we are his sheep (John 10:3–4; Hebrews 13:20).
- He is the true Vine and we are the branches (John 15:5).
- He is the Cornerstone and we are God's building (1 Peter 2:4–8).
- He is our High Priest and we are royal priests (Hebrews 4:14–5:10; 1 Peter 2:9; Revelation 1:6).
- He is the Bridegroom and we are his chosen bride (2 Corinthians 11:2; Ephesians 5:25–27; Revelation 19:6–8).

Points to Remember

- ☑ From the time of humanity's failure, God promised that a Restorer would come who would reverse the effects of Adam's sin.

- ☑ God's promised Deliverer was Jesus, the Son of Man and the Son of God.

- ☑ Jesus restored our friendship with God not by wearing a crown but by dying on a cross.

- ☑ Through Jesus' death, we can be made "at one" with God.

- ☑ Jesus died as our substitute on the cross. The death we deserved, he was willing to endure.

- ☑ God's just anger against my sin was poured out on someone else — on God's own Son, Jesus.

- ☑ Because Jesus paid our debt of sin, we are free from its penalty — free to serve God.

- ☑ All of Jesus' claims were verified by his resurrection from the dead.

- ☑ Forty days after his resurrection, Jesus ascended to heaven to the place of authority at God's right hand.

- ☑ Jesus is in heaven today as our Defender, our Priest with God, and our coming King.

- ☑ All we must do to possess God's gift of eternal life is receive it.

CHAPTER 8

Your Life's Greatest Change: Salvation

Your Life's Greatest Change: Salvation

▶ God to the rescue!

▶ Find out if you are born again (or want to be).

▶ Discover some of the big words of the Bible and what they mean.

▶ Be amazed at God's amazing grace and love to you!

A New Beginning

The human story began in the garden of Eden with Adam and Eve's failure and the resulting inability in every one of us to meet God's perfect standard. That story led us straight to Jesus, the Restorer, the one God promised to send, the one who would win back what Adam lost—and Jesus changed everything! The first book of the Bible opened with the words, "In the beginning God created the heavens and the earth" (Genesis 1:1). The gospel of John in the New Testament promised a new beginning: "In the beginning was the Word [Jesus]" (1:1). Jesus is the Redeemer everyone has been waiting for!

Restoring the friendship between God and humanity required a terrible price. Someone had to pay sin's penalty. God is holy and just. His justice demands that the debt of sin had to be paid. The amazing thing is that God paid the penalty himself. The very person we had offended stepped down from heaven's glory and died on a Roman cross in our place. Because Jesus died, we are free.

Only one problem remained. The penalty of sin had been paid, but somehow human beings needed to be persuaded to accept the freedom and friendship that God was offering—and persuading lost, rebellious people was no easy task! We have a powerful inner bent toward rebellion. The Bible says we are all like sheep who by nature and by choice want to wander from God (Isaiah 53:6; 1 Peter 2:25). Left to ourselves we will always choose the darkness of sin over the light of God. How does God rescue people who are separated from him? We call this work of God *salvation*. God in grace saves us from the power and penalty of sin.

Becoming a Christian

The new beginning of the Christian experience starts when a person believes in Jesus and receives God's salvation. There's nothing automatic or hereditary about that process. You are not delivered from sin's penalty because you live in a mostly Christian nation or because you were baptized or confirmed or raised in a Christian church. You need to do something personally, individually, to become a Christian.

It Begins with Faith

We become Christians by trusting in Jesus and in his death on the cross as the only way to friendship with God. John Stott, a prominent Christian leader, said it this way: "I must do more than acknowledge I needed a Savior, more even than acknowledge that Jesus Christ was the Savior I needed; it was necessary to accept him as *my* Savior" (*Basic Christianity* [Downers Grove, Ill.: InterVarsity, 1971], 122).

The Bible uses the word *faith* to describe what it means to trust in Jesus. Faith is far more than just believing that God exists or that Jesus is real. At least three elements combine in genuine faith:

- *Faith is knowing certain facts about the Christian message* — that God is holy, that we are separated from God by our sin, that Jesus died as a perfect sacrifice and rose from the dead as triumphant Lord, that we are only brought into a right relationship with God through the death and resurrection of Jesus.
- *Faith is believing these facts to be true.* We acknowledge that what God says about our separation from him and about Jesus' work of redemption is correct.
- *Faith is receiving and resting on these facts as true about me personally.* I give up every other way of trying to be right with God and personally trust Jesus alone to save me. I commit myself fully to him as Savior and King.

Faith is coming to the end of your own efforts and your own resources and crying out to God to deliver you from the guilt and penalty of sin. It is staking everything, including your eternal destiny, on Jesus and his death on the cross for you.

The Bible's clearest, simplest message is to believe in Jesus:

- "Everyone who believes in [Jesus] receives forgiveness of sins through his name" (Acts 10:43).
- "If you declare with your mouth, 'Jesus is Lord,' and believe in your heart that God raised him from the dead, you will be saved" (Romans 10:9).
- "To all who did receive [Jesus], to those who believed in his name, he gave the right to become children of God" (John 1:12).
- "God so loved the world that he gave his one and only Son, that whoever believes in him shall not perish but have eternal life" (John 3:16).

Turning Life Around

The Bible also associates the word *repent* with the act of becoming a Christian. Repentance means to change your mind. When we believe in Jesus, we change our minds about several key issues.

- *We change our minds about **ourselves***. Instead of seeing ourselves as basically good people on our way to heaven, we see ourselves as God sees us and as the Bible describes us—lost, separated from God, under sin's condemnation.
- *We change our minds about **God***. He's not the kindly old grandfather who overlooks sin. Nor is he the angry tyrant ready to club us for our wrong. He is a holy, pure God who out of grace has done all that is required to rescue us from sin and death.
- *We change our minds about **Jesus** too*. He is more than just a religious teacher or a plastic figurine in a nativity scene. He is our Savior, our Restorer, our Lord.

Here are a few passages from the Bible that link repentance and faith:

- "The time has come .... The kingdom of God has come near. Repent and believe the good news!" (Jesus in Mark 1:15).
- "I have declared to both Jews and Greeks that they must turn to God in repentance and have faith in our Lord Jesus" (Paul in Acts 20:21).
- "Repent, then, and turn to God, so that your sins may be wiped out" (Peter in Acts 3:19).

Changed minds lead to changed actions. Instead of excusing our sin, we admit it and ask God to forgive us and cleanse us. Instead of rejecting Jesus, we now declare our trust in him and express our commitment to follow him. Instead of relying on religious rituals or church affiliation or our own efforts at doing good deeds to make us right with God, we trust in Jesus alone to make us right before God.

The key question is this: What is your relationship with Jesus? If you have received him into your life by faith and are trusting in his death on the cross for forgiveness before God, you are a Christian, a child of God,

If you have not yet become a Christian and want to do so, you could pray this prayer with sincere faith:

> Lord God, I come into your presence. I admit I have broken your law. I know that there is a deep selfishness within me and that by myself I cannot love you as I should. I realize my personal need for Jesus Christ.
>
> I turn away from everything that is wrong in my life. I am truly sorry that I have not lived life your way but mine.
>
> I thank you, Lord, that in your great love you have made the way open for me to come back to you. I realize that it is only the death of Christ that can bring me back to you. I want to respond to your goodness.
>
> I thank you that Jesus Christ died on the cross for me. Give me faith to believe that Jesus died to forgive *my* sin, that he took on himself the punishment that was due *me*, and that he can make me clean from all the guilt of my sin.
>
> I trust my whole life to you. I humbly yet confidently look to Jesus right now. Come to me as my Savior to rescue me from death and hell. Come to me as my Lord to direct my life toward God and heaven.
>
> I want to give my whole being—my heart, mind, and will—to you, Lord Jesus, right now. Jesus Christ, I take you to be my God. I want to follow you for the rest of my life. Amen.
>
> Martin Manser, *Prayers for Good Times and Grim* (Oxford: Monarch, 2008), 187.
> Used by permission.

If you have prayed this prayer, you have made the most crucial spiritual decision in your life. It's important that you tell a Christian friend about your faith as soon as you can so that you can be helped and encouraged to grow in your walk with Christ.

a believer in the Lord Jesus. If you have not by an act of faith received Jesus into your life, why not believe in him right now? You don't need a priest or a pastor or a church to believe. You can become a Christian right where you are by putting this book down and crying out to God in faith to save you. He promises to receive all who willingly come to him in faith. That act of belief will change your life forever.

A New Birth

What is so amazing about God's gift of salvation is that all we do is receive it! Jesus already paid the price, and we can't add anything to his redeeming work—so the gift is ours to receive. When we believe in Jesus, God continues to work in powerful ways. We don't just have a religious encounter and then go on our way. An encounter with Jesus changes everything about us spiritually.

One remarkable change is that the believing person is given new life. To use the Bible's description, we are *born again* or *regenerated*.

Bible Networking

Ephesians 2:1 – 10 (*The Message*)

It wasn't so long ago that you were mired in that old stagnant life of sin. You let the world, which doesn't know the first thing about living, tell you how to live. You filled your lungs with polluted unbelief, and then exhaled disobedience. We all did it, all of us doing what we felt like doing, when we felt like doing it, all of us in the same boat. It's a wonder God didn't lose his temper and do away with the whole lot of us. Instead, immense in mercy and with an incredible love, he embraced us. He took our sin-dead lives and made us alive in Christ. He did all this on his own, with no help from us! Then he picked us up and set us down in highest heaven in company with Jesus, our Messiah.

Now God has us where he wants us, with all the time in this world and the next to shower grace and kindness upon us in Christ Jesus. Saving is all his idea, and all his work. All we do is trust him enough to let him do it. It's God's gift from start to finish! We don't play the major role. If we did, we'd probably go around bragging that we'd done the whole thing! No, we neither make nor save ourselves. God does both the making and saving. He creates each of us by Christ Jesus to join him in the work he does, the good work he has gotten ready for us to do, work we had better be doing.

Jesus talked about a new birth in a conversation he had one night with a prominent Jewish leader named Nicodemus. Jesus told him that he had to be born again in order to enter the kingdom of God (John 3:3, 5). Entrance into the realm of friendship with God is gained by a spiritual experience that comes from above. We believe, but God the Holy Spirit is the one who gives us new life. Jesus said that flesh gives birth to flesh; the Spirit, however, gives new life to our spirits (John 3:6).

We were all born the first time by a natural birth. We were conceived and born from two human parents. The problem is we were born wrong the first time. We were born with the same bent toward sin that our parents were born with. No amount of education or resolution or human effort will ever change that old human spirit. It takes a radical inner transformation to alter our course. It takes a second birth, a new birth of our spirit, a birth from above.

The new birth makes us into new beings. The old "you" dies and a new "you" is formed. It's not a physical transformation. Your body, hair color, waistline, ethnic background all stay the same. Even your basic personality type stays the same (although God may want to change certain aspects of that). The transformation is spiritual. You have new desires, new interests, a new outlook, new capacities. Your goal is now to please and honor Christ in your life, not focus solely on yourself. Here's a good verse to highlight in your Bible and in your mind: "If anyone is in Christ, he is a new creation; the old has gone, the new has come!" (2 Corinthians 5:17 NIV).

Just as at our first birth we received our parents' natures, at our second birth we receive a new nature, a godly nature. We "participate in the divine nature" (2 Peter 1:4). The old sin-controlled nature is still around, but we now have the capacity to overcome its power and to live in such a way that we honor God. The Holy Spirit lives in us and gives our new nature the power to overcome the drag of the old life.

People who have not believed in Jesus sometimes think they have to change their lives before they can become a Christian. They have old habits or sinful attitudes they think they have to give up. That kind of radical change seems so difficult that they walk away in defeat. The good news is that Jesus accepts us just the way we are—but he loves us too much to leave us that way. Once we believe, we realize that the ability and desire to change come from the Holy Spirit—not from our own resources but from God's power. He makes us new and keeps working to make us more and more like Jesus. The process begins the moment we are born again.

What God Says about You

You don't have to think about our sin and God's salvation very long before you encounter a real problem. We are guilty by nature and by choice of sin; God is holy and pure and cannot approve what is evil. But God offers forgiveness and restored friendship to all who will believe in Jesus. How can God pardon those who are guilty? How can God set us free when we deserve his condemnation? The answer is found in one of the Bible's big words—*justification*.

I grew up hearing justification explained like this: God justifies the believing sinner—that is, God treats me "just as if" I had never sinned. Unfortunately, this easy-to-remember phrase is not an accurate under-

Help File

THREE TOOLS FOR NEW LIFE

A Christian's new life comes from God—and God uses three tools to bring new life to our spirits.

- *God uses the message about Jesus, the gospel.* We believe in Jesus when we hear the message of his death and resurrection and understand his love and grace extended to us. That message about Jesus is called the *gospel*—it is good news to all who hear! Listen to the words of Paul: "I am not ashamed of the gospel, because it is the power of God that brings salvation to everyone who believes" (Romans 1:16).

- *God uses the Holy Spirit* to convince us of the truth of the message and to draw us to faith in Jesus. We are born of the Spirit (John 3:6). God the Holy Spirit produces the new life in us. The apostle Paul makes this clear in Titus 3:5–6: "[God] saved us, not because of righteous things we had done, but because of his mercy. He saved us through the washing of rebirth and renewal by the Holy Spirit, whom he

poured out on us generously through Jesus Christ our Savior."

- *God also uses human messengers* to share the message about Jesus. God could have sent angels to tell every person about his forgiveness but he sent his followers into all the world to proclaim the gospel (Mark 16:15). Occasionally a person will pick up a Gideon Bible in a motel room or find a small pamphlet that explains who Jesus is and how we can be rescued through him. That person is led to believe just by reading God's Word! More often, people believe in Jesus because a neighbor or friend shares the message—or they hear a pastor explain the gospel in a church service, or an evangelist on television calls them to receive Christ as Savior. "How can they believe in the one of whom they have not heard?" Paul wrote. "And how can they hear without someone preaching to them?" (Romans 10:14). God has entrusted his wonderful message of grace to us.

standing of justification. God never looks at us as though we had never sinned. God has found all of us guilty of violating his law and defaming his holy character. Justification is God's declaration that guilty men and women are put in a right relationship with God because of Jesus' death on the cross. The Bible says that those who believe in Jesus "are justified freely by [God's] grace through the redemption that came by Christ Jesus" (Romans 3:24). We do not work to be declared right with God. All our efforts are worthless when it comes to earning merit with God. We are justified freely—as a gift—by God's grace.

The amazing thing is that God extends his grace to *guilty* people. We all are sinners who deserve God's judgment. But Jesus made it possible for God to declare guilty sinners to be righteous—not innocent, but in a right standing with God. Here's how it happens: Our sin and its penalty were transferred to Jesus, and Jesus' right standing with God the Father was transferred to us. God made Jesus to be sin in our place. The penalty I deserved was fully paid, but not by me. Jesus paid my penalty on the cross. So God can remove the sentence of judgment against me and place it on Jesus. In return, God takes Jesus' right standing before God and places it on me. I am now a child of God, guilty but forgiven—and not just forgiven, but also declared to be right with God.

Why does God make such a dramatic transfer? Because I have done so many good things? No. Because I have become a church member or become baptized or given money to a good cause? No. I'm a guilty rebel, remember? God makes that transfer when I believe in Jesus. We are justified through faith alone in Christ alone by grace alone.

Don't just take my word for it. Here's what the Bible says:

- "We maintain that a person is justified by faith apart from observing the law" (Romans 3:28).
- "A person is not justified by observing the law [i.e., keeping religious rules], but by faith in Jesus Christ. So we, too, have put our faith in Christ Jesus that we may be justified by faith in Christ and not by observing the law" (Galatians 2:16).
- "Clearly no one is justified before God by the law, because 'the righteous will live by faith'" (Galatians 3:11).

Get the picture? We are not made right with God by keeping a list of rules—even God's rules! We are not saved by our own attempts at righteous deeds. We are made right with God only through faith in Jesus. It's that simple.

Bible Networking

Romans 5:17

If, by the trespass of the one man, death reigned through that one man, how much more will those who receive God's abundant provision of grace and of the gift of righteousness reign in life through the one man, Jesus Christ!

Philippians 3:9

[I desire to be found in Christ,] not having a righteousness of my own that comes from the law, but that which is through faith in Christ—the righteousness that comes from God on the basis of faith.

Enjoying the Benefits

God's act in declaring the believer to be in the right produces some astonishing benefits:

- *We have peace with God.* "Since we have been justified through faith, we have peace with God through our Lord Jesus Christ" (Romans 5:1). The war is over! God is not sitting up in heaven, fuming over your sin. The penalty has been paid; God's justice has been satisfied. God is free to welcome us into his presence.
- *We are free from condemnation.* Since God, the highest authority in the universe, declares us to be in the right with him, who can possibly bring any accusation against us? "Who then can condemn? No one. Christ Jesus who died—more than that, who was raised to life—is at the right hand of God and is also interceding for us" (Romans 8:34).

  Satan loves to accuse us, other people may remind us of our past life, and our own mind certainly does a good job of dredging up old failures—but God answers all of these accusations with one word: *justified!*
- *We are cleansed from sin.* Even when we sin after our salvation, God has promised to forgive us. "The blood of Jesus, his Son, purifies us from all sin" (1 John 1:7). This truth certainly doesn't give us permission to sin. It just opens the door for cleansing when we do.

- *We are made God's heirs.* "Being justified by his grace we might become heirs according to the hope of eternal life" (Titus 3:7 ESV). We have "an inheritance that can never perish, spoil or fade. This inheritance is kept in heaven for you" (1 Peter 1:4).

We all stand before God's throne condemned, but those who believe in Jesus find themselves declared in a right standing and relationship with God. The penalty we deserved is placed on someone else, and we are set free. Then, to our complete astonishment, God steps down from his throne and embraces us as his own dear children. He makes us the recipients of eternal life and heirs of the glory of heaven. And we did nothing to earn or deserve God's gift. We only came with empty hands and by faith received the gift God offered. I hope I never recover from the awesome wonder of God's grace!

Restoring the Friendship

I participated in a wedding recently that involved a bride and a groom—but also their children and grandchildren! The couple had separated and divorced several years earlier. Then, by God's grace, the old conflicts began to be resolved and old wounds were bathed in forgiveness. In time, the marriage and the family were put back together.

When Adam and Eve disobeyed God, they were removed from the garden of Eden, from the place of close friendship and access to God.

In Other Words

Since there is no righteousness in us, we can be justified only by a righteousness that comes from somewhere outside us. The righteousness of God is God's own righteousness, which he grants to us by virtue of our own union with Jesus Christ.

Philip Ryken, in *The Message of Salvation* (Downer's Grove, Ill.: InterVarsity, 2001), 196.

When God justifies sinners, he is not declaring bad people to be good, or saying that they are not sinners after all. He is pronouncing them legally righteous, free from any liability to the broken law, because he himself in his Son has borne the penalty of their law breaking.

John Stott, in *The Cross of Christ* (Downers Grove, Ill.: InterVarsity, 1986), 190.

A POWERFUL PARABLE

Jesus told a stunning story of reconciliation. A son asked his rich father for his share of the inheritance and then proceeded to run away and squander it all. Eventually, in desperation, the son returned to his father, fully prepared to be a servant in his father's house. The father saw his son coming and ran to meet him. There was no lecture, no probation, no grudge. Instead the father threw a party. The son who was lost had been found!

When we return to God, he doesn't sit around nursing hard feelings toward us for our years of rebellion. He welcomes us home, and the angels rejoice. God runs to meet us!

(You can read the story of the prodigal son in Luke 15:11–24.)

From that time on, they approached God only through a sacrifice. The way into God's immediate presence was barred by a powerful, holy angel. All of Adam's descendants faced the same problem—our sin broke any possibility of friendship with God. The Bible says that on our side of the relationship we were enemies of God, alienated from him, totally unresponsive.

God, however, determined to do something about our separation. Through Jesus and through Jesus' death on the cross, we can be reconciled with God. Our strained and estranged relationship is completely transformed into a close and intimate friendship. Here's how the New Testament describes God's work: "All this is from God, who reconciled us to himself through Christ ... God was reconciling the world to himself in Christ, not counting people's sins against them" (2 Corinthians 5:18–19).

The entire work of reconciliation came from God's side—and he didn't wait until we wanted to be his friends or decided to be his friends. We were his enemies! "When we were still powerless, Christ died for the ungodly" (Romans 5:6). Jesus did not die for people who loved him and served him. He died for his enemies, for those who were hostile to God. We had no desire, no inclination, and no power to restore the friendship between ourselves and God.

What we needed was someone who could intervene with us—someone who both understood God and his holy character and could also identify with us and our struggles. Only one person was qualified to step between us and make peace—Jesus, God the Son and the Son of Man, fully God and fully human. God could have said, "I won't forgive you until you apologize for your sin." If he had waited for us to apologize, we all would have continued on our downward way. Instead, God in love sent Jesus to pay the price of our sin and to remove the barrier between us. God is now free to forgive all who will receive his forgiveness. God isn't reluctant to forgive; he joyfully welcomes us back.

Enjoying the Benefits

Because God has reconciled us to himself, we enjoy some amazing benefits:

- *We stop being God's enemy and become God's friend.* The hostility between us has ended. God has made peace with us. The battle is over.
- *We are at peace with other Christians.* Not only has the war ended between us and God; we are also brought into unity with other Christians.
- *We are God's ambassadors to the world.* God's work doesn't end just because we have been restored to his friendship. He sends us out into a hostile world and gives us a job to do. We are commissioned to call others to the same friendship with God that we enjoy.

Bible Networking

Ephesians 2:17

[Jesus] came and preached peace to you who were far away and peace to those who were near.

2 Corinthians 5:20

We are therefore Christ's ambassadors, as though God were making his appeal through us. We implore you on Christ's behalf: Be reconciled to God.

Matthew 5:9

Blessed are the peacemakers,
for they will be called children of God.

Adopted by the Father

The Bible uses several family-centered images to describe our new relationship to God. We've already seen that when we believe in Jesus as Savior we are born again. We become a child of God by spiritual birth. The relationship between Jesus and his followers is also pictured as a marriage—Jesus is the groom, those who believe in him are his bride.

A third family image comes from the process of adoption. In human adoption we take an outsider and make him or her a member of the family. Divine adoption is different. We are already made a member of God's family by spiritual birth, so God's adoption is not designed to make us a member of God's family. God's adoption raises the status of someone who is already a family member. Divine adoption advances us to the position of an adult. We receive all of the privileges of a mature son or daughter.

Bible Networking

Galatians 3:24 – 26

The law was put in charge of us until Christ came that we might be justified by faith. Now that this faith has come, we are no longer under the supervision of the law.

So in Christ Jesus you are all children of God through faith.

Romans 8:15

The Spirit you received does not make you slaves, so that you live in fear again; rather, the Spirit you received brought about your adoption to sonship. And by him we cry, *"Abba*, Father."

2 Corinthians 6:1 – 2

As God's co-workers we urge you not to receive God's grace in vain. For he says,

> "In the time of my favor I heard you,
>   and in the day of salvation I helped you."

I tell you, now is the time of God's favor, now is the day of salvation.

In Other Words

Those who refuse to confess their sins and to be reconciled to God through Jesus have heard the message of reconciliation in vain. And the danger is that they may never hear it again. Now is the time of God's favor for every sinner who trusts in the cross of Christ. Now is the day of salvation for everyone who repents and receives Jesus Christ as Savior. But the day of salvation will not last forever. Soon the sun will set on the horizon of eternity, and for those who are not reconciled to God, all will be dark.

Philip Ryken, in *The Message of Salvation* (Downers Grove, Ill.: InterVarsity, 2001), 129.

God adopts us so that he may bring us up in his family likeness, so that people will look at us and give glory to him.

Robert Horn, in *Go Free! The Meaning of Justification* (Downers Grove, Ill.: InterVarsity, 1976), 63.

Enjoying the Benefits

I find at least four benefits that come to every adopted son or daughter of God:

- *An adopted heir is free from being treated like a little child.* When we were very young, our parents had a list of rules for us. We ate meals when we were told to eat. We went to bed at a certain time. We were *not* allowed to watch some television programs or movies. Our parents had rules that we were responsible to obey. But as we grew into adulthood, more and more responsibility was transferred to us. We began to choose the clothes we wore to school. We began to drive, and so we could do what we wanted to do rather than simply going with our parents. Eventually we reached mature adulthood and made all our choices. That is the spiritual freedom we have as Christians. We don't live under the law (external rules) any longer; we now live under the direction of the Holy Spirit (internal motivation). We serve God, not because we are forced to, but because we want to. We begin our Christian lives as spiritual infants, but God expects us to grow quickly into spiritually mature adults—and God has given us the position to match.

- *An adopted heir can come to the Father with confidence.* My son came to me recently with a personal problem. He was embarrassed to talk to me, but he knew I would listen and would love him in spite of his struggle. As believers we can come to the Father with any problem. "The Spirit you received brought about your adoption to sonship and by him we cry, 'Abba, Father'" (Romans 8:15). The word *Abba* is an Aramaic word of endearment for a father. It means "Dad" or "Papa" or whatever word you used to speak most lovingly to your father. We have the privilege of speaking to God the Father in the most intimate and personal way.

- *An adopted heir receives good gifts from the Father.* Just as we love to give gifts to our children and grandchildren, God loves to give good things to his spiritual children. For example, he gave us the Holy Spirit to live in us and to guide and to help us. "Because you are sons, God sent the Spirit of his Son into our hearts, the Spirit who calls out, 'Abba, Father.' So you are no longer a slave, but a son; and since you are a son, God has made you also an heir" (Galatians 4:6–7 NIV).

- *An adopted heir is disciplined by the Father.* This doesn't sound like much of a benefit, but it is! We think of discipline as a negative, but discipline is the evidence of the depth of God's love for us. "The Lord disciplines those he loves, and he chastens everyone he accepts as his child" (Hebrews 12:6). Discipline is an evidence of our relationship with God. I may reprimand other children who do something wrong, but I don't discipline them. I only discipline my own child. I do it out of love; I do it because I want the best for my child. God does the same thing—except God knows perfectly what is best for us. He may take us through difficult experiences and may never explain himself. What anchors our soul is the confidence that God is working to bring us to maturity. "God disciplines us for our good, that we may share in his holiness" (Hebrews 12:10).

Taking It to Heart

I hope you have seen yourself as you have read this chapter. I hope as we have explored these great truths that your heart has been stirred.

Points to Remember

☑ Restoring the friendship between God and humanity required a terrible price to be paid: the death of Jesus on the cross.

☑ God in grace has made a way for us to be delivered from the power and penalty of sin.

☑ We become a Christian by trusting completely in Jesus and in his death on the cross to make us right with God.

☑ Repentance happens when I change my mind—about myself, about God, and about Jesus.

☑ Our first birth was wrong; we need a second birth from God.

☑ When we believe in Jesus, God declares us to be in the right with him. The penalty of our sin has been paid in full!

☑ Because we are justified by faith, we have peace with God.

☑ Friendship with God has been restored by Jesus' sacrifice of himself on the cross.

☑ We are born into God's family by the new birth; we are raised to the level of a mature adult by God's work of adoption.

☑ We can speak to God in the most intimate way about our deepest needs.

☑ The best day to believe in Jesus is today!

But maybe you felt like you were reading about someone else and not yourself. Maybe you thought you were a Christian because you went to church or were baptized or attended confirmation classes. But now as you see the blessings that God gives to his own children, you realize that you don't share in these blessings. Your faith is simply an outward profession, but there is no inner reality or personal relationship with God.

The Bible calls us to believe in Jesus—to accept his claims as true and to personally receive the forgiveness and cleansing that he offers. Salvation is the free gift of God, but it must be received. God won't force himself on you. When we believe, God gives us all the blessings this chapter has described. Enjoy them, live in their security and under their protection, thank God for them, share the message with others. Jesus did not come to condemn us. We had already done that on our own. Jesus came to rescue us—not just as slaves set free but as sons and daughters of God forever.

CAN OUR SALVATION BE LOST?

Is it possible to believe in Jesus and be saved and then sometime, somehow to lose that salvation? Christians have given two different answers to this question. Some believe the gift of salvation can never be lost, while others believe it can.

Before we jump into the debate, let's cover a few ground rules.

- Bible-believing, committed Christians stand on both sides of this issue. We may disagree, but we are brothers and sisters in Christ.
- We are talking about *genuine* believers, not merely professing believers. Both sides would agree that just going through a ritual or walking to a church altar does not save anyone. We are saved only through genuine faith in Jesus alone.
- The issue of our security in Christ or the assurance of a believer goes much deeper than whether we can lose our salvation. Your position on that question reflects a wider perspective on the whole subject of salvation.

Those who believe that a genuine Christian will never lose his or her salvation are usually called Calvinists. The title comes from John Calvin, a Swiss reformer, who set down a particular view of salvation that many Christians believe is most consistent with biblical truth. The main points of Calvinism are summarized with the letters of the word *tulip.*

- *Total depravity.* Calvinists believe that human beings are completely without ability or desire to seek for God or respond to God on their own. God must always initiate the work of grace to draw people to Jesus in faith.
- *Unconditional election.* Every person is separated from God by sin, but God is determined to save some in order to display his glory. So God chooses some to be saved. He does not choose because of something good or attractive in us. There is nothing good or perfect in us. God chooses those whom he will save based purely on his sovereign decision.
- *Limited atonement.* God determined to provide redemption for the elect (for those he has chosen to save) by sending Jesus to die for their sins. Not all Calvinists hold this view. Some believe that Jesus' death had the potential to save all human beings, but his redemption is applied only to those God has chosen.
- *Irresistible grace.* Since God has determined to save those whom he has chosen, God works in their hearts so that each of them and all of them come to believe in Jesus. They cannot resist or refuse God's offer of salvation. God's chosen ones willingly believe but only because God works in their hearts to draw them and to make them willing.
- *Perseverance of the believer.* God will not fail to bring his chosen ones to heaven. A person will genuinely believe in Jesus only if he or she is chosen, and if God has determined to bring the elect to heaven, genuine Christians cannot lose their salvation.

The other position on how salvation works is called the Arminian view, named after Jacob Arminius, a Dutch theologian who disagreed with John Calvin's view. The Arminian position was refined by John Wesley during the eighteenth-century revivals. The view is often described as "Wesleyan Arminianism."

- *Total depravity and God's grace.* Arminians believe that we are all lost and dead in sin, just like the Calvinists believe. Salvation is all of God's initiative and God's grace. But Arminians believe that God works in every human being to give them the capacity to accept or to reject Jesus' offer of forgiveness. When a person hears and understands the message of salvation, the Holy Spirit works in that person's heart in such a way that he or she has the ability to choose to receive or to choose to reject Jesus' offer.
- *Election based on foreknowledge.* God's election or choice of those who will be saved is based on God's knowledge of who will believe and will remain faithful to Jesus. Since God sees the future perfectly, he knew before creation who would eventually believe in Jesus and who would not believe.
- *Unlimited atonement.* When Jesus died on the cross, the payment was sufficient to cover the sins of the world. The offer of salvation is valid even if a person refuses to believe.
- *Resistible grace.* Arminians believe that a person can hear and understand the gospel message and still refuse to believe. God works in their hearts to draw them to faith, but each person makes the choice to believe or to refuse to believe.
- *Assurance of salvation.* Those who believe in Jesus can be assured of their salvation, but they are called to continue to walk in obedience and faith. Arminians believe that a genuine Christian can turn away and stop believing in Jesus, and at that point the person is no longer a Christian. Calvinists usually talk about "the security of the believer" (i.e., salvation cannot be lost); Arminians use the phrase "the assurance of salvation" (i.e., Christians can have confidence in salvation as long as they continue to believe).

So which are you? Most Reformed, Presbyterian, Sovereign Grace, and Bible churches are firmly Calvinistic. Wesleyan, Methodist, Nazarene, Missionary, and Assembly of God churches are Arminian. Many Baptists believe in "the security of the believer" but reject the other aspects of Calvinistic teaching and come closer on some points to the Arminian view.

The main point to keep in mind is that both views are held by committed, Bible-believing Christians—and neither view answers all our questions! There is nothing wrong with being firmly convinced of one view or the other. Just hold your view with a measure of humility and grace toward those who disagree. Whichever view you hold and defend, all of us as Christians would agree that the Bible calls us to stay close to Christ, to remain faithful to him, and to follow him passionately. A system of theology doesn't save us; only Jesus saves.

CHAPTER 9

The Faith Journey: The Christian Life

The Faith Journey: The Christian Life

- ▶ What do we do after we believe?
- ▶ Find out what being holy is all about.
- ▶ Enroll in God's "gifted" class!
- ▶ Making it all the way to heaven!

The First Step

The Christian life begins with a step of faith. We put our trust in Jesus as Savior and Lord and King. In that instant we are made new. We pass in a heartbeat from death to life. But the first step of faith leads to a walk of obedience and trust. The journey begins with a decisive act, but we don't sit down just inside the door of God's kingdom. We go on in our walk with the Lord. We grow up into spiritual maturity. We take a second step and a third and a four-thousandth step on a journey through life toward an eternity in Christ's presence.

Salvation is a work totally of God's grace. We receive God's gift of eternal life, but we contribute nothing to our salvation. Living the Christian life, however, is something else. *We* participate in spiritual growth, *we* obey God's Word, *we* seek to please the Lord in all we do. But we are not left to do this on our own. We have help in that process. God the Holy Spirit lives in us. He gives us the resources, the energy, and the desire to follow Jesus and to pursue spiritual maturity. "It is God who works in you to will and to act in order to fulfill his good purpose" (Philippians 2:13). We have help, but we also choose as Christians either to submit ourselves to God or to follow our own desires.

The goal in the journey of faith is to become more and more like Jesus. The saying has been used so much that it's almost worn-out—"What would Jesus do?" As trite as the question is, it's still a powerful challenge to the growing Christian. How much am I like Jesus? How much of his character do people see in me?

The transformation that takes place in the Christian's life after salvation is called *sanctification*. The word itself means "to be made holy"—not the pious, holier-than-thou attitude we see displayed sometimes, but the positive, joyful walk of submission to God that we see in Jesus. How does that process of sanctification happen? What's my part in it and what's God's part? That's what we want to explore in the next section of this book. If you are saved, and that's as far as you want to go in your spiritual walk, this chapter won't challenge you much. On the other hand, if you are ready to break out of the spiritual rut you are in, this part of our study together will spark a fire in your heart. Fan the flame—and get ready to see some dramatic changes in your life.

Past, Present, Future

The Bible talks about sanctification, the process of being made like Jesus, in three ways.

- Christians *have been saved* in the past from the penalty of sin (that's the first stage).
- Christians *are being saved* in the present from the power of sin (that's the second stage).
- Christians *will be saved* in the future from the presence of sin (the final stage).

Help File

A BELIEVER'S RÉSUMÉ

The New Testament uses several words and phrases to describe a Christian. Each one emphasizes a different facet of our salvation.

- children of God (John 1:12; Galatians 3:26)
- athletes (1 Corinthians 9:24; 2 Timothy 2:5)
- citizens of heaven (Philippians 3:20; Hebrews 12:22)
- followers/disciples of Jesus (Acts 21:16)
- saints (Ephesians 1:18–19 NIV)
- servants (Colossians 4:7)
- sheep/flock (John 10:15–16)
- soldiers (Ephesians 6:13; 2 Timothy 2:4)
- brothers and sisters (James 1:2)
- heirs of God and co-heirs with Christ (Romans 8:17)
- priests (Hebrews 10:19–22; 1 Peter 2:9)

Made Holy in Christ

When we believed in Jesus, in that moment of faith our sins were forgiven. The penalty of spiritual death that had been declared against us was removed. The condemnation of our sin was placed on Jesus and his right standing before God was declared over us. That act of God in removing sin's penalty from us is called *initial sanctification* or *positional sanctification*. God sets us apart (which is what the word *holy* or *sanctified* means) as his own people.

Because believers are inwardly separated from the old sinful nature by God's grace, even immature and erring believers can be referred to as *saints* (literally, "holy ones") or as *God's people*. When the apostle Paul wrote his letter to the wayward Christians at Corinth, he called them "those sanctified in Christ Jesus and called to be his holy people" (1 Corinthians 1:2). Paul spoke that way not because the Corinthian Christians were growing into spiritual maturity and Christlikeness (most of them weren't!), but because of their positional holiness — their right standing before God based on Christ's justifying work. The Corinthians were new creatures in Christ. They had died to sin and been raised to a new life in Christ. Later on in the Corinthian letter, after reminding the Corinthians of their sinful lives before they believed in Jesus, Paul says, "And that is what some of you were. But you were washed, you were sanctified, you were justified in the name of the Lord Jesus Christ and by the Spirit of our God" (1 Corinthians 6:11).

Initial sanctification gives us a position of being set apart as God's own people, declared holy and in right standing with God. That first work is a work totally from God and is based totally on Jesus Christ's work on the cross.

The Day-to-Day Process

Being made new inwardly is just the first step, however. The challenge of the Christian life is to become on the outside what God has made us on the inside. That outward transformation takes time and effort and a desire to live obediently before God. The process of becoming holy (set apart from sin and to God) is called *progressive sanctification*. All of us are somewhere in the process of becoming like Jesus.

In the Old Testament, God revealed himself to be a holy God — and he called his people to mirror his holy character: "I am the LORD your God; consecrate yourselves and be holy, because I am holy" (Leviticus

11:44). That call to holiness is repeated in the New Testament: "Just as he who called you is holy, so be holy in all you do; for it is written: 'Be holy, because I am holy'" (1 Peter 1:15–16).

The New Testament also makes the point that becoming like Jesus is a gradual and progressive work. A few verses will show this clearly:

- Peter commands Christians to "grow [present tense command] in the grace and knowledge of our Lord and Savior Jesus Christ" (2 Peter 3:18).
- Paul writes that "inwardly we are being renewed day by day" (2 Corinthians 4:16). It's a process going on day by day.
- The author of Hebrews places our positional sanctification (at salvation) alongside our progressive sanctification (which is ongoing): "By one sacrifice [Christ] has made perfect forever those who are being made holy" (Hebrews 10:14).

The Bible also emphasizes that the process of becoming more and more like Christ involves struggle, sometimes intense struggle, against the drag of the old sinful nature that still is part of our life in these bodies. "The sinful nature desires what is contrary to the Spirit, and the Spirit what is contrary to the sinful nature. They are in conflict with each other, so that you do not do what you want" (Galatians 5:17 NIV).

In Other Words

Though the saints do not live in sin, it still lives in them, and sometimes it becomes very active and powerful.

> Charles Horne, in *The Doctrine of Salvation* (Chicago: Moody, 1984), 73.

Much of the New Testament is taken up with instructing believers in various churches on how they should grow in likeness to Christ. All the moral exhortations and commands in the New Testament epistles apply here, because they all exhort believers to one aspect or another of greater sanctification in their lives. It is the expectation of all the New Testament authors that our sanctification will increase throughout our Christian life.

> Wayne Grudem, in *Bible Doctrine* (Grand Rapids: Zondervan, 1999), 328.

Bible Networking

2 Corinthians 3:18

We all, who with unveiled faces contemplate the Lord's glory, are being transformed into his image with ever-increasing glory, which comes from the Lord, who is the Spirit.

Colossians 3:5 – 10

Put to death, therefore, whatever belongs to your earthly nature: sexual immorality, impurity, lust, evil desires and greed, which is idolatry. Because of these, the wrath of God is coming. You used to walk in these ways, in the life you once lived. But now you must also rid yourselves of all such things as these: anger, rage, malice, slander, and filthy language from your lips. Do not lie to each other, since you have taken off your old self with its practices and have put on the new self, which is being renewed in knowledge in the image of its Creator.

As Christians, we grow in our spiritual development in many different ways:

- by abiding in (staying close to) Christ (John 15:4, 7)
- by longing for the spiritual milk of God's Word (1 Peter 2:2)
- by living in the light of God's presence (1 John 1:7)
- by continuing to obey Jesus' teaching (John 14:23)
- by purifying ourselves from sin (1 John 3:3)
- by holding true to our commitment of faith in Jesus (Revelation 2:25; 3:11)

The Final Cleansing

Christians are called to grow toward maturity and holiness. This struggle away from the old life and toward Christlikeness is going on every day to some degree. Sometimes we wonder if we will ever reach a level of spiritual growth when the power of sin can't grab on to us anymore. The Bible is emphatic in its declaration that it is possible, at least for a time, to live without sinning (1 John 2:1; 3:6), but most of us haven't been at that level very often. Nor can we say that we are without sin or above the capacity to sin (1 John 1:8).

So will we ever reach the complete perfection of Jesus? The Bible's answer is that we will reach perfection some day. God is committed to it in every believer! Paul says, "Those God foreknew he also predestined to be conformed to the image of his Son" (Romans 8:29). When God saved you, he committed himself to seeing this process of being conformed to the image of Jesus Christ completed in you.

While we certainly can grow toward this image in this life, the fullness of our sanctification comes only when we leave this sin-prone body behind and are taken into the presence of Christ. "We know that when Christ appears, we shall be like him, for we shall see him as he is" (1 John 3:2). When we die and go to heaven or when Jesus returns, we will be removed not just from sin's penalty and sin's power but from sin's presence. We will be "blameless and holy in the presence of our God" (1 Thessalonians 3:13).

How in the World Can I Be Holy?

Almost all Christians would agree (with minor tweaks) with the three-stage view of sanctification I've just presented. There would be some wide disagreement, however (are you surprised?), on how sanctification actually works out in the Christian experience. I will outline some of the main views and then give you suggestions on how to sort it out in your own spiritual walk.

Is sanctification a crisis or a process?

I believe the Bible teaches that it is a process—we gradually become more like Jesus Christ. There are, however, certain times when the implications of our following Jesus come home to us in an intense manner, making a significant impact on our lives, giving us a fresh sense of assurance, and helping us make great leaps forward. I recall one time when I was seeking God that I suddenly and unexpectedly heard a gentle whisper, "You are my son." I knew the Scriptures that promised this, but now I heard the Holy Spirit speaking to me. Just today, as I was writing this, a friend emailed me to say that while he was praying for me, he kept getting the words "I am with you" over and over. So he emailed me with the thought—which again brought a needed sense of encouragement to me.

Bible Networking

1 Thessalonians 5:23 – 24

May God himself, the God of peace, sanctify you through and through. May your whole spirit, soul and body be kept blameless at the coming of our Lord Jesus Christ. The one who calls you is faithful, and he will do it.

Philippians 1:6

Being confident of this, that he who began a good work in you will carry it on to completion until the day of Christ Jesus.

Ephesians 2:10

We are God's handiwork, created in Christ Jesus to do good works, which God prepared in advance for us to do.

We Become Holy by a Gradual Process

Many Christians believe that sanctification is a process that ebbs and flows in a believer all throughout life. We are steadily making progress toward Christlikeness as we commit ourselves to God in obedience (our part) and as God works in us to give us the desire for a walk of holiness (God's part). Salvation by God's grace breaks the power of sin over us, but we still struggle with the flesh or the sinful nature. The Christian according to this view does not reach entire sanctification until the Christian is in Christ's presence.

The "gradual process throughout life" view is held by most Reformed, Lutheran, Presbyterian, Bible, and Baptist churches.

- "To be washed with Christ's Spirit means ... that more and more I become dead to sin and increasingly live a holy and blameless life" (Heidelberg Catechism Answer 70).
- "This restoration [to the image of Christ] does not take place in one moment or one day or one year; but through continual and sometimes even slow advances God wipes out in his elect the corruptions of the flesh,... that they may know ... that this warfare

will end only at death" (John Calvin, *Institutes of the Christian Religion*, Book III, chapter III, paragraph 9).

We Become Holy through the Sacraments

Roman Catholic theology teaches that we become holy by means of the sacraments that God has provided. It begins with (1) the sacrament of baptism, which (in this view) removes the guilt of original sin. The process continues through (2) confirmation and (3) participation in the Eucharist (the body and blood of Christ). These three sacraments impart the gift of sanctifying grace to those who receive them in faith. Christians cooperate with this grace by obeying God's commands set down in Scripture or established by the authority of the church. If a person commits a mortal sin, that person forfeits eternal life until he or she performs the sacrament of penance. Heartfelt penance restores a believer to a place of baptismal righteousness.

We Become Holy through a Second Work of God's Grace

Many Christians in the Wesleyan/Holiness tradition (including the Free Methodist Church, Church of the Nazarene, and other holiness denominations) believe that holiness begins at the moment of salvation but is perfected by an instantaneous work of the Holy Spirit called *the second blessing* or *the second work of grace*. Those who hold this view claim that sometime after salvation a Christian should experience a work of such transforming power that he or she enters the realm of *entire sanctification* or (as John Wesley preferred to call it) *perfect love*. This work enables the Christian to live without willful sin, and it fills the heart with perfect love for God and other people.

- "So long as [a Christian] believes in God through Christ and loves him and is pouring out his heart before him, he cannot voluntarily transgress any command of God, either by speaking or acting what he knows God has forbidden" (John Wesley, "Sermon 19: 'The Great Privilege of Those That Are Born of God'").

Fully sanctified believers have not reached the perfection of God himself but possess a relative perfection, a freedom from disobeying the known will of God. The believer may still make mistakes or errors from ignorance and may still experience temptation. The wholly sanctified person is considered faultless, not sinless.

- "Let us purify ourselves from everything that contaminates body and spirit, *perfecting holiness* out of reverence for God" (2 Corinthians 7:1, italics added).
- "Be perfect, therefore, as your heavenly Father is perfect" (Matthew 5:48).

Some Christians who stand in the holiness tradition have rejected the idea of "entire sanctification" but still see the importance of crisis events in pushing us forward in our walk with the Lord. They would say that a Christian not only experiences a *second* work of the Spirit but a third and fourth and fifth work as well. The believer comes to a point of conviction about a certain area of his or her Christian life and the Holy Spirit uses that crisis to push them forward in their commitment and obedience to the Lord. The normal gradual forward progress is marked by small leaps to new levels of holy living.

We Become Holy through a Work of Spirit Baptism

Some branches of Pentecostalism believe that the Spirit works in three separate instantaneous acts to produce holiness in the believer—a regenerating work of salvation, a second sanctifying work to purify the believer's heart, and a third empowering work of Spirit baptism. In the third work the Holy Spirit takes full possession of the purified believer, and speaking in tongues is the evidence of this work. More mainline Pentecostal groups, such as Assemblies of God, do not advocate entire sanctification but do hold to a postconversion baptism by the Spirit marked by speaking in tongues. This baptism experience empowers the believer for ministry and should be earnestly pursued by every believer.

- "There are two distinct moments [for the Christian]: conversion and baptism with the Spirit. They may be separated from each other by years, although both belong to the full life of the Christian" (J. Rodman Williams, *The Pentecostal Reality*).

Finding the Right Path to Holiness

Reading through the different views might be helpful, but I come away asking, "Which way is right? How can I strive after godliness in my own life right now?" I think these suggestions will help us *all* move forward in our spiritual growth.

- *Study* the position your own church holds on the issue of sanctification. Ask your pastor for some help. Read your denomination's doctrinal statement and explore the verses of Scripture used to support that position.
- *Seek* to be filled with the Spirit. We are never commanded in the Bible to be baptized with the Spirit or to speak in tongues; we *are* commanded to be filled with the Spirit and to walk in obedience to God's Word. "Do not get drunk on wine .... Instead, be filled with the Spirit" (Ephesians 5:18). Just as alcohol "controls" a person who is drunk, the Spirit is to direct us as Christians. As we submit ourselves to him, he produces his transforming work in us.
- *Strive* after holiness. We have a part in sanctification too. As God teaches you truth in his Word, work to practice that truth in your life. Believe it and do it. As the Holy Spirit convicts you about an attitude or a behavior that does not reflect the Spirit of Christ, seek to change that attitude or action with the Spirit's help. Ask a spiritual friend or mentor to evaluate your progress as a Christian. Are you growing in Christlikeness, or are you standing still or even falling back?

One warning needs to be added. It's easy to fall into a legalistic approach to sanctification. We can be tempted to believe that following a list of Christian rules and traditions will lead to Christlike character—that simply *acting* holy will make us holy. The Bible absolutely rejects this approach to sanctification. We are made holy only by the inner work of the Holy Spirit as we commit ourselves to his direction and are obedient to God's Word.

Life in the Spirit

As we Christians grow in our spiritual lives, we are like trees. Hanging from the limbs of our lives is the evidence of the Spirit's presence—aspects the Bible calls "the fruit of the Spirit."

> The fruit of the Spirit is love, joy, peace, patience, kindness, goodness, faithfulness, gentleness and self-control.
>
> Galatians 5:22–23

Those qualities emerge and mature in us as we are guided by the Holy Spirit into Christlikeness. Not each aspect may be present to the same degree in an individual's life, but all of them together are the evidence of the Spirit's presence and control.

Every believer is also equipped for ministry and spiritual service with one or more *gifts* of the Spirit. These are abilities that the Spirit gives to believers for the purpose of strengthening and building up the church. We are not gifted by the Spirit to take center stage and run the whole show! Our gifts are interlocked with the gifts of others so that the needs of the body of Christ are met as we serve together.

> There are different kinds of gifts, but the same Spirit distributes them....
> Now to each one the manifestation of the Spirit is given for the common good.
>
> 1 Corinthians 12:4, 7

A lot has been written and taught about how to discover what your spiritual gifts are. The interesting thing is that the Bible never commands us to discover our gifts. It just says we have them and calls us to use these gifts to build up other believers. I think the best way to figure out what your gifts are is just to start serving the Lord where he gives you the opportunity. You will soon find an area of ministry that you enjoy and in which you are effective. That is the area of your giftedness. God the Spirit has equipped you in that area not for personal acclaim but for ministry to brothers and sisters in Christ.

Following the Spirit

Life in the Spirit as a Christian involves obedience, humility, ministry, and spiritual growth. It's an ongoing, everyday adventure of following

SPIRITUAL GIFTS

If you want to explore the key teaching of the Bible on spiritual gifts, check out the following passages:

- 1 Corinthians 12–14
- Romans 12:6–8
- Ephesians 4:11
- 1 Peter 4:11

Which of the gifts listed do you think you have? Which do you know you don't have? How are you using your gift or gifts?

Jesus and being directed by the Holy Spirit. The walk of faith is God's desire for every Christian. Jude, in his little New Testament "postcard," summarizes our part in the life of faith: "You, dear friends, by building yourselves up in your most holy faith and praying in the Holy Spirit, keep yourselves in God's love as you wait for the mercy of our Lord Jesus Christ to bring you to eternal life" (verses 20–21).

SIGNS AND WONDERS

A news item flashed across the Internet in July 2008 that a pastor in Kentucky was arrested when dozens of poisonous snakes were found in his possession. The snakes, he explained, were used in worship in his church. These folks took the words of Mark 16:17–18 as an invitation to literally pick up rattlesnakes and copperheads: "These signs will accompany those who believe: ... they will pick up snakes with their hands." Most Christians are not ready to take these verses to that extreme. There is a debate within Christian churches, however, about whether we should see spectacular signs and miracles today like the ones the apostles saw in the book of Acts.

One side in the debate believes that public signs and wonders have ceased. God may still work miraculously in quiet ways to heal a Christian or to protect someone from harm, but for the most part, the miraculous works were confined to the age of the New Testament. This also includes the more miraculous spiritual gifts such as discerning of spirits or speaking in tongues (spontaneously speaking in a language unknown to the speaker or in a special prayer language). Those sign gifts were for the benefit of the early "immature" church, before the New Testament was completed. Today (according to this view) we have the self-affirming written Word of God and no longer need to rely on sign gifts to know God's will.

Other Christians, of course, take exception to this position and say that God has given these gifts to be exercised throughout the church age. The only reason we don't see more wonders is the lack of faith on the part of so many Christians. Pentecostal and charismatic churches strongly defend the full range of sign gifts, especially speaking in tongues, as appropriate for the twenty-first-century church.

I join many Christians in taking a more moderating approach. I would say that God can heal and often does heal miraculously. He doesn't do it for public spectacle but as a quiet ministry to a believer in need. God may also choose to protect a believer through a work of his power—or provide for a believer's need in a way no one can explain or predict. Many Christians would also be open to the exercise of sign gifts today but would not believe, for example, that every Christian must speak in tongues or even that sign gifts are an essential part of public worship. We rely on the written Word of God to guide us, but we are also open to the Spirit's presence and power.

Do we "rest in Christ" to bring us to maturity—or do we "strive after godliness" with our own efforts? The New Testament emphasizes both! Paul puts both ideas together in Colossians 1:29—"I labor, struggling with all his energy, which so powerfully works in me" (NIV). We rest in Jesus Christ and his resources; yet it is we who labor and struggle. We commit ourselves to Christ and remain close to him and obey him. We are active in putting to death our old sinful nature. We do all these things, but not in our own power or strength. We depend constantly on the Holy Spirit and his help. Maybe some of us who are more activistic need to learn to rest more in Christ, and some of us who enjoy being still and resting need to get up and be more active!

God doesn't force this kind of life on us, of course. The Bible tells us that it's possible by our disobedience or carelessness to live outside of fellowship with the Lord. We are warned to not grieve the Holy Spirit (Ephesians 4:30) and to not put out the Holy Spirit's fire in our lives

Bible Networking

Romans 8:30

And those [God] predestined, he also called; those he called, he also justified; those he justified, he also glorified.

1 Corinthians 15:25 – 26

[Christ] must reign until he has put all his enemies under his feet. The last enemy to be destroyed is death.

1 Corinthians 15:42 – 44

So it will be with the resurrection of the dead. The body that is sown is perishable, it is raised imperishable; it is sown in dishonor, it is raised in glory; it is sown in weakness, it is raised in power; it is sown a natural body, it is raised a spiritual body.

Points to Remember

- ☑ Salvation is totally God's work of grace; Christian growth is a cooperative work between God and us.

- ☑ The goal of the Christian journey is to become more and more like Jesus.

- ☑ Sanctification is the process of being set apart *from* sin and set apart *to* God—becoming on the outside what God has made us on the inside.

- ☑ Initial sanctification occurs at salvation and sets us free from the slavery of the old life. Progressive sanctification is the process of transformation into the image of Christ. Final sanctification comes when we see Christ and are completely set free from the presence of sin.

- ☑ Christians have different views on how the work of sanctification takes place in a Christian's life.

- ☑ Every believer has been given spiritual gifts to use in serving others and in building up other believers.

- ☑ We will spend eternity as complete, redeemed human beings—with resurrected bodies and purified spirits.

(1 Thessalonians 5:19). It is possible to live for a season in disobedience to God and his Word.

We may give up on God for a time, but God never gives up on us. The Holy Spirit will convict us of sin and disobedience. He will bring circumstances into our lives to discipline us (Hebrews 12:4–11). The Spirit's desire is not to push us away but to pull us back in repentance and love. The little book of Jude reminds us that God "is able to keep you from stumbling and to present you before his glorious presence without fault and with great joy" (Jude 24). Peter adds that we "through faith are shielded by God's power until the coming of the salvation that is ready to be revealed in the last time" (1 Peter 1:5). The Holy Spirit desires my spiritual maturity far more than I do, and he will do whatever it takes to move me toward the goal of Christlikeness.

Enduring to the End

The goal of walking in obedience to Jesus is that we will be found blameless in him when Jesus returns or when we pass from this life into Jesus' presence. As we've already seen, Christians disagree on whether genuine believers can ever lose their salvation, but we can all agree that believers who persevere in faith will experience the final stage of sanctification—the complete transformation of being fully redeemed in heaven with Jesus. This final stage is called *glorification*—our removal from sin's presence and ultimately the resurrection and purification of our bodies. We will spend eternity with the Lord as glorified, complete human beings, body and spirit.

In Other Words

We will live in bodies that have all the excellent qualities God created us to have, and thereby we will forever be living proof of the wisdom of God in making a material creation that from the beginning was "very good" (Genesis 1:31). We will live as resurrected believers in those new bodies, and they will be suitable for inhabiting the "new heavens and a new earth, in which righteousness dwells" (2 Peter 3:13 [NASB]).

Wayne Grudem, in *Bible Doctrine* (Grand Rapids: Zondervan, 1999), 358.

Several years ago I conducted a funeral for a man who had alienated almost everyone in his family. None of his sons would talk to me about their father, for he had spent most of his life making all of them miserable. He was an angry, bitter old man who took out his anger on everyone around him. When it came to God and the Bible, the man's attitude was pretty much the same. He didn't care for either.

After the funeral a little boy came up to me and asked, "Is my grandpa in heaven?" I don't know where my response came from except to say it came from the Holy Spirit. I simply told the little boy, "Your grandpa is in God's hands now, and he will do what is right.". . . The God we love and trust will always do what is right.

Mark Tabb, in *Theology: Think for Yourself about What You Believe* (Colorado Springs: NavPress, 2006), 265.

CHAPTER 10

The Good, the Bad, and the Ugly: The Spirit World

The Good, the Bad, and the Ugly: The Spirit World

▶ Meet some amazing servants of God—and some ardent enemies of every Christian!
▶ Learn how angels came into existence and what happened next.
▶ Discover how your spiritual enemy works.
▶ Find out what resources are available to you in the spiritual battle.

Angels around Us

Throughout the vast reaches of God's universe, in a realm unseen through telescopes or microscopes, fantastic, powerful beings live. They move at the speed of light to carry out the wishes of their master. They inhabit the highest heaven, the atmosphere of earth, and the pit of hell. They are involved in international political affairs and are sensitive to the smallest concerns of children. These beings are called *angels.*

The Bible reveals an amazing amount of information about angels. Just over half the biblical books (34 out of 66) refer to angels. The word *angel* appears more than 250 times in the Bible. Our English word comes directly from the New Testament Greek word *angelos.* The corresponding word in the Hebrew Old Testament is *malʾāk.* Both mean "messenger." Occasionally the words are used of a human messenger, but most often they refer to a supernatural being.

The fact that angels are "messengers" gives us an important clue about their place in God's order of things. Angels don't act independently; they act under the authority of a leader. That's why angels seem to be organized in military fashion. They are an army with various levels and ranks of authority and power. They exist to serve, to follow orders, not to pursue their own will but the will of the one who rules over them.

The main point to remember about angels is that they fall into two categories—good, pure angels who do the bidding of God and sinful, corrupt angels who seek to deceive and destroy.

Creation Morning

Angels have not always been in existence. They are created beings. In the book of Job God says that the angels were present when the earth's foundations were laid (Job 38:7). Moses made it clear that everything God created was made within the six days of creation week (Exodus 20:11). Since the earth was created first and since angels were present when the earth was formed, angels must have been created just moments before God's creation of the earth. Some Christians believe that angels existed long before the earth was formed, but the biblical evidence seems to place their creation in the context of Genesis 1:1: "In the beginning God created the heavens [including the angels] and the earth."

God created the angels individually. Angels do not reproduce, so there are no baby angels or families of angels. The angels were created fully mature, knowledgeable, and holy. They didn't need to grow up or learn or develop. They were naive and untested by experience,

Help File

ANGELIC TITLES

The writers of Scripture use several terms to refer to angels, each one highlighting an aspect of the nature or work of angels.

- God's angels are called his "hosts" or army (1 Kings 22:19; Psalms 103:20–21; 148:2; Luke 2:13).
- They are also called "the chariots of God" (Psalm 68:17) because of their swift power and disciplined organization.
- The prophet Daniel describes angels as "messengers" or watchmen who act as God's agents in the affairs of human governments (Daniel 4:13, 17, 23).

- The phrase *sons of God* occurs several times in the Old Testament as a general term for all angels, good and evil (Genesis 6:2; Job 1:6; 2:1 NASB).
- God's angels are called "holy ones" (Psalm 89:7; Daniel 8:13; Zechariah 14:5) and "sons of the mighty" (Psalm 89:6 NASB).

Only three angels are named in the Bible: Gabriel (Daniel 8:15; 9:21–22; Luke 1:11, 19, 26–38), Michael (Daniel 10:21; 12:1; Jude 9; Revelation 12:7–10), and Lucifer or Satan (Isaiah 14:3 KJV; Revelation 12:9).

but angels could immediately function in their full capacity as God's servants.

The Bible speaks about the creation of the angels in Psalm 148—"At [the LORD's] command they were created" (verse 5). God the Creator spoke one word of command and brought millions of angels into existence. At the end of creation week God looked at everything he had made (which was, well, everything—including angels), and he declared it all to be "very good" (Genesis 1:31). Angels were originally created as pure, holy servants of God—beings with incredible power and dazzling majesty.

I Saw a Strong Angel

Angels excel in strength. God repeatedly entrusts these mighty ones with duties that require swift execution and supernatural power. In the days of David, for example, one angel destroyed 70,000 people in Israel in a single day (2 Samuel 24:15–16). Angels can direct the forces of nature, throw great boulders into the sea, and shut the mouths of ravenous lions (Revelation 7:1; 16:5; 18:21; Daniel 6:22).

Not only are angels more powerful than humans, but some angels are more powerful than other angels. In his tiny New Testament book, Jude tells us that two angels, Satan and Michael, argued over the body

Bible Networking

Exodus 20:11

In six days the LORD made the heavens and the earth, the sea, and all that is in them, but he rested on the seventh day.

Job 38:4, 7

Where were you when I laid the earth's foundation?
    Tell me, if you understand....
while the morning stars sang together
    and all the angels shouted for joy?

of Moses. Michael had been sent by God to bury the body, but Satan wanted to claim the body for himself. Michael, a powerful angel, did not dare to pronounce judgment himself on Satan, so he enlisted an even greater power than either himself or Satan by saying, "The *Lord* rebuke you!" (Jude 9, italics added). Unable to stand against that authority, Satan fled and Michael buried Moses.

While angels possess great power, they are not all-powerful. They have definite limitations.

- *Angels are limited in their presence.* One angel cannot be present everywhere at the same time. He is limited to one place at one time. That includes Satan too! Satan has to gather information and do his work through other angels. In contrast, God may choose at times to work through angels, but he is not dependent on them.
- *Angels are limited in knowledge.* Angels may have great ability to know certain things about people or events, but they don't come close to possessing God's knowledge.
- *Angels have limitations in strength as well.* As powerful as Satan is, his final end has already been determined by God.

God is more powerful than any angel. The Christian faith is not dualistic. We do not see a good God on one side and an equally strong evil Devil on the other side. We are not waiting nervously to see which side will win this cosmic battle. The victory already belongs to God. His power is unlimited; an angel's power is limited. Angels are creatures; God is the Creator.

GETTING ANGELS' WINGS

A popular misconception is that God "promotes" Christians who have died and makes them into angels. This idea appears to have come from a misreading of Mark 12:25. In that verse Jesus does not say that when the dead rise, they will *be* angels in heaven. He says they will be *like* angels in this one respect—they will not reproduce in heaven. Human beings remain human beings forever. God created angels as a separate, distinct group of beings in his kingdom. You may *think* it would be cool to be an angel, but be happy you are human. We are a little *lower* than the angels right now in terms of glory and strength, but as redeemed children of God, our glory will surpass even the angels!

AN ANGEL'S RÉSUMÉ

This summary of the characteristics of angels is drawn from the Bible:

- They are inconceivably powerful.
  (Genesis 19:13; Psalm 103:20–21; Revelation 7:11; 16:8–9)
- They are instantly obedient to God.
  (Psalm 91:11–12; Matthew 26:53)
- They are innumerable (to us!).
  (2 Kings 6:16–17; Daniel 7:10; Revelation 5:11)
- They are all-wise (but not all-knowing).
  (2 Samuel 14:17–20)
- They are pure, holy, before God.
  (Matthew 28:3; Acts 10:22)
- They are dazzling in appearance—glorious and shining creatures.
  (Daniel 10:6; Luke 9:26; Revelation 10:1)
- They are humble. They refuse human worship.
  (Isaiah 6:2; Revelation 19:10)
- They possess personality.
  (Daniel 8:16; 12:1; Revelation 9:11)
- They cannot die.
  (Luke 20:35–36)
- They can travel rapidly from one place to another.
  (Daniel 9:21)
- They can become visible in human form.
  (Genesis 19:1, 5; Judges 13:3, 6; Hebrews 13:2)
- They are able to observe human beings.
  (Ecclesiastes 5:6; 1 Corinthians 4:9; 11:10)
- They cannot reproduce.
  (Matthew 22:30; Luke 20:35–36)
- They exercise special protective care over little children and over God's people.
  (Matthew 18:10; Psalm 91:11)
- They escort the spirits of believers to heaven after death.
  (Luke 16:22)
- Sinful angels will not be redeemed. Jesus died for human sin, not angelic sin.
  (Ephesians 3:15; Hebrews 2:14–17; 1 Peter 1:12)

A Falling Star

When God made the angels, he created them as holy beings. God is not the source of moral evil, so everything he made was good. The holy character of the angels, however, was untested. Their loyalty to God had never been challenged until one powerful angel allowed pride to enter his heart. This single angel failed the test of loyalty to God and rebelled, and in his rebellion he put all the other angels to the test. Would they be loyal to God, or would they join in the rebellion?

The original angel to rebel against God was a powerful, beautiful angel named *Helel* in Hebrew. It means "shining one" or "daystar." In the Authorized or King James Version of the Bible, the angel's name is translated *Lucifer* (Latin for "light bearer").

Lucifer, like all the angels, was created during the first day of creation week. He saw God lay the foundations of the earth and rejoiced as God formed the universe. Lucifer may have occupied a place of honor above the throne of God. At least through the six days of creation week Lucifer maintained his place of majesty and glory. But shortly after the sixth day, that same honor overflowed into pride and an obsession to become like God.

Isaiah the prophet poetically describes Lucifer's change of focus from God to himself. The prophet begins talking about the king of Babylon, but his mind then turns to the evil master behind the wicked human king. Isaiah takes up a taunt against Satan himself:

> How you have fallen from heaven,
>   morning star, son of the dawn!
> You have been cut down to the earth ...!
> You said in your heart,
>   "I will ascend to heaven;
> I will raise my throne
>   above the stars of God ....
> I will ascend above the tops of the clouds;
>   I will make myself like the Most High."
>
> Isaiah 14:12–14

Lucifer became so proud of his beauty and position that he deceived himself into thinking he could actually overthrow the sovereign Ruler of the universe. He thought he could replace God or at least rise to a level equal with him. His goal was to be like God. To accomplish that,

SATAN'S NAMES

The Bible uses a variety of names and descriptive titles for the enemy of God:

- Satan ("adversary") (2 Corinthians 11:14)
- Devil ("slanderer") (1 Peter 5:8)
- the evil one (Matthew 13:19)
- the enemy (Matthew 13:39)
- a liar (John 8:44)
- the tempter (1 Thessalonians 3:5)
- a murderer from the beginning (John 8:44)
- Beelzebub ("lord of the flies," "lord of the demons") (Matthew 10:25 NIV)
- prince of this world (John 14:30)
- the great dragon (Revelation 12:9)
- the ancient serpent (Revelation 12:9)
- the ruler of the kingdom of the air (Ephesians 2:2)
- the god of this age (2 Corinthians 4:4)
- Belial ("worthless") (2 Corinthians 6:15)
- the accuser (Revelation 12:10)
- the Destroyer (Revelation 9:11)

Does this sound like someone you would want to invite over for a barbeque?

THE ORIGIN OF EVIL

One of the toughest philosophical questions surrounding the Christian faith is the problem of the origin of evil. If God is good and if God's creation is good, where did evil come from? When Adam and Eve sinned in the garden of Eden, there was a tempter to deceive them. When we sin, we have three enemies encouraging us: "the world" provides the opportunity for sin, "the devil" plays on our weaknesses, and our own sinful desires—"the flesh"—rise up and urge us on. But Satan had no sinful world to lure him, no tempter to push him, and no innate sinful nature to overpower him. Where, then, did moral evil originate? The Bible doesn't explain this fully, but it does tell us that, just as sin entered the human race through Adam, sin entered the angelic realm as rebellious pride was born in the will and in the heart of one angel.

Lucifer had to either raise himself to God's level or somehow bring God down to his. He has been trying to do both ever since.

The moment Lucifer said in his heart, "I will make myself like the Most High," he fell into moral sin. He stopped being a holy angel and became an evil angel. His power was intact. His brilliant mind was intact. He lost his exalted position, of course, but he was determined to make his own way in the universe. Lucifer, the daystar, became Satan, which means "the adversary, the accuser." His nature was totally corrupted with evil.

Satan's Kingdom

Because God has a kingdom, Satan (if he was going to be like God) needed a kingdom too. In God's kingdom, God ruled over both angels and humans. So Satan set out to fill his kingdom with both angelic and human subjects. Satan, however, had a problem. God had the ability to create personal beings to populate his kingdom; Satan, as a creature, did not. The most Satan could hope for was to persuade or deceive some of God's angels and some of God's humans into joining him.

The Bible describes Satan's deception of human beings in Genesis 3. Like the angels, our parents, Adam and Eve, were created in purity, but this purity had been untested by any challenge. God placed one test in the garden of Eden—Adam and Eve were not to eat the fruit from the

In Other Words

Pride entered Lucifer's heart.
The excellent captain came to believe he was being cheated somehow. He didn't merely want to play a noble role in the Story; he wanted the Story to be about him. He coveted the throne; he wanted to be the star. He wanted the worship and adoration for himself.

John Eldredge, in *Epic* (Nashville: Nelson, 2004), 35.

There are two equal and opposite errors into which our race can fall about the devils. One is to disbelieve in their existence. The other is to believe, and to feel an excessive and unhealthy interest in them. They themselves are equally pleased by both errors.

C. S. Lewis, in *The Screwtape Letters* (New York: Macmillan, 1943), 9.

tree of the knowledge of good and evil (Genesis 2:16–17). Satan, disguised as a serpent, persuaded Eve to eat its fruit. When she offered some to Adam, he ate too. They failed God's test, and as a result they became sinners. Human beings become part of God's kingdom only through Christ's redemptive power.

Satan's deception of the other angels is not recorded in Scripture, but we know that other angels followed him. God apparently allowed Satan to approach and test the other angels. Many were deceived and became part of Satan's rebellious kingdom. We don't know whether all the angels were tested at one time or whether it is possible today for a holy angel to become sinful. We do know that by the time Satan is excluded from heaven and confined to the earth in Revelation 12, one-third of the angels will have chosen to follow him.

Those angels who followed Satan experienced a falling away from God into a state of sin, just as Satan had. They have been confirmed in their sinfulness. In contrast, the angels who passed the test and who maintain their loyalty to God are confirmed in their holiness.

So we have two clearly distinct groups of angels in existence: good angels—God's holy angels—and evil, fallen angels controlled by Satan. Evil angels are also called *demons* or *evil spirits*. I think all these terms refer to the angels who are under Satan's power and who submit to his will.

Doing Satan's Work

The angels operating under Satan's direction are busy! Their major function is to "demonize" human beings. Demonic activity toward men and women who have not believed in Jesus can range from temptation to sin to emotional and spiritual oppression.

Demons may actually dwell in some people and control them. Demon-possession might be laughed at in modern society, but the Bible teaches that such control by evil angels is possible. Mark 5:1–18 gives a chilling example of a "demon-possessed man." The man was totally controlled not just by one but by many demons. Only the authority of Jesus can overcome a demon who oppresses someone.

Demons attack Christians too! I don't believe a demon can control a believer because we have the Holy Spirit living in us, but demons can certainly wage war against us. The apostle Paul reminds us that we are in a struggle against "spiritual forces of evil" (Ephesians 6:12). I think Satan and his angels use three main methods of attack against Christians:

Bible Networking

Colossians 1:13

[God] has rescued us from the dominion of darkness and brought us into the kingdom of the Son he loves.

Revelation 12:3 – 4

Then another sign appeared in heaven: an enormous red dragon with seven heads and ten horns and seven crowns on its heads. Its tail swept a third of the stars out of the sky and flung them to the earth.

- *Demons try to deceive us.* Satan will disguise himself as an angel of light if it will lead someone away from God's truth (2 Corinthians 11:14).
- *Demons try to discourage us.* Paul, in 2 Corinthians 2:11, says that Satan concocts all kinds of schemes against us. He (and his angels) look each one over very carefully. They lay cunning plans against us. They will do whatever they can to make us feel defeated or discouraged.
- *Demons love to accuse us.* Satan is called "the accuser of our brothers and sisters" (Revelation 12:10). Satan actually spends a lot of time in God's presence, accusing us before God. He will do the same thing in our hearts and minds. Satan's angels like nothing more than to remind us of old sins and failures. Those sins may be long-forgiven in God's mind, but Satan uses them to attack us, to silence us, to make us feel unworthy of God's goodness.

Resisting Satan's Power

The Bible also gives us some practical direction on counteracting Satan's attacks. Probably the most direct advice comes from the book of James: "Resist the devil, and he will flee from you" (4:7). We can stand against Satan, not in our own power, but in the authority of Jesus. When he or his flunkies attack, we can stand firm in God's truth and God's grace.

In Other Words

When Jesus says to Peter, "Get behind me, Satan! You are a hindrance to me; for you are not on the side of God, but of men" (Matthew 16:23 [RSV]), he recognizes that Peter's attempt to keep him from suffering and dying on the cross is really an attempt to keep Jesus from obedience to the Father's plan. Jesus realizes that opposition ultimately comes not from Peter, but from Satan himself.

Wayne Grudem, in *Bible Doctrine* (Grand Rapids: Zondervan, 1999), 176.

Protection [from angels] begins early in life and continues throughout life. . . . This protection seems to extend to physical help. Our spiritual help comes from the indwelling Christ and the Holy Spirit. . . . Even though it is an argument from silence, there is not one verse that suggests we should pray to angels for help. We pray to the Father, and he sends angels.

Elmer Towns, in *Concise Bible Doctrines* (Chattanooga, Tenn.: AMG, 2006), 282.

When the apostle Paul talks in Ephesians about the spiritual warfare being waged against us, he gives us four resources available to every Christian for overcoming the enemy's assault.

- The first resource is the *armor of God*—spiritual protection developed as we walk in conscious obedience to God. "Therefore," Paul counsels, since we are engaged in this ongoing spiritual struggle, "put on the full armor of God, so that when the day of evil comes, you may be able to stand your ground" (Ephesians 6:13). It's only by obeying the Lord that we can benefit from the spiritual armor he provides. We can't be careless about how we live and expect protection from demonic attack.
- Our second resource in the struggle is the *sword of the Spirit*, which is the Word of God (Ephesians 6:17). The only fighting weapon in our armory is a sword—God's Word, the Bible. As we grow in our understanding of God's truth, we become better equipped to strike back at Satan's attacks.

- The most neglected spiritual resource is *prayer*—"Pray in the Spirit on all occasions with all kinds of prayers and requests" (Ephesians 6:18). Our prayers in times of spiritual struggle or oppression may be short or long, silent or vocal, calm petitions or shrieks of pain, but we *must* pray.
- Our fourth supernatural resource is *the Holy Spirit*. Paul challenges us to pray "in the Spirit" (Ephesians 6:18). The Spirit of God, who resides in us, is far wiser and stronger than all the enemy's hosts standing against us.

None of these resources seem particularly spectacular. They may not be included in some of the more exciting stories about spiritual warfare that you hear in church or on Christian television. But these are the resources God has promised to bless. Far too often, when we find ourselves under fire, we focus on the fierceness of the attack or on the strength of the enemy rather than on the powerful resources that are available to us.

Where in the Universe Is Satan Now?

If you think that Satan and his angels live in the regions of hell, shoveling coal into a cosmic furnace, your belief comes more from comic

Sometimes when I am trying to focus my heart and mind on the Lord, I find myself attacked by powerful wrong thoughts that crowd in on my mind, seemingly coming from nowhere. Sometimes the attack is sustained, playing for example on some of my natural weaknesses; at other times it is sudden and short-lived—but it is always severe.

I am learning to look to the Lord at these times, calling on him in prayer and trying to exercise the faith that can extinguish *all* the flaming arrows of the evil one (Ephesians 6:16). It also helps to remind myself of specific verses in the Bible, speaking God's Word to myself, reminding myself of the greatness and holiness of God and of who I am in Christ. I find that another help in times of attack is to be watchful, as Jesus commanded: "Watch and pray so that you will not fall into temptation" (Matthew 26:41). I fill my mind with good things, being careful about what television programs I watch and what websites I visit. The Enemy will do his best to distract us from pursuing lives devoted to the Lord. His attacks have to be met with guarded hearts and minds.

Bible Networking

Hebrews 9:12

[Christ] did not enter [heaven] by means of the blood of goats and calves; but he entered the Most Holy Place once for all by his own blood, thus obtaining eternal redemption.

1 John 2:1 – 2

My dear children, I write this to you so that you will not sin. But if anybody does sin, we have an advocate with the Father—Jesus Christ, the Righteous One. He is the atoning sacrifice for our sins, and not only for ours but also for the sins of the whole world.

---

strips than from the Bible. As strange as it may sound, sinful angels inhabit the heavens. The Bible uses the word *heaven* in three ways. The first heaven is the air, the atmosphere around the earth. Jesus in Matthew 6:26 said, "Look at the birds of the air [literally, of the heaven]." Birds fly in the first heaven. The second heaven is what we call space. Psalm 8:3 reads, "When I consider your heavens, . . . the moon and the stars." The third heaven is the place where God dwells. When Stephen, an early Christian, was being stoned for his faith, he "looked up to heaven and saw the glory of God, and Jesus standing at the right hand of God" (Acts 7:55). The third heaven is the place where Jesus is today. It is also the place where holy angels live. They surround God's throne, waiting to be sent on any mission God desires.

The fallen, sinful angels do not live in God's heaven. They lived there once but no longer. Satan and his angels dwell primarily in the first heaven—in the atmosphere of the earth. Jesus made an interesting statement in the book of Revelation to the church in the city of Pergamum. He said, "I know where you live—where Satan has his throne . . . in your city—where Satan lives" (Revelation 2:13). Satan undoubtedly has a place today somewhere in the earthly realm where he lives.

In the book of Job, God asks Satan, "Where have you come from?" Satan answers, "From roaming through the earth and going back and forth in it" (Job 1:7; 2:2). Satan dwells on the earth and in the atmosphere around the earth.

- ☑ The Bible has a lot to say about angels.
- ☑ Angels fall into two categories—good, holy angels who do God's bidding, and corrupt, evil angels who do Satan's bidding.
- ☑ Angels were created by God individually and fully mature. Angels do not reproduce.
- ☑ Angels are powerful beings—more powerful than humans, and some angels are more powerful than other angels.
- ☑ Human beings never become angels. We remain human forever.
- ☑ Sin began in the heart of one angel who was lifted up with pride and who wanted to be like God.
- ☑ Satan tries to mimic or imitate God. Satan's kingdom (like God's) has both human and angelic inhabitants.
- ☑ Fallen angels (demons) have joined Satan's rebellion against God, and they seek to "demonize" human beings.
- ☑ The Bible's direction for dealing with Satan's attacks is to "resist the devil."
- ☑ God provides abundant resources to protect us and to equip us to stand against Satan's assault.
- ☑ God's angels dwell in heaven in God's presence. Satan and his angels dwell in the atmosphere of earth but (for a time) have access to God in order to accuse Christians.
- ☑ Satan and his angels will spend eternity in the lake of fire.

The other fact that becomes clear as you read the account in the book of Job is that Satan has access to God's heaven. He may go there because God summons him there (as in the scenes that open the book of Job), or Satan may go there to accuse a believer before God. The book of Revelation says that Satan accuses believers "before our God day and night" (Revelation 12:10). I don't think that means Satan is *always* there, but he has access at any time to bring an accusation.

What a depressing thought! Satan can stand before God at any time and raise an accusation against me. What gives me comfort and encouragement is to know that my High Priest is continually and eternally in God's presence as well, praying for me constantly. When Satan brings an accusation, we have an advocate, a defense lawyer, who pleads our case before the Father. Satan may accuse us day and night, but he never wins a case!

Satan's End

The most compelling fact to remember about Satan is that *he is a defeated enemy*. Jesus' death on the cross conquered sin and death forever. It also doomed Satan to an eternity of judgment. Satan is not in hell today. He is not the king of hell. Satan hates hell because it is the place where he will spend eternity.

At the final wrap-up of human history, that old enemy of God and God's people will bow his knee in submission to Jesus Christ, and he will confess that Jesus is Lord (Philippians 2:10–11). Then God will kick him into absolute darkness forever.

> The devil, who deceived them, was thrown into the lake of burning sulfur .... [He] will be tormented day and night for ever and ever.
> Revelation 20:10

The lake of fire, eternal hell, was created and prepared by God as a place of eternal confinement for the Devil and his angels (Matthew 25:41). That's important to remember in a world that seems to be more and more dominated by evil and violence. God's ultimate victory over all the works of the Devil has never been in doubt. Some day soon, Satan's reign will give way to God's reign.

Help File

ANGELS IN WORSHIP

Wonderful guests are present every week in our Sunday worship services, yet we almost never recognize them. As Christians gather to worship the Lord, we not only join with millions of other Christians; we also join with the hosts of angels in heaven giving praise and honor to God.

One of the great ancient declarations of faith, called *Te Deum* in Latin, beautifully expresses the attitude of our hearts as we, with all of God's angels, come joyfully and confidently before God in worship:

We praise Thee, O God;
we acknowledge Thee to be the Lord.

All the earth doth worship Thee,
the Father everlasting.
To Thee all angels cry aloud;
the heavens and all the powers therein.
To Thee cherubim[*] and seraphim[*] continually do cry.
Holy, Holy, Holy Lord God of Sabaoth[**].
Heaven and earth are full of the majesty of Thy glory.

[*] Cherubim (Ezekiel 1; 10:20) and seraphim (Isaiah 6:1–7) are types of angels.

[**] Lord God of Sabaoth means "Lord God of hosts"; *Sabaoth* is the Hebrew word for hosts or armies.

In Other Words

By his death and resurrection, Jesus conquered the power of death and Satan. By his name the apostles healed the sick and cast out demons, for there is no name above that of Jesus. Christians wage an important spiritual war, in which they are called to put into effect the victory Jesus Christ has already won. As they demonstrate his power over evil spirits, they will weaken Satan's rule and strengthen God's kingdom.

Tite Tíenou, in *Exploring the Christian Faith* (Nashville: Nelson, 1996), 139.

Digging Deeper

If you want to learn more about angels, check out:

✗ C. Fred Dickson, *Angels: Elect and Evil.* Chicago: Moody, 1995.

Douglas Connelly has written a LifeGuide Bible Study on *Angels* (InterVarsity, 2004). It's an exploration of some of the key passages in the Bible on angels.

CHAPTER 11

Welcome to the Family: The Church

Welcome to the Family: The Church

- ▶ Where is *your* church?
- ▶ Discover why the church is so important in God's program.
- ▶ Find out if communion is just a tiny meal—or something more significant.
- ▶ Line up to be baptized!

"Here's the Church, Here's the Steeple . . ."

In virtually every community you can find strange-looking buildings. They may be small or as large as a soccer stadium. They usually have a steeple on the roof or a cross on the front. Stained-glass windows set them off from other buildings. When we drive by, we instantly recognize the building as a church. If someone says to us, "What church do you go to?" we respond with a location: "My church is on the corner of Main and Elm."

Sometimes we refer to a cluster of like-minded congregations or a denomination as a church. You may be part of the United Methodist Church or the Missionary Church or the Southern Baptist Church—or the Finnish Apostolic Lutheran Church!

At other times we may use the word *church* to mean institutional Christianity in general. We may say, "The church doesn't have much influence in our society," or "The church is working to become more in touch with the culture."

What is surprising is that the Bible never uses the word *church* in any of those ways. You never read in Scripture of a church building, a denomination, or the church's influence in society. The New Testament always uses the word *church* to refer to *people*. The church is the body of genuine believers in Jesus.

The Bible uses the term *church* in two ways—one universal and one local. The universal church is the entire body of genuine Christians in every part of the world and throughout the entire church age. Jesus said, "I will build my church" (Matthew 16:18). He was not talking about bricks and mortar but about a body of believers who would be united by their loyalty to and faith in Jesus. The apostle Paul wrote, "Christ loved the church and gave himself up for her to make her holy, ... and to present her to himself as a radiant church" (Ephesians 5:25–27). Paul was not talking about one congregation or one denomination. He was talking about the one true church over which Jesus reigns as Head and Lord.

The Bible also uses the word *church* to refer to a visible expression of the universal church—a localized church, one congregation of believers. When Paul wrote a letter to the Christians living in the city of Thessalonica, he wrote "to the church of the Thessalonians" (1 Thessalonians 1:1). In his letter to the Corinthian Christians, Paul combined both ideas:

> To the church of God in Corinth [a local group meeting as a
> congregation], ... together with all those everywhere who call on the
> name of our Lord Jesus Christ [the universal group of all believers].
> 1 Corinthians 1:2

The *building* where my congregation meets on Sunday is not the church; the *people* are the church. When the people leave to go about their lives, the church is scattered out in the neighborhoods and schools and businesses of my community, where we are called to be fully committed followers of Jesus.

When Jesus went back to heaven, he did not leave behind a denomination or a creed or system of thought. He left behind a visible community—the church, a called-out group of people who would take his light and truth to the world.

What's in It for Me?

Christians believe that spiritually healthy followers of Jesus have some connection with *both* expressions of the church. We are part of the universal church purely by God's grace, by virtue of our faith in Jesus, and because of our participation in his salvation provided through his death on the cross. But it's not really enough to say, "I don't belong to any visible church. I'm just a member of the invisible, universal church."

Some Christians are pretty disillusioned with the organized church. They've been wounded or burned-out or have been victims of spiritual abuse. But you can't escape the witness of the New Testament that true Christians were always part of the visible community of believers with appropriate leadership and organization to do God's work in the world. Has the organized church become too rigid at times—or too disconnected from biblical principles? Yes, but that doesn't mean we can bail out. We either work to change it, or we find a congregation that holds more closely to biblical truth.

The New Testament never makes a division between the universal community and the local gathered community. The writers of Scripture thought of only one church because there is only one Lord who rules over it—Jesus Christ.

Snapshots of the Church

The Bible uses several images to describe the church and to help us understand how we are to function together.

- The image used most often in the New Testament is the church as the *body* of Christ. It means more than just a collection of individuals, like the student body at your local high school. The term *body* points out that the church is a spiritual organism, a living unity connected to the Head, Jesus Christ.

  "Just as each of us has one body with many members, and these members do not all have the same function, so in Christ we, though

Bible Networking

Ephesians 4:4 – 6

There is one body and one Spirit, just as you were called to one hope when you were called; one Lord, one faith, one baptism; one God and Father of all, who is over all and through all and in all.

Colossians 1:18 – 19

[The Son] is the head of the body, the church; he is the beginning and the firstborn from among the dead, so that in everything he might have the supremacy. For God was pleased to have all his fullness dwell in him.

many, form one body, and each member belongs to all the others"
(Romans 12:4–5).

- The church is also pictured as a *family*, which suggests that the
church is a fellowship of love and acceptance. The church is God's
way of meeting a deep-seated need in the human heart—the need
to belong.

    "You are no longer foreigners and strangers, but fellow citizens
    with God's people and also members of his household" (Ephesians
    2:19).

- The church is also pictured as God's *building*, as the *temple* of
the Holy Spirit. This image stresses our unity in Christ. We aren't
several factions in competition but one structure centered on God's
glory. When the congregation gathers for worship, we become
God's temple. The cornerstone is Jesus, and the foundation is the
Word of God given through Christ's apostles and prophets.

    "Don't you know that you yourselves are God's temple and that
    God's Spirit dwells in your midst? If anyone destroys God's temple,
    God will destroy that person; for God's temple is sacred, and you
    together are that temple" (1 Corinthians 3:16–17).

- The most intimate description of the church is when we are
called the *bride* of Christ. Christians today are "engaged" to
Jesus (2 Corinthians 11:2), but the day will come when Jesus will
"marry" his bride and celebrate that event at the wedding supper
of the Lamb (Revelation 19:9). When God's work of preparation
is completed, we will be presented to Christ "as a radiant church,
without stain or wrinkle or any other blemish, but holy and blameless" (Ephesians 5:27).

- The apostle Peter pictures the church as "a chosen people, a royal
priesthood, a holy nation, God's special possession" (1 Peter 2:9).
In Old Testament Israel, individual believers had to approach God
through a specially chosen family, the descendants of Aaron who
were priests. In the church age, all believers have access to God
through one priest, Jesus our High Priest.

The one conclusion we can draw from all these images is that God
has called us out as his own people to live distinctive lives before
the world. The church is designed to give visible expression to God's
grace and compassion and justice. Our focus is not to be inward with
an isolated "fortress" mentality but outward to a world that needs to
hear—and see—the grace of God in action.

Church with a Mission

Jesus established the church with clear purposes in mind. It was not just a Sunday social club. Christians gathered as a body for a reason. Church services may be formal or informal, the music may be traditional or contemporary, the dress code may be suits and dresses or jeans and sandals, but several elements identify a biblical church.

- *Worship and prayer.* The church meets for worship. We gather to lift up Jesus as Savior and Lord and to exalt him together. A Christian can worship God at any time and in any place, but there is something powerful about worship with other believers. The "audience" in worship is not the congregation; the primary focus is on the Lord. The question to ask as you leave a church service is not, Did I get anything out of it? but Was Jesus pleased with my adoration of him?
- *Instruction.* New Testament Christians also met to be taught the truth of God's Word. Teaching is designed to stimulate spiritual maturity and to produce godliness in a believer's walk in the world. The sermon is the primary vehicle for instruction in the church.
- *Fellowship.* The church also gathers for mutual encouragement and love. We pray for each other, serve each other, help those with spiritual or physical needs, and demonstrate our care for each other.
- *Service.* The gathering of believers also allows Christians to use their spiritual gifts to build up and bless other believers. You may have the gift of teaching or of helping or of administration or of healing. When the church meets, the exercise of your gifts is vital to the spiritual health of the body.

In Other Words

As the bride of Christ, part of our job is to constantly invite people to come and experience what we've found in Christ. This fellowship we enjoy with one another and with Jesus is open to anyone. This should be the one place where every wall sin builds between people is broken down. Race, gender, national origin, economic class, and anything else you can imagine — none of it matters. All that matters is a thirst for God.

Mark Tabb, in *Theology: Think for Yourself What You Believe* (Colorado Springs: NavPress, 2006), 222–23.

Great Debates!

UNION OR UNITY?

The New Testament repeatedly emphasizes the one-ness of those who have believed in Jesus. We are *one* body, under *one* head, Christ Jesus, and are filled with *one* Spirit. Jesus even made our one-ness part of his prayer in John 17: "I pray also for those who will believe in me ..., that all of them may be one" (17:20–21).

We all agree that Jesus prayed for our unity, but the Christian church seems to be anything but unified. Hundreds of denominations exist, and thousands of churches would call themselves "nondenominational"—unattached to any denomination. Even the larger church is divided between the Roman Catholic branch, the Orthodox churches, and Protestant churches. How are we "one" in Christ?

Some Christians have worked hard to promote union—the joining of denominations into one large institution. Other Christians are not bothered as much by divisions and denominations. They see our unity as a spiritual reality focused on our loyalty to Christ and our commitment to the basic truths of the Bible. Christians from many traditions can gather for a conference or a concert and sense a "oneness," a unity in the Spirit with those around them.

The believers in the New Testament never seemed to meet together for the purpose of evangelism. The focus of the church gathered was worship and spiritual growth; the focus of the church scattered was evangelism. We don't stop being the church when we leave the worship service on Sunday morning. Instead we are scattered like powerful seeds into the world, where we seek to proclaim the good news that Jesus is willing to rescue all who come to him in faith.

Water and Wine: Baptism and the Lord's Supper

Christians have some practices that may seem a little weird to a non-Christian or even to a new Christian. We call these practices *ordinances* or *sacraments*. The word *sacrament* has come to mean "a channel of grace." Some Christians believe we receive a measure of God's grace by participating in these religious practices. The Roman Catholic Church, for example, recognizes seven sacraments: baptism, the Eucharist (receiving the bread and the wine), confirmation, penance for sin, anointing with oil for sickness or at death, holy orders (entering a religious order as a priest or a nun), and marriage. Protestants have historically recognized only two practices as sacraments—baptism and the Lord's Supper (receiving the bread and the wine). Many Protestants prefer to call them *ordinances*, which means "a command." They see them as commands to the church rather than as channels of grace. We are saved by God's grace alone through faith alone, not by participating in religious activities.

More Than Getting Wet

While we may share in the Lord's Supper many times in our Christian life, usually we are baptized only once. The command to be baptized is very clear. Jesus' final words to his disciples before he ascended into heaven were these: "Go and make disciples of all nations, baptizing them in the name of the Father and of the Son and of the Holy Spirit, and teaching them to obey everything I have commanded you" (Matthew 28:19–20). In the book of Acts as the Christian community began to form and grow, those who became Christians were baptized (Acts 2:41; 8:36).

Again, however, Christians disagree on what baptism means and how baptism should be performed.

Help File

BIBLICAL "ONE ANOTHERS"

The New Testament is pretty clear on the responsibilities we have as believers to others in the church family.

- Accept one another (Romans 15:7).
- Bear with one another in love (Ephesians 4:2).
- Love each other (John 15:12).
- Stop passing judgment on one another (Romans 14:13).
- Instruct one another (Romans 15:14).
- Be devoted to one another in love (Romans 12:10).
- Honor one another above yourselves (Romans 12:10).
- Greet one another (2 Corinthians 13:12).
- Serve one another humbly in love (Galatians 5:13).
- Be kind and compassionate to one another, forgiving each other (Ephesians 4:32).
- Submit to one another (Ephesians 5:21).
- Encourage one another (1 Thessalonians 4:18).
- Live in peace with each other (1 Thessalonians 5:13).
- Confess your sins to each other (James 5:16).
- Pray for each other (James 5:16).
- Offer hospitality to one another (1 Peter 4:9).
- Clothe yourselves with humility toward one another (1 Peter 5:5).
- Carry each other's burdens (Galatians 6:2).

CHURCH GOVERNMENT

The church as the body of Christ is a living organism—but in its visible form in the world it also requires organization. Christians have developed different forms of organizational government, but their aim in each case is to be guided by the true Head of the church, Jesus Christ. Three main types of church government have emerged over the centuries.

- *Episcopal.* This form of church authority is based on the Greek word *episkopos*, meaning "overseer" or "bishop." These are churches directed by bishops or a hierarchy of church leaders. The United Methodist Church uses a very simple form of bishop authority. Each bishop oversees a cluster of churches and assists the pastors of those churches. The Roman Catholic Church has a very complex hierarchical leadership, with final authority resting with the bishop of Rome, the pope.

- *Presbyterian.* The title for this form of church government comes from another New Testament Greek word—*presbyteros*, meaning "elder." In this system spiritual leaders from the congregation are chosen to sit with the pastor in a council of elders to direct the ministry of the church. Above the local church council are various other levels of presbytery or synod, where higher levels of authority in a denomination reside.

- *Congregational.* In this form of government, final authority rests not with one leader or a council of leaders but with the entire local congregation. A congregation may select a church council or board to make most decisions, but weightier decisions come to the congregation for discussion and decision. Most Baptist and Bible churches are congregational in their government.

It might be helpful to explore the form of government followed at the church you attend—and on what biblical authority that government rests!

There are three basic positions on what baptism means.

- *Baptism is a channel of saving grace.* Many Christians believe that baptism is linked to salvation. The Roman Catholic Church teaches that if an infant is baptized, the guilt of original sin is removed. Baptism, in effect, guarantees the child's salvation until he or she reaches the age when he or she can exercise personal faith and receive the sacraments of the church. Lutherans also practice infant baptism but put a larger emphasis on the presence of faith in the parents or the godparents to stand in the place of the child's faith until the child is confirmed in his or her own belief as a young adult.

To worship is to quicken the conscience by the holiness of God, to feed the mind with the truth of God, to purge the imagination by the beauty of God, to open the heart to the love of God, and to devote the will to the purpose of God.

William Temple, former Archbishop of Canterbury, in *Readings in John's Gospel* (London: Macmillan, 1945), 68.

The Church of Christ believes that baptism is an essential element in salvation, but they only baptize believers, not infants. Those who profess faith in Jesus are usually baptized on the same day.

- *Baptism is a sign and seal of God's covenant.* Many Reformed, Anglican, and Presbyterian churches baptize infants as a sign that the child is part of God's covenant people. They see New Testament baptism in the same light as Old Testament circumcision. It is an act of entrance into God's covenant promises.
- *Baptism is an outward picture of our salvation.* Baptists, Wesleyans, charismatics, and many other Christians view baptism as an outward sign of our inward cleansing. The cleansing occurs when we believe in Jesus and are indwelt by the Holy Spirit. Baptism is simply a picture of that inward reality. Only those old enough to understand and believe the message about Jesus are baptized, not infants.

Even the form of baptism varies from church to church. Three forms (the traditional word is *modes*) are practiced today.

- *Sprinkling.* In the early church, baptismal water was sprinkled over those too sick or too weak to be immersed in water in a river or a pool. Gradually, sprinkling was adopted by some churches as the appropriate form, particularly those churches that baptized infants.
- *Pouring.* In this form of baptism, water is poured three times over the head of the one being baptized—once for each member of the Trinity. Many Mennonite churches practice pouring as their form of baptism.

- *Immersion.* The evidence seems to indicate that the earliest form or mode of baptism practiced in the church was immersion, which meant completely submerging a person in water. The New Testament word for *baptize* (in Greek, *baptizō*) meant "to dip or drown." Jesus was baptized by John in the Jordan River and came "up out of the water" (Mark 1:10). Many Christians believe that immersion best pictures our death, burial, and resurrection with Christ (Romans 6:3–4).

More Than a Meal

The night before his arrest and crucifixion, Jesus ate a meal with his closest followers. During the meal, Jesus took a flat loaf of bread, he blessed it, he broke it in pieces, and then he gave it to his followers to eat. "This is my body," Jesus said. "Eat this in remembrance of me." Later Jesus took a cup of wine and blessed it. Then he told them to drink from it. "This is my blood," Jesus told them. "Drink this in remembrance of me." Jesus also told his followers to continue to observe this ceremony until he returns from heaven.

Christians all agree on the importance of the ceremony we call the Lord's Supper. Some churches call it the Eucharist (pronounced **you-kar-ist**, based on the Greek word *eucharistia*, "giving of thanks"); others call it Communion or the Lord's Table. Some Christians share in the bread and cup every week; some less often. The basic elements of the observance, however, are the same.

For me, being a part of a local community of believers is vital.

Soon after I became a Christian, I spent a year in Germany. On my first day at the local Baptist church, I was invited back to lunch by some of the people in that congregation, and I discovered the warmth of true Christian fellowship. Later, when I moved home, I was invited to someone's house for coffee after a service, and I have stayed at the same church for over thirty years!

We've had our ups and downs, of course, such as changes in the style of worship, not being voted onto the leadership team, and going for a few years without a senior pastor, but for me the church remains fundamentally about being a group of people who are committed to one another through thick and thin.

Key Passages on the Lord's Supper

- Matthew 26:26–29
- Mark 14:22–25
- Luke 22:14–22
- 1 Corinthians 11:23–26

What Christians disagree about is the meaning of the Lord's Supper. Four distinct views have emerged over the centuries of the church age:

- *The bread and wine become the body and blood of Jesus.* The Roman Catholic Church teaches that, when the priest elevates the bread (the host) and the wine in the service of the Mass, those elements miraculously change substance and become the literal body and blood of Jesus. They may still look and taste like bread and wine, but the person of faith will receive them as the life-giving body and blood of Jesus. This view is referred to as *transubstantiation*—i.e., the substance is changed.
- *The body and blood of Christ are present in the bread and the wine.* The Lutheran view of the Lord's Supper is referred to as *consubstantiation*, meaning "with the substance." Their view is that Jesus' body and blood are actually present in the bread and wine, but the substance of the elements does not change. The body and blood of Jesus is present in or with or alongside the bread and the wine. For Lutherans, the Lord's Supper is not a re-sacrifice for sin (as in the Catholic Mass), but we do receive real spiritual benefits from eating and drinking the elements in faith.
- *Jesus' spiritual presence is in the bread and the wine.* Many Reformed churches reject the idea of the real presence of Jesus' body and blood in the Communion elements, but they believe that his spiritual presence resides in the bread and the wine. Because of the mystical presence of Christ in the elements, those who receive the bread and the wine receive a measure of grace from them.

- *The bread and the wine are symbols of Jesus' body and blood.* The memorial view of the Lord's Supper is held by most evangelical Christians. They believe that there is no actual or spiritual presence of Jesus in the bread and the wine, but that the elements remind us of Jesus' body and blood. The observance of the Lord's Supper is designed to draw us back to the cross and Jesus' death in

In Other Words

Roman Catholic Transubstantiation View

The Mass with its colorful vestments and vivid ceremonies is a dramatic reenactment in an unbloody manner of the sacrifice of Christ on Calvary.

John O'Brien, in *The Faith of Millions* (Huntington, Ind.: Our Sunday Visitor, 1974), 382.

Lutheran Consubstantiation View

What is the Sacrament of the Altar?

It is the true body and blood of our Lord Jesus Christ, under the bread and wine, for us Christians to eat and to drink, instituted by Christ himself.

Martin Luther, in The Small Catechism Part V.

Spiritual Presence View

Christ is also spiritually present in a special way as we partake of the bread and wine. . . . We meet him at his table, to which he comes to give himself to us. As we receive the elements of bread and wine in the presence of Christ, so we partake of him and all his benefits.

Wayne Grudem, in *Bible Doctrine* (Grand Rapids: Zondervan, 1999), 392.

Memorial View

Christ is present in the [Lord's] Supper not in the bread and wine but in his people as they gather to break the bread and drink from the cup. Their symbolic action is not simply a memory device but a way of making the past event of Christ's death present and real for the family of faith.

Bruce Shelley, in *The Church: God's People* (Wheaton, Ill.: Victor, 1978), 80.

☑ The church is not a building or an institution. The church is the body of genuine believers in Jesus.

☑ The New Testament uses the term *church* in two ways—the universal church of all Christians and the local church of Christians in a particular place.

☑ The church is the *body* of Christ, the *family* of God, the *temple* of the Holy Spirit, and the *bride* of Christ.

☑ The church meets for worship, instruction, and fellowship; the church scatters for evangelism and ministry.

☑ Christians practice water baptism and the Lord's Supper as part of their worship.

☑ Christians have different views on what the bread and the wine of the Lord's Supper mean and what baptism signifies.

☑ The church takes its direction from the Head of the church, Jesus Christ.

our place. We remember his sacrifice with adoration and gratitude and renewed commitment.

People with a Purpose

When Jesus went back to heaven, he left his work in the hands of a small group of faithful followers. The apostle Paul said that God determined to demonstrate his wisdom and power by using weak and simple people to do God's work (1 Corinthians 1:27–29). A few times in history the church has been powerful and wealthy; most of the time the church has looked weak and fragile. But Jesus has continued to build his church. It's not the institutional church that concerns Jesus. He's far more concerned about his body, the spiritual church. *That* church will ultimately be revealed as the glorious sons and daughters of God.

The church has a very clear purpose on earth. We gather in cathedrals or in chapels or in homes or in caves for worship and teaching and fellowship. Then we scatter into the world to live as distinctive followers of Christ Jesus. Along the way, we tell people about the One who loves them and who opened the way for them to be restored to friendship with God. We stand for justice and goodness in a world bent on oppression and greed. We help the poor, love the unlovely, open our arms to the lost, visit those who are sick, and bring a message of hope to the hopeless. Everything we do as Christians we do for the honor and glory of Jesus.

If you want to know more about your own church tradition and heritage, talk to your pastor or priest about books or resources that will help you get a deeper insight into your beliefs and practices. Focus on the biblical foundations of your church. Talk to people in your congregation about the history of your own church. If you are not part of a congregation of believers, visit some churches. Find a church that honors Jesus and that believes the Bible, and become part of the fellowship.

CHAPTER 12

A New World Coming: The Future

A New World Coming: The Future

▶ God knows the future—but has he told us?
▶ Find out where Christians agree on the future—and why sometimes they disagree.
▶ Meet an evil world ruler and discover what "666" is all about.
▶ Learn what heaven will be like and what we'll do there.

The End Is Near (or Something Like That)

We all want to know the future. Think about your own life—your job, your friends, your marriage, your investments. We could have fabulous success and avoid a lot of problems if we could just get a glimpse of what the future holds.

The Bible has quite a bit to say about the future, but the problem is that the information seems to be a confusing mix of mysterious symbols and weird visions. The preachers and pundits who study biblical prophecy seem to end up with differing views and strange charts and sometimes pretty wild claims. Most people (including a lot of Christians) find prophecy too difficult and too far-out. So they just walk away from it all.

The purpose of this chapter is not to confuse you even more! Prophecy is an important part of God's truth. My intention is to help you see the big picture. Yes, we will look at various viewpoints—and, yes, it can be tough to keep it all straight. But the benefit is that you will grow in your understanding *and* in your confidence in God. God knows the future. God in his wisdom has told us how the story ends. Now he wants you to rest in him for *your* future.

Prophecy's Big Picture

Probably no area of biblical truth prompts more disagreement among Christians than the study of God's plan for the wrap-up of the human story. Books are written, seminars are held, conferences are convened—all to defend one view or one position as the correct one. Looking at all the debates surrounding biblical prophecy, there's one thing we can easily lose sight of, however: *Christians agree on many of the big issues of biblical prophecy.* I find at least six broad areas of agreement when it comes to God's plan for the future.

- *God created human beings to live forever.* Christians believe that human beings live on beyond the point of physical death. The body may die, but the human spirit or soul continues to exist.
- *Human beings experience conscious existence between physical death and the resurrection of the body.* Christians believe that at death those people who have believed in Jesus in this life enter a state of rest and joy in the presence of Jesus. Those who have refused to believe in Jesus enter a state of separation from him. All those who have died are consciously aware of where they are and what is going on around them.
- *The bodies of human beings will be raised from the dead.* All human beings, whether believers or unbelievers, will be raised from the dead. In the future our spirits will be reunited with our resurrected bodies. The bodies of believers in Jesus will experience the resurrection to life in a body forever free from sickness or pain or death. The bodies of unbelievers will experience the

Help File

ABUNDANT EVIDENCE

Once you start looking seriously at prophecy, you will be amazed at how much of the Bible refers to the future. One respected Bible scholar has calculated that 27 percent of the Bible contains information that relates to the future. Only four books of the Bible contain nothing directly predictive (Ruth and Song of Songs in the Old Testament; Philemon and 3 John in the New). The remaining sixty-two books include at least some prophetic material. (These figures all come from J. Barton Payne, *Encyclopedia of Biblical Prophecy* [New York: Harper & Row, 1973].)

The Bible contains approximately 2,500 predictions about events that were future when the predictions were recorded or spoken. Two thousand of those predictions have been fulfilled in every detail. (What are the odds?) We can conclude that 500 biblical predictions are about events yet to happen.

The theological term for the study of what the Bible teaches about the future is *eschatology* (ess-ka-**tol**-o-gy). It means "the study of last things"—the last events on the time line of human history.

resurrection to condemnation. Their bodies will be raised to stand in judgment before God.

- *All human beings will stand before God to give an account of their lives.* Unbelievers will face God and hear God's sentence of eternal separation. There will be no excuse for their rejection of God's gift of salvation. Believers in Jesus will give an account too. We will be rewarded according to the faithfulness of our lives to Jesus.
- *Jesus will return.* All Christians agree that Jesus will return to earth a second time. The Bible is so clear on the *fact* of Jesus' return that there is no real debate about it.
- *An eternal heaven will be prepared for those who believe in Jesus as Savior; eternal separation from Jesus will be the destiny of those who refuse God's grace.* There is no disagreement among Christians that we will all experience eternity. We look for a new heaven and a new earth of peace and joy forever.

On the big issues, Christians agree! It doesn't matter what your denomination or tradition is, if your church takes the Bible seriously, these six declarations are believed and taught. Christians also agree

Bible Networking

Psalm 10:16

The LORD is King for ever and ever.

1 Chronicles 29:11 – 12

Yours, LORD, is the greatness and the power
    and the glory and the majesty and the splendor,
    for everything in heaven and earth is yours.
Yours, LORD, is the kingdom;
    you are exalted as head over all.
Wealth and honor come from you;
    you are the ruler of all things.
In your hands are strength and power
    to exalt and give strength to all.

that the Bible contains a number of prophecies that have yet to be fulfilled. We are certain of those events, but disagreements arise over the sequence and timing and nature of those events.

What I try to keep in mind as I think about biblical prophecy is that committed, Bible-believing Christians hold views about future events that are different from mine. In fact, the two authors of this book take differing viewpoints on exactly how the future will unfold. So explore the options and hold a position with conviction, but add a good dose of humility in the mix as well. Some day God will do his work of bringing human history to an end, and we will all agree on one more issue: We will all say that God was right, and *all* of us (to some degree) were wrong.

Thy Kingdom Come

The mother of all controversies with respect to biblical prophecy is the debate over the kingdom. Endless rows of long, boring books have been written on exactly when Christ's kingdom begins, what it is like, who is included, when it will end, and if we are in it now or if we have to wait a while. It's enough to make you want to skip the subject completely. But don't do it! The kingdom is an important biblical promise, and we really need to work at understanding it.

On two points all Christians agree! First, Christians believe that Jesus will return in the future as the Judge of all humanity. He will return physically and visibly in power and majesty. The second point we all agree on is that Jesus is the King. He is the anointed Ruler of everything. No one and nothing are outside his knowledge, control, and care.

Bible Networking

Ephesians 1:20 – 22

[God] raised Christ from the dead and seated him at his right hand in the heavenly realms, far above all rule and authority, power and dominion, and every name that can be invoked, not only in the present age but also in the one to come. And God placed all things under his feet and appointed him to be head over everything for the church, which is his body, the fullness of him who fills everything in every way.

You may not be convinced that Jesus is King over all when you read the headlines or hear the daily news reports of violence and cruelty and war. That's why we need to read more than just the newspaper. God does reign, but he is allowing an evil world to run its course.

Jesus reigns over an eternal kingdom. If that's the case, what's the problem? Why such a big debate about the kingdom of God? The debate arises from passages of Scripture that describe the kingdom. Are we to take these passages in a literal sense as pointing to an actual visible kingdom on earth—or do the kingdom passages describe a spiritual reality that transcends the visible world?

The one Bible passage quoted in every discussion of the kingdom is Revelation 20:1–6:

> And I saw an angel coming down out of heaven, having the key to the Abyss and holding in his hand a great chain. He seized the dragon, that ancient serpent, who is the devil, or Satan, and bound him for a thousand years. He threw him into the Abyss, and locked and sealed it over him, to keep him from deceiving the nations anymore until the thousand years were ended. After that, he must be set free for a short time.
>
> I saw thrones on which were seated those who had been given authority to judge. And I saw the souls of those who had been beheaded because of their testimony about Jesus and because of the word of God. They had not worshiped the beast or his image and had not received his mark on their foreheads or their hands. They came to life and reigned with Christ a thousand years. (The rest of the dead did not come to life until the thousand years were ended.) This is the first resurrection. Blessed and holy are those who have part in the first resurrection. The second death has no power over them, but they will be priests of God and of Christ and will reign with him for a thousand years.

Here's the question: When will we "reign with him for a thousand years"? When will we see that visible kingdom come—or can we see it today if we look in the right places? That's the heart of the big debate—what does the promised kingdom of God look like, and when does it come?

Christians have given two basic answers to these questions. The advocates of each position believe that the Bible promises a kingdom. The disagreement comes with respect to *when* the kingdom comes in the plan of God. Each of these views on the kingdom is a "millennial" view—i.e., each focuses on the promised one-thousand-year (= millennium) reign of Jesus Christ.

View #1 of the Kingdom: "We're in It Today!"

Christians who hold this view of the kingdom of God call themselves *amillennialists*. Putting the letter *a* in front of the word *millennium* makes it mean "no millennium." Simply stated, they believe that there will be no *future* thousand-year reign of Christ on earth. Instead Christ reigns right now in heaven and in his church on earth. We are in Christ's kingdom today.

Amillennialists base their position on the following arguments:

- Jesus could return at any time. When he returns, Jesus will bring human history to an end in one big bang. Jesus will come to earth, all human beings who ever lived will be resurrected (their bodies raised back to life), every person will be judged by God, and each will be sent to his or her eternal destiny. There will be no literal, physical thousand-year kingdom on earth.

- The "one thousand years" of Jesus' reign mentioned in Revelation 20 is to be understood as a symbolic number, not a literal number. Nowhere else in the Bible is one thousand years mentioned as the length of the kingdom. John was using a large, round number to convey the idea of "a long time" to his readers. He did not expect them to take it literally.

- God did make promises to Israel in the Old Testament about an earthly kingdom of peace and prosperity. When Israel rejected Jesus as their Messiah, however, God transferred those promises to the Christian community—to the church, to a *new* Israel. All God's promises are being fulfilled spiritually today. We will see the literal fulfillment of those promises in God's *eternal* kingdom on a new earth.

- Satan has been "bound" in this age, just as Revelation 20:1–3 predicted. That doesn't mean that Satan is inactive. He still opposes the work of God, but he can no longer deceive the nations or stand against the power of the gospel message. Near the end of this present age, Satan will be unfettered for a short time, and he will deceive the nations to fight against the Lord and his people (Revelation 20:7–10). Christ will destroy those who come against him when he returns in glory. Satan will then be confined to an eternal lake of fire.

MAJOR PLAYERS

The amillennial view of God's kingdom is held by the Roman Catholic Church, Eastern Orthodox churches, and many Protestants and evangelicals. The foundations of this view are usually traced back to Augustine, a fifth-century church leader and teacher (AD 354–430). The Protestant reformers John Calvin and Martin Luther also taught an amillennial view.

- Jesus made it clear throughout his ministry that the kingdom of God "has come near" (Matthew 4:17) and that some of his own disciples would "not taste death before they see the Son of Man coming in his kingdom" (Matthew 16:28). Was Jesus mistaken, or did the kingdom actually begin on the day of Pentecost when the Holy Spirit began to form the Christian community—the church? The kingdom can't be "near" if we've waited two thousand years to see it.

- Those who expect a visible kingdom on earth have missed the point of Romans 14:17: "The kingdom of God is not a matter of eating and drinking [literal activities], but of righteousness, peace and joy in the Holy Spirit [spiritual qualities]." Jesus reigns over his kingdom right now. He reigns in heaven over the spirits of Christians who have died, and they reign with him, just as Revelation 20 predicted. Jesus reigns on earth in his church and in the hearts of Christians.

View #2 of the Kingdom: "Jesus Will Bring It!"

The *premillennial* view of the kingdom of God holds that Jesus will return to earth *before* the Kingdom Age. Premillennialists believe that Jesus will reign over a visible, earthly kingdom for one thousand years. The kingdom will arrive suddenly and powerfully when Jesus returns from heaven and destroys his enemies. Satan will be removed from the earth during the kingdom, and the effects of sin's curse will be lifted. Believers from the Old Testament and Christians from the present age will be resurrected and will reign with Jesus over the earth.

Premillennialists would agree with their amillennial friends that Jesus reigns over his church in this age and that he rules in the hearts of his people. They would make it clear, however, that Jesus' reign today is not to be confused with the future fullness of the kingdom when Jesus will rule on earth as King for a thousand years.

Premillennialists use these arguments to bolster and defend their position:

- Premillennialism takes Revelation 20:1–6 at face value. Six times in this passage the Bible says that Jesus will rule over a kingdom that lasts one thousand years. Also in Revelation, John makes it clear that the kingdom is established *after* Jesus' return to earth in power and glory (Revelation 19:11–21).
- Premils accept the fact that the kingdom is said to be one thousand years in length only in Revelation 20. But they add that the *concept* of a visible kingdom on earth is taught throughout the Bible. God promised Abraham (the human father of the nation of Israel, the Jews) the land of Canaan as a permanent dwelling place (Genesis 12:1–3; 15:18–19). The Jews have held the land at various times but never permanently. God also promised King David that his kingdom would last forever and that one of David's descendants would sit on Israel's throne forever (2 Samuel 7:12–16; 1 Chronicles 28:5, 7). Both promises are fulfilled completely in the future kingdom.
- Jesus came the first time proclaiming that the kingdom of God was near. He was not offering a *different* kingdom from the one God had promised in the Old Testament but the *same* kingdom. When Israel as a whole rejected Jesus as their promised King, God

In Other Words

An Amillennialist Speaks

There is no indication in these verses [Revelation 20:1–6] that John is describing an earthly millennial reign. The scene is set in heaven. Nothing is said in verses 4–6 about the earth, about Palestine as the center of this reign, about the Jews. Nothing is said here about believers who are still on earth during this millennial reign — the vision deals exclusively with believers who have died. This millennial reign is not something to be looked for in the future; it is going on now and will be until Christ returns.

Anthony Hoekema, in *The Bible and the Future* (Grand Rapids: Eerdmans, 1979), 235.

postponed the complete establishment of the visible kingdom until Jesus' second coming. Christians enjoy some of the aspects of the kingdom today, but the fullness of the kingdom will only come when Jesus the King returns to the earth.

- Some premillennialists distinguish between *Israel* (the people descended from Abraham through his son Isaac and his grandson Jacob; the Jews) and the *church* (all individuals who have received Jesus as Savior and Lord). The church (in their view) is *not* the new Israel.

The future kingdom will be a time of peace and prosperity—exactly what God, in his Old Testament promises, pictured the kingdom to be. Think about these incredible benefits:

- War will disappear, and the industries of war will be focused on peaceful pursuits (Isaiah 2:4; 9:7; Zechariah 9:10).
- Social justice, moral purity, and racial harmony will permeate the fabric of human culture (Psalm 72:1–4, 12–14; Isaiah 42:3).
- Physical deformity and disease will be eradicated (Isaiah 33:24; 35:5–6; 61:1–2).
- Long life will be the norm (Isaiah 65:20–22).
- The earth will be abundantly productive (Psalm 72:16; Isaiah 35:1–2; Amos 9:13).
- The knowledge of the one true God will extend to every person in every nation (Isaiah 66:23).

MAJOR PLAYERS

The view that Jesus will return to reign over a thousand-year kingdom was the view of the early church. Almost all the church leaders in the first three centuries after Jesus' resurrection held to a premillennial view. The fifth-century leader, Augustine, was the one who suggested that the kingdom of God was a spiritual kingdom made visible in the early church (the amillennial view). His view soon replaced premillennialism as the majority view. Premillennialism made a comeback in the middle of the nineteenth century and is currently a widely held view (especially in the United States) among Baptist, Bible-church, and nondenominational believers; many charismatics; and many churches in the Wesleyan tradition. Some well-known premillennialists are Chuck Swindoll, John MacArthur, Charles Ryrie, and Wayne Grudem. The *Scofield Reference Bible* and the *Ryrie Study Bible* are strongly premillennial in their interpretation of biblical prophecy.

In Other Words

A Premillennialist (or Two) Speaks

Premillennialism generally holds to a revival of the Jewish nation and their repossession of their ancient land when Christ returns. Satan will be bound and a kingdom of righteousness, peace, and tranquillity will ensue.

John Walvoord, in *The Millennial Kingdom* (Grand Rapids: Zondervan, 1959), 5.

I and every other completely orthodox Christian feel certain that there will be a resurrection of the flesh, followed by one thousand years in the rebuilt, embellished, and enlarged city of Jerusalem, as was announced by the prophets Ezekiel, Isaiah, and others.

Justin Martyr (AD 100–165), an early Christian teacher, in *Dialogue with Trypho*, 80.

Jesus' reign will be a "forever" reign because his reign over a *restored* earth in the kingdom will be extended to his reign over a *new* earth for eternity (Revelation 21–22).

Keeping Perspective

Remember that each of these positions on the millennium is held by sincere, committed Christians who believe they are interpreting the Bible correctly. We may not agree on how the future will unfold, but we can certainly learn significant truths from each other.

Premillennialists can learn to live more courageously as inhabitants of Christ's kingdom today. We don't just wait for things to get better in the Kingdom Age; we work hard at pursuing kingdom ideals such as justice and peace in the world around us right now.

Amillennialists can learn to rejoice in God's promises and to look expectantly for the day when Jesus will return in majesty to reclaim his creation. We focus on building Christ's kingdom now, but we don't forget about the future glory.

Every Christian can use today to tell others about Jesus' love. God patiently waits for men and women to believe in Jesus and be saved, but someday soon his waiting will end and Jesus will return. He won't come quietly to a stable in Bethlehem this time. He will come in power and majesty. Everyone on earth will see him, and humanity's day will give way to the glorious day of the Lord.

Descent into Darkness: The Tribulation

In addition to the millennium or the age of God's kingdom, the Bible also describes a period of time called *the Tribulation*—a time of intense judgment from God and escalating evil on the earth. Jesus said, "Then there will be great distress, unequaled from the beginning of the world until now—and never to be equaled again" (Matthew 24:21).

Christians agree that the Tribulation is real; what they don't agree on (are you surprised?) is *when* the Tribulation will come. I will try to explain the three main views on the Tribulation. Even if you already have a conviction on this issue, it widens your understanding to grapple with the other views.

Possibility #1: The Tribulation Is Past

Some Christians believe that the predictions in the New Testament about a time of great distress were fulfilled very soon after they were

The return of Jesus Christ is the final high point of human history. He will return at the end—like at the end of a play, when the author walks onto the stage. The world *is* going somewhere. History *will* come to a close. And as the final curtain falls, the author will walk onto the world's stage.

When I first became a Christian, I did a double take when I heard sermons on Jesus' return. Obviously Jesus had entered our world the first time, but now someone says he is coming back. What a crackpot idea! Then I heard more and more people talking about it. Then I got my Bible out and found it was true.

Am I excited by it? A day is coming when the dead of all the ages will be raised. Christians will be given new bodies that will not weaken or decay or die. We will be like Jesus! Does this excite us? Are we stirred, exhilarated, thrilled at the prospect?

written. In their view, the Tribulation is not some future period of time but a series of events that happened in the past—about forty years after Jesus' death and resurrection.

In AD 70 the armies of the Roman Empire crushed a Jewish rebellion in Judea, the land where Jesus had lived. The Romans devastated the land, killed hundreds of thousands of Jews, and leveled the city of Jerusalem. The temple where Jesus had taught was burned to the ground.

This destruction was God's judgment on Israel for rejecting Jesus as her promised Messiah. Some in Israel had believed in Jesus, but the nation as a whole had not. Some Christians see this horrific destruction as the fulfillment of the biblical prophecies of a great Tribulation.

The position that the Tribulation happened in the past is called the *preterist* view. The term comes from a Latin word that means "past." The reformer John Calvin (1509–1564) held this view. The main contemporary defenders of the "tribulation is past" view are R. C. Sproul, Kenneth Gentry, and Hank Hanegraaff.

Possibility #2: The Tribulation Is Timeless

Another approach to understanding what the Bible says about the Tribulation is to apply those predictions to the ongoing conflict between good and evil. This view is referred to as the *idealist* position. Those Christians who hold this view argue that the symbols used in the book of Revelation, for example, do not represent any single event in the past or in the future but themes and trends in any age. Satan is constantly attacking God's people, and somewhere, even in our world today, Tribulation-like persecution is going on. Prophecy speaks to each generation in its own situation. William Hendriksen and Michael Wilcock are two of the best-known advocates of the idealist or spiritual view of Revelation.

Possibility #3: The Tribulation Is Future

The third view of when and how the Tribulation fits in God's plan is the *futurist* position. Christians who take this perspective believe that the Bible's predictions about the Tribulation will all come to pass in a future period of intense judgment from God. Futurists take the statements of Revelation in a very literal sense as accurate descriptions of judgment and persecution yet to come to the world. The popular Left Behind novels by Tim LaHaye and Jerry Jenkins were written from the futurist perspective. John Walvoord, John MacArthur, Charles Ryrie, and Chuck Swindoll all teach that the Tribulation is a time yet to come on the earth.

Searching for Common Ground

Once again we have a situation in which sincere Christians hold each of the three views of the time and nature of the Tribulation. So which view is right? Is it possible that each view has something significant to teach us?

Those who believe that the Tribulation happened in the first century when Jerusalem was destroyed emphasize God's powerful works of judgment in the past. But does the past tell the whole story? Maybe the past "distress" was *pre-fillment* of the Bible's predictions about the Tribulation, but the *full-fillment* is yet to come. And while the futurist may enjoy studying the sequence of events in that future time as they are laid out in Scripture, maybe we also need to let prophecy speak more directly to our lives today, as the idealist suggests. It's one thing to discuss how believers will survive in the Tribulation; it's something else to survive persecution and slavery in Sudan today or to stand for Christ against the official opposition of the North Korean government. We can forget sometimes that brothers and sisters in Christ may be experiencing the equivalent of the Tribulation right now.

Enter the Beast: The Antichrist

We've seen some pretty nasty leaders come and go in the last two thousand years—men and women who rise to power and leave a legacy of

Bible Networking

Most of what we know about the Antichrist comes from three essential go-to sections of the Bible:

- Daniel 11:36–12:1
- 2 Thessalonians 2:1–10
- Revelation 13:1–9

oppression, war, and murder. The Bible talks about one world ruler as more evil than all the rest. He's called the beast or the Antichrist.

Your view of who this leader is and when he appears on the world scene is determined by your view of when the Tribulation period occurs. Those Christians who think the Tribulation occurred in the past, in the events of the Roman destruction of the land of Israel in AD 70, point to Emperor Nero as the Antichrist. The writer of the book of Revelation used a "code" that the readers of his day would readily understand. "A beast coming out of the sea" in Revelation 13:1 was the "beastly" Roman emperor who was persecuting Christians.

If you take a more symbolic view of the Tribulation and believe it could take place any time Christians are persecuted, the Antichrist becomes a dictator or any government authority that attacks Christians. In the New Testament era the beast was the Roman Empire. Today oppression may arise from a militant Islamic government or a purely secularist regime that is bent on destroying the Christian witness within the borders of its influence.

Help File

666

The "mark of the beast" has become a universal symbol of terror and oppression—but what is it? The apostle John in the book of Revelation (13:16) says that a mark (literally, a brand; think *tattoo*) will be placed on the right hand or forehead of those who pledge their loyalty to the Antichrist. This mark will be required to get a job, buy food, or get a driver's license during the time of the Antichrist's oppression.

John adds one more puzzling remark about the mark—it will be the name of the beast (the Antichrist) or the number of his name.

> This calls for wisdom. Let those who have insight calculate the number of the beast, for it is the number of a man. That number is 666.
> Revelation 13:18

John is referring to the ancient practice of assigning numbers to various letters of the alphabet and then calculating the "number" of a person's name. The Antichrist's name computes to 666—but in what language and using what numerical system?

Christians have found "666" everywhere. One "prophetic scholar" figured out that Ronald Wilson Reagan was the Antichrist because he had six letters in each of his three names. In 1965 one Bible teacher confidently declared that John F. Kennedy was the Antichrist because he received 666 votes at the Democratic presidential convention. I think it's safe to say that no one has been able to figure this out conclusively.

Christians who believe the Tribulation is still to come think the Antichrist is a future world leader who will rise to prominence in the Western world and who will eventually dominate virtually the entire earth. He will set himself up as a "god" to be worshiped and will order the death of anyone who refuses to bow to his authority.

The Great Disappearance: The Rapture

The rapture is a future event predicted in the Bible in which Jesus will return from heaven and gather his followers and take them into heaven. If you've never heard of the rapture, it may sound a little weird, but I want you to know that Christians didn't just dream this up. We believe in the rapture because the Bible clearly teaches that it will happen.

Help File

PRE-TRIB, POST-TRIB, MID-TRIB, OR NO-TRIB

Many Christians believe that Jesus will return to earth in one big bang! He will come to wrap up human history in one powerful event. Amillennialists, for example, do not distinguish between the rapture (when Christians are resurrected and given eternal bodies) and the return of Jesus to the earth. These are simply different aspects of one climactic event—the second coming of Jesus.

Premillennialists tend to make more of a distinction. They believe Jesus' second coming has two separate phases—the rapture of Christians and the return of Jesus in power and majesty. Many premillennialists also separate these two aspects in time. Some believe that Jesus will return in the air for his church *before* the seven-year period of the Tribulation begins. That view is called the pre-tribulation rapture. At the end of the Tribulation, Jesus will return with his church to the earth to destroy his enemies and set up his kingdom.

Other premillennialists disagree. They think the rapture will take place near the middle of the Tribulation before the final (and worst) series of judgments from God. Their view is referred to as the mid-tribulation rapture or the pre-wrath rapture. (Confused yet?) A third group holds to a post-tribulational rapture in which Jesus comes *for* his church near the end of the Tribulation and then returns almost immediately *with* his church to inaugurate the kingdom.

Those who hold each of these positions make persuasive arguments for their particular view. You might want to invest some time in coming to your own conclusion based on the biblical evidence. Just be sure to hold that view with a degree of humility and grace. Committed, Christ-loving, Bible-honoring Christians hold each of these views, and we will all share heaven together!

Bible Networking

Jesus in John 14:3

If I go and prepare a place for you, I will come back and take you to be with me that you also may be where I am.

Paul in 1 Corinthians 15:51 – 52

Listen, I tell you a mystery: We will not all sleep, but we will all be changed—in a flash, in the twinkling of an eye, at the last trumpet. For the trumpet will sound, the dead will be raised imperishable, and we will be changed.

The passage quoted most often about the rapture is found in 1 Thessalonians:

> The Lord himself will come down from heaven, with a loud command, with the voice of the archangel and with the trumpet call of God, and the dead in Christ will rise first. After that, we who are still alive and are left will be caught up together with them in the clouds to meet the Lord in the air. And so we will be with the Lord forever.
> 1 Thessalonians 4:16 – 17

Christians are in agreement about the *fact* of the rapture, because the Bible talks directly about it. Disagreement emerges when we begin

Digging Deeper

Here are two resources that will help you explore biblical prophecy in greater depth:

✗ Douglas Connelly, *The Book of Revelation for Blockheads.* Grand Rapids: Zondervan, 2008.

✗ J. Daniel Hayes, J. Scott Duvall, and C. Marvin Pate, *Dictionary of Biblical Prophecy and End Times.* Grand Rapids: Zondervan, 2007.

JESUS IS COMING! OCTOBER 21 — OR MAYBE . . .

On New Year's Eve, AD 999, Pope Sylvester II celebrated what he thought would be the last Mass in history. Based on Revelation 20:7–8, he thought Jesus would return at the end of a one-thousand-year Church Age. As midnight approached in Rome, Pope Sylvester raised his hands to heaven. The bells rang in the year 1000, but Jesus did not return.

Edgar Whisenant predicted that Jesus would return in September 1988. Several million copies of his book, *88 Reasons Why the Rapture Will Be in 1988*, were sold. When September 1988, passed, Whisenant published a revised edition of his book and reset the date for October 3, 1989. Not as many copies were sold of that book!

In 1990, Elizabeth Clare Prophet, a New Age visionary who claims to communicate directly with Jesus and Buddha, issued a call to her followers to come to the "Church Universal and Triumphant" compound in Montana. She predicted that a nuclear war would destroy everyone except her faithful flock. Thousands of people sold their possessions and moved to Paradise Valley. When the date of history's final war passed without incident, the cult leader claimed that her prayers had averted the disaster.

Joseph Smith, the founder of Mormonism, wrote this prediction in his diary, dated April 6, 1843: "I prophesy in the name of the Lord God—and let it be written: That the Son of Man will not come in the heavens till I am 85 years old, 48 years hence, or about 1890." Joseph Smith was shot to death in 1844—one year after making the prediction.

to talk about *when* the rapture will take place. While there are clear statements in the Bible about what the rapture will be like, there is no clear, definitive statement telling us when it will occur.

The Future Gets Personal: Death and What Comes After

The Bible has a lot to say about *your* future too—a future that extends far beyond your life here on earth. The doorway to this future is an experience most of us don't like to think about—we call it *death*.

Information about death is not hard to find. Just visit your local bookstore or tune in to a television talk show. Someone will be there who has "died" and come back to life. The guest will be happy to tell you about the dark tunnel or the bright light. Information about death is not the problem. The problem is *reliable* information about death and about what happens beyond death's door.

Thankfully, there is one person who has passed through death and come back to tell us about it—and his word can be trusted! Jesus Christ walked into the jaws of death, stripped it of its power, and conquered it forever through his resurrection. In addition, Jesus beamed a clear, bright light into the darkness beyond death, and he lets us see what's waiting for us there. The Bible tells us what death is like by painting some pictures—not with watercolors but with words. Each image is designed to bring us peace and comfort as we think about death. If you are terrified by the thought of death, begin to replace those fearful images with God's pictures of what death will bring.

- The Bible most often pictures death as *sleep* (Psalm 13:3; John 11:11–13; 1 Corinthians 15:51). Death, like sleep, is temporary and ends in a great awakening. We don't fear sleep; we embrace it, and we eagerly anticipate a new day.
- Jesus described his death as an *exodus*, a joyful liberation (Luke 9:31). Our death is not a descent into oblivion but a joy-filled release from the pain and disappointment of life.

Help File

WHAT ABOUT PEOPLE WHO HAVE NEVER HEARD?

One of the difficult issues Christians struggle with is this: What will God do with people who have never heard the message about Jesus? If we must believe in Jesus and his sacrificial death in order to be saved, how can a person be condemned for not believing what they have never heard?

The Bible doesn't answer every question on this issue, but it is clear that every person will stand before God and all who have not believed in Jesus will be condemned. The apostle Paul says that there is enough spiritual "light" in the created world and in the human awareness of right and wrong (the conscience) to make every person accountable before God (Romans 1:20; 2:14–15). Even those who have never heard the message of the gospel know that God exists and that they are morally responsible to him. God's law is written on their hearts.

Do those who have never heard respond positively to the spiritual light they have? It's possible, but instead they usually turn to false gods and carve idols out of wood and stone to worship. I am prone to believe that those who *do* respond to the light of creation and conscience will receive more light. God in his sovereign plan will see to it that somehow they will hear the message and have the opportunity to believe.

Salvation is only offered in this life, however. The Bible never gives any hint or any hope of a second chance to believe and be saved after death.

WHAT OTHER OPTIONS DO I HAVE?

Not everyone agrees on what happens after we die. Just ask the people you work with what they think. If you ask ten people, you'll end up with eleven opinions. Here are some of the more popular alternative views:

- *Reincarnation.* The belief that human beings are reborn to earthly existence after death is not new. The idea of reincarnation first appeared in early Hindu writings about 1000 BC. But biblical Christianity has always rejected reincarnation—with very good reason. Human beings are not progressing upward toward God through a long cycle of rebirths. The Bible says we are lost and far from God. What redeems us from this dreadful situation is not our repeated attempts at living a good life but the grace and mercy of God.
- *Soul sleep.* Some religious groups teach that at death the soul or spirit sleeps, just as the body sleeps. Both spirit and body are awakened at the resurrection. The New Testament, however, makes it clear that our spirits exist in consciousness between death and the resurrection. In Philippians 1:23–24, Paul makes a dramatic distinction between being "in the body" here on earth and being "with Christ" after death.
- *Annihilation.* Many people in our world think that when we die, we cease to exist. The Bible clearly contradicts this view. A few Christian theologians believe that the traditional concept of eternal suffering in hell should be replaced by the view that unbelievers simply cease to exist. In their view, God's judgment is not literal punishment but instead an act that brings eternal consequences.

- Death is also compared to *taking down a tent.* Our bodies are our temporary dwelling places—"the earthly tent we live in" (2 Corinthians 5:1). In these bodies we are subject to disease and distress and despair. But as Christians we can be confident that when this earthly tent is folded up in death, "we have a building from God, an eternal house in heaven, not built by human hands" (2 Corinthians 5:1).
- One of the most comforting pictures of death in the Bible is that of *coming home.* When our spirit separates from our body in death, we find ourselves "at home with the Lord" (2 Corinthians 5:8). For the Christian, home is a place we've never been.
- The apostle Paul thought of death as a *departure* (Philippians 1:22–24; 2 Timothy 4:6). We pull up the anchor, untie the ropes

holding us to this life, and sail away. It's not a departure to an unknown destination. We depart to be with Christ forever.

The Bible doesn't promise this kind of death to everyone. These pictures and promises are for those who have believed in Jesus Christ as Savior. If you have never personally trusted Jesus, you *should* be terrified of death. You will face death all alone, and you will find yourself in an eternity separated from God. The good news is that you don't have to live in fear of death. God offers you eternal life right now if you in faith receive Jesus as your Savior and Lord. Eternal life doesn't start after you die; you experience a whole new kind of life the moment you believe.

Judgment Day

Christians believe that every person faces a future evaluation before God—and no one will be able to avoid it! The judge in charge will know every fact fully and honestly. The hidden motives and intentions behind every act and every word will be obvious to him. No legal technicality will get a person off the hook. The final judgment will be absolutely just and without appeal. Some people face this future day with joy; many face it with dread.

God the Father has given the responsibility of judging human beings to one person—to God the Son, Jesus Christ (John 5:22, 27, 30). The Father did that so the judgment would be fair. If God the Father was the judge, human beings could say, "You don't know what it's like to live in this world

Bible Networking

John 5:27

[God] has given [Jesus] the authority to judge because he is the Son of Man.

Acts 17:31

[God] has set a day when he will judge the world with justice by the man [Jesus] he has appointed. He has given proof of this to everyone by raising him from the dead.

of temptation and struggle." No one can say that to Jesus because he has been here. He has lived life as a human. He faced everything we face. As a result, Jesus can be a sympathetic, understanding judge.

The Bible talks about several times of judgment in God's plan, but two judgments stand out.

The Judgment Seat of Christ

In the future, every believer, one by one, will stand before the Savior who died for us.

> We must all appear before the judgment seat of Christ, that everyone may receive what is due them for the things done while in the body, whether good or bad.
>
> 2 Corinthians 5:10

Keep several facts in mind as you think about that future day. First, Jesus' evaluation of our lives is *not* to determine whether we enter heaven or not. The issue of our eternal destiny was settled when we believed in Jesus and received eternal life by grace alone. Second, we will not face condemnation or punishment for our sins when we stand before Jesus because God has promised that no condemnation will ever fall on those who are in Christ Jesus by faith (John 5:21; Romans 8:1). The final fact to remember is that this evaluation will focus on what we did in life with the gifts, resources, and opportunities God gave us. The

Bible Networking

Essential Reading on the Judgment Seat of Christ

- 1 Corinthians 3:1–15
- 2 Timothy 4:7–8
- James 5:8–9
- 1 John 2:28
- Matthew 20:1–16
- Matthew 25:14–30
- Romans 14:10, 12
- 2 Corinthians 5:10
- 1 Corinthians 9:24–27
- Philippians 3:14

Imagine staring into the face of Christ. Just the two of you — one-on-one! Your entire life is present before you. In a flash you see what he sees. No hiding. No opportunity to put a better spin on what you did. No attorney to represent you. The look in his eyes says it all. Like it or not, that is precisely where you and I shall be someday.

Erwin Lutzer, in *Your Eternal Reward* (Chicago: Moody, 1998), 23.

outcome of this evaluation will be either reward from Jesus or the loss of reward that could have been ours.

Some Christians are bothered by the idea of rewards or crowns for faithful obedience to Christ, but the apostle Paul certainly wasn't ashamed to strive for rewards. He served Christ first and foremost out of love for Christ, but he also had a burning passion to receive Christ's approval on a life lived faithfully and courageously.

The Judgment of All Unbelievers

Almost at the end of the book of Revelation, the apostle John saw an overwhelming scene unfold before him. Jesus the King is seated on a great white throne, and all the dead are raised back to life and stand before him. Some Christians believe this includes every person who ever lived; other Christians conclude that believers have been raised to life and have given account to Christ before this, so this must be a judgment of unbelievers only. Whichever position you take, the emphasis of the account in Revelation 20 is on the destiny of those who have refused to believe in Jesus as Savior and Lord.

Unbelievers who stand at the great white throne are not judged to see whether they might get another chance at heaven. They made that decision when they chose to live their own way rather than God's way. The books are opened and they are judged "according to what they had done" (Revelation 20:12), but the works recorded will do nothing more than confirm their choice to reject all that God offered to them in grace. God's

Points to Remember

☑ The Bible is the only reliable source of information from God about the future.

☑ Christians agree on most of the "big issues" related to the future. Disagreements arise over matters of interpretation and the timing of certain events.

☑ Jesus reigns as King over the kingdom of God!

☑ The Bible describes a time of God's judgment on the world called the Tribulation—but did it come in the past, is it going on now, or is it yet to come?

☑ The mark of the beast will identify followers of the Antichrist.

☑ The rapture is a future event in which Jesus will return from heaven to gather his followers out of the world.

☑ If someone claims to know the date of Jesus' return, back away slowly! That information has not been revealed to anyone.

☑ Death for the Christian is like going home.

☑ Every human being will some day stand before Jesus the Judge. The lives of Christians will be evaluated at the judgment seat of Christ. Those who have refused to believe in Jesus will face God's condemnation.

☑ The final "heaven" will be on a new earth where we will enjoy God's presence forever.

☑ Prepare for heaven now!

final judgment will conclude with an act of ultimate separation. Every unbeliever's knee will bow to Jesus, and every individual will confess that Jesus is Lord, and then every person who has rejected God's grace will be ushered into the lake of fire. Jesus even gave us the words that will seal their destiny: "Depart from me, you who are cursed, into the eternal fire prepared for the devil and his angels" (Matthew 25:41).

Is it fair and just for God to do that? It is! All of us are guilty before God—and God always does what is right. The Lord gave this assurance to Abraham way back in the book of Genesis when Abraham questioned the rightness of destroying Sodom: "Will not the Judge of all the earth do right?" (Genesis 18:25).

Heaven and That Other Place

The Bible describes only two places where human beings will spend eternity—a place of fellowship with God and a place of separation from him. Those who decide to exclude the Lord from their lives in this life will get what they want—no relationship with the Lord forever. But those who by faith receive

Jesus into their lives on earth will spend eternity with him in a place we call heaven.

When a believer dies today, his or her spirit goes to be with Christ in "heaven." Jesus said he was going to the Father's house when he left earth (John 14:1–3). Jesus has prepared that place just for us. It's a place of comfort and joy and peace. We'll see Jesus when we get there, but we won't run up and slap him on the back! We will fall at his feet in humble adoration and worship. We will see those believers who have died before us as well. They are already there, worshiping, rejoicing, waiting for God's purposes to be completely fulfilled.

The Father's house, however, is not the final heaven. After earth's history comes to an end and all judgment has been completed, Jesus will create a new heaven and a new earth as our eternal dwelling place. Some Christians think this present earth will be cleansed with fire and restored to its original beauty. Other Christians believe the current earth will dissolve and a whole new entity will be created. Whatever approach Jesus uses, we will step onto a magnificent earth, filled with beauty and wonder—an earth centered on a fabulous city, the new Jerusalem, that descends from heaven (Revelation 21:2–3).

Sadly, some people don't get very excited when they think about heaven. They view it as an eternal church service—or a cosmic rest home, where we sit on clouds and strum harps! Pain and sorrow are gone, but it sounds kind of boring. Actually, heaven will be a place of

Bible Networking

Revelation 21:1–4

Then I saw "a new heaven and a new earth," for the first heaven and the first earth had passed away, and there was no longer any sea. I saw the Holy City, the new Jerusalem, coming down out of heaven from God, prepared as a bride beautifully dressed for her husband. And I heard a loud voice from the throne saying, "Look! God's dwelling place is now among the people, and he will dwell with them. They will be his people, and God himself will be with them and be their God. He will wipe every tear from their eyes. There will be no more death or mourning or crying or pain, for the old order of things has passed away."

complete fulfillment and limitless opportunities. At least five activities will fill our lives in heaven.

- *Worship.* We *will* spend time "in church," but it will be joyous, spontaneous, completely natural worship. We won't be distracted by time, we won't get tired physically, and we won't be inhibited in our worship by what is acceptable in our particular church tradition.
- *Ministry.* The apostle John tells us eight times in the book of Revelation that part of our activity in heaven will be to serve God—"[God's] servants will serve him" (Revelation 22:3). The work God gives us will be enriching, challenging, and far more fulfilling than anything we have experienced in this life.
- *Fellowship.* Eternity will give us the time to enjoy the company of millions of believers—and Jesus himself (Hebrews 12:22–23).
- *Learning.* We won't know everything when we get to heaven—but we will have a boundless capacity to learn. The Bible says that in the coming ages God will allow us to fully explore the wonders of "the incomparable riches of his grace" (Ephesians 2:7).
- *Rest.* Heaven will be a place of complete and perfect wholeness. We will enjoy the empowering, energizing rest found in God's presence alone.

Sounds like a place you want to go to, doesn't it? But God hasn't told us about heaven's glory so we will dress in white robes and sit on a

Help File

YOU DON'T REALLY BELIEVE IN HELL, DO YOU?

It might surprise you to know that Jesus talked more about hell than he did about heaven. Jesus was never afraid or ashamed of the subject. He made it clear to his followers, his listeners, and his enemies that he believed in a place of judgment called *hell*.

Some people believe that God is too loving to send a person to hell. The God of the Bible, however, is not only loving but also holy and just. His love does not cancel out his holy hatred of sin and his promises to judge those who reject him.

To be honest, I am very disturbed by the idea of hell. If the Bible did not make such clear declarations about the reality of hell, I would want to find some other destiny for those who refuse God's grace. But Jesus, who is the truth, said it was a real place. He didn't try to frighten people with that fact; he tried to warn them. And he offered himself in order to provide an alternative to hell.

mountaintop waiting for Jesus to return. He's told us what lies ahead so that we will live courageous, faithful lives here and now.

> So then, dear friends, since you are looking forward to this [new heaven and new earth], make every effort to be found spotless, blameless and at peace with [God].
>
> 2 Peter 3:14

Living Now in the Light of Forever

The biblical unfolding of future events should prompt some very personal response in our hearts and lives. We look forward to eternity with anticipation, but we aren't called to just sit in church until Jesus comes. God has told us about the future in order to change the way we live.

Let me give you a few practical suggestions to pursue as you look toward heaven yet to come:

- *Be sure you are in a right relationship with God.* As Peter wrote, "[The Lord] is patient with you, not wanting anyone [your name fits over "anyone"] to perish, but everyone [that's you again] to come to repentance" (2 Peter 3:9).
- *Focus on Jesus Christ.* It's possible to get so caught up in the details of biblical prophecy that we miss the central event. At the heart of our hope for the future is nothing less than the expectation of the personal appearing of the Lord Jesus. Keep your eyes on him.
- *Build up fellow believers.* Paul taught about the rapture so Christians would encourage each other with its truth (1 Thessalonians 4:18). Help make Christ's church all that it should be—holy and pure, ready for the Bridegroom.
- *Pursue holiness.* Begin to put aside those old habits and attitudes and behaviors that God has been speaking to you about for so long. Determine to walk in obedience to the Lord.
- *Pray.* Jesus included the future in the model prayer—"Your kingdom come" (Matthew 6:10). We keep asking Jesus to bring his kingdom to fulfillment.
- *Practice your praise.* Heaven is a place of joyful worship. We might as well get warmed up here on earth!
- *Stay awake spiritually.* We are not to become so engrossed in the everyday affairs of life that Jesus' coming catches us off guard

(Matthew 24:36–44). Don't forget that your future destiny is as a citizen of heaven. So keep persevering in the faith. Faithfully obey Jesus, and be actively involved in whatever work he has called you to do.

- *Finish life well.* We have a goal to pursue. God doesn't want us always to be looking back; we have our eyes on the prize of finishing well and hearing our Savior say, "You have done well."

If you want to explore some of the key Bible passages about heaven, check out the LifeGuide Bible Study *Heaven,* written by Douglas Connelly and published by InterVarsity Press.

CHAPTER 13

On a Mission:
Where We Go from Here

On a Mission: Where We Go from Here

▶ Discover what Jesus wants every Christian to do.

▶ Is Jesus the only way to heaven?

▶ Find out where you are going on the journey—and what to do next.

Jesus' Final Command

Just before Jesus returned to heaven after his resurrection, he gave a command to his followers that still stands today as a powerful challenge:

> "Go and make disciples of all nations, baptizing them in the name of the Father and of Son and of the Holy Spirit, and teaching them to obey everything I have commanded you. And surely I am with you always, to the very end of the age."
>
> Matthew 28:19–20

This wasn't just Jesus' instruction to the original group of followers; this command remains in effect until the end of the age, until the day Jesus returns. Once we become Christians, the person who died for us and who reigns over us as King gives us a very clear directive—while you are going from place to place in this world, be intentional about making disciples. We call the passage in Matthew 28 the "Great Commission." The words embody Jesus' directive to the church for this entire age.

Jesus has entrusted to us the work of telling others about him. He could have used angels to do it. Jesus could have appeared personally to every person. Instead he committed the future of his whole program to eleven followers originally—and through them to us. We are to "make disciples." That involves more than just sharing the message about Jesus

Mahatma Gandhi in *Hind Swaraj or Indian Home Rule*

The various religions are like different roads converging on the same point. What difference does it make if we follow different routes, provided we arrive at the same destination?

Jesus in John 14:6 and John 6:40

I am the way and the truth and the life. No one comes to the Father except through me.

My Father's will is that everyone who looks to the Son and believes in him shall have eternal life.

and his offer of salvation. It starts with *evangelism*—sharing the good news that God has opened the way for us to be delivered from the penalty of sin and to be set free forever. Evangelism—leading people to Christ, or winning people to Christ—is essential, but it's only the first step in our responsibility to them.

Beyond the point of faith in Jesus, we are called to bring new Christians to the place where they are growing spiritually and where they are living in obedience to Jesus' commands. Making disciples means new believers are being baptized as a witness to their faith and new life. It means bringing them to the place where they are following Jesus as fully committed disciples. Then it also becomes their responsibility to begin the process of making disciples in their own lives. Disciples make disciples who also make disciples.

That's not a job just for pastors or Christian leaders; it's a call to all of us who believe in Jesus. Christians are people who are convinced that they have found the truth, and we want everyone to hear the message. Christians are criticized sometimes for being so "evangelistic" and for thinking they have the only way to God. We think that way because that's exactly what Jesus taught. He is *the* truth and *the* way. No one is able to come to God except one way—through Jesus (John 14:6). Those who accuse Christians of being narrow need to know that we are just agreeing with Jesus. There are not many paths to God; there is only one.

The Ends of the Earth

Christians take Jesus' words so seriously that we cross cultures and oceans and national boundaries to tell people about the salvation that God offers in Jesus. In the years after Jesus' death and resurrection, Christian missionaries moved through the Roman Empire with the message of God's grace. Dozens, then hundreds, then thousands of people believed in Jesus and became followers of him. It wasn't long until Christians moved beyond the boundaries of Roman authority to Persia and India and Africa.

Through the centuries of the Christian age, men and women have been compelled by Jesus' offer of forgiveness to all who will believe to learn new languages and to live in a new culture so they can share that message with those who have never heard it. Even today, across every continent, in cities, in rural areas, in remote regions, the message continues to be spread. It's not just missionaries who are on a mission; every Christian has the mission—to live as salt and light in the world, to tell people about Jesus and his love, to help new believers grow into committed disciples.

So, What about You?

As I see it four kinds of people will read this book:

Thinking about It

You might be exploring the Christian faith out of curiosity or interest (or you have to write a paper for a religion class), but you have never made a decision to believe in Jesus. I want to congratulate you for reading this far! I hope some of your questions have been answered. I even hope you get a good grade on your religion paper!

What I hope most is that you will seriously consider becoming a Christian. You don't need a pastor or priest or church in order for you to make that decision. In the solitude of your own heart, you can say, "Jesus, I believe in you. I receive you as my Savior. I believe you died for my sin and rose again from the dead, and I trust you for my life and my eternity right now."

Jesus promises that he will receive *all* who come to him in faith. If you have genuinely believed, you have passed from death to life—eternal life. Now is when you might want to talk with a pastor or another Christian, who will help you grow in your life with Christ. You've made the most important decision of your life—so keep following Jesus.

In the future new creation, justice will reign, and there will be true love and understanding and peace. This shows us the kind of society, the community, that God wants to develop right now. Standing for and working toward social justice in our own age and in the present world glorifies God. God's new community is more than seeing an individual make a response to God through Jesus Christ. We are to be salt and light in our neighborhood, having an influence on the city or town or village where we live. You may be on the local school board or a member of a neighborhood association or the leader of the local Lions Club. Wherever you are, God calls you to leave a mark for good and for God.

A Newbie

Maybe you have just recently believed in Jesus, and you've picked up this book (or been given this book) to help you get grounded in your new life. I'm humbled that you made this choice—and I hope the book has helped you understand the basics of the Christian faith. I would encourage you to read the book again in a few months. You will be surprised how much more you will learn.

I would also encourage you to get connected with a group of Christians in a local church. Visit several churches, and you will find one that fits with you in terms of style of worship, dress code, and size of congregation. The most important things are that the church is committed to Jesus

Bible Networking

Paul in 2 Corinthians 5:20

We are therefore Christ's ambassadors, as though God were making his appeal through us. We implore you on Christ's behalf: be reconciled to God.

Jesus in Acts 1:8

You will receive power when the Holy Spirit comes on you; and you will be my witnesses in Jerusalem, and in all Judea and Samaria, and to the ends of the earth.

Points to Remember

- ☑ Jesus gave his followers the "Great Commission" just before he returned to heaven.

- ☑ Jesus has entrusted to us the work of telling others about him.

- ☑ Christians believe that Jesus is the only way to God because that's exactly what Jesus taught.

- ☑ The love of Christ for lost men and women compels us to take the message to the entire world.

- ☑ Keep following Jesus!

and that they teach the Bible, God's truth. If you have a few Christian friends, start to get together to study the Bible and to encourage each other. I've written a Bible study guide that should help you move forward in your commitment to the Lord. The guide is called *Following Jesus* (by Douglas Connelly, published by InterVarsity Press). Don't just sit down inside the door of God's kingdom. Start down the path to maturity.

Sitting on the Sidelines

You may have accepted Jesus several years ago, but if you are honest, you haven't done much for him lately. You've been burned—or you are burned-out—and you are sitting on the sidelines. I'm glad you are reading, and I hope this book has stirred a fresh desire in you to get back in the race. The Lord promises to receive you and restore you, even if you have walked away from him for a while. He won't give up on you!

Maybe the best thing to do is to set this book aside for a while so you can speak directly to the Lord. Reaffirm your faith and love for Jesus. Express your sorrow for drifting away or walking away. Renew your commitment to follow Jesus fully. Then find another believer at church who will be a spiritual mentor and friend to you. Ask that person to hold you accountable for spiritual growth and faithfulness in your life. That simple act will pay big dividends in your spiritual bank account.

A Veteran

You may be reading this book with many years of faithful Christian ministry under your Bible belt. Good for you! That shows me you are still growing. It's easy when we've followed Jesus for a while to slip into a spiritual fog and just drift along. We tend to rely on what we've learned long ago rather than on a fresh experience of God's grace today. You have demonstrated that you haven't developed hardening of the spiritual arteries.

My suggestion to the veteran Christian is to find another believer to mentor and to encourage. Pray for God's direction, and look around at church or in your small group fellowship. Meet that person where they are and seek to spur him or her on in his or her walk with the Lord. You might suggest that you work through this book together. Memorize some of the key Bible verses. Talk about the issues that are raised. Dig deeper, reach higher, push harder in the life of holy living.

Wherever you find yourself on the spiritual path, keep following Jesus! He's the Beginning of the Christian faith and the End of it. He's the Source of life, the Sustainer of faith, and the Goal of all we do.

Jesus will be the theme of our song for ever and ever!

> "Worthy is the lamb, who was slain,
>   to receive power and wealth and wisdom and strength
>   and honor and glory and praise!"
>
>   Revelation 5:12

A Word of Thanks—and a Word about the Authors

A Word of Thanks—from Douglas Connelly

No book is written alone. That is true of this book more than others, since Martin and I worked on this together—writing, reading, suggesting, debating. I've appreciated working with him. The folks at Zondervan (as always) have been great encouragers and have exercised incredible patience with this book. Thanks to David Frees, Dirk Buursma, Rob Monacelli, Tammy Johnson, Ben Fetterley, Jesse Hillman, and Fred Jensen.

I also want to thank Bonnie Schreck, who took my handwritten scribbles and translated them into computer pages. My church family at Parkside Community Church has been very supportive of this project and is a great blessing in our lives. My deepest gratitude goes to my family—Karen most of all—for their love, patience, and passionate encouragement.

A Word of Thanks—from Martin H. Manser

I want to thank Stan Gundry of Zondervan for his belief in this book as a valuable contribution to the Blockheads series and our editors David Frees and Dirk Buursma for their encouragement at every stage of the book's development.

I also want to express my gratitude to Stuart Olyott, Michael Herbert, and Robert Hicks for their notes and writings that have helped me in writing parts of the text.

I have used parts of this material in my home church of Southcourt Baptist Church, Aylesbury, England, and also in courses I have led on Christianity at Aylesbury College (Buckinghamshire New University).

I would like to thank my family and friends—especially my wife, Yusandra—for their support and encouragement.

A Word about Douglas Connelly

Douglas Connelly is the senior pastor of Parkside Community Church in Sterling Heights, Michigan. He is a graduate of Grace Theological Seminary in Winona Lake, Indiana (MDiv, ThM), and is the author of more than twenty books and Bible study guides. He has written *The Bible for Blockheads*, *The Book of Revelation for Blockheads*, and *Amazing Discoveries That Unlock the Bible* (all by Zondervan). Doug and his wife, Karen, have three children and five grandchildren.

A Word about Martin H. Manser

Martin H. Manser (*www.martinmanser.com*) was born in 1952 in Bromley, England. He was educated at Manchester Grammar School and Eltham College. He received a BA Honours degree in linguistics after studying at the Universities of York (England) and Regensburg (Germany) and went on to gain an M.Phil. degree. Since 1980 he has worked on a wide range of reference books with a contemporary appeal. He has also compiled and edited many titles that encourage Bible reading, including the *NIV Thematic Reference Bible*, the *Zondervan Dictionary of Bible Themes*, and the Lion *Book of Bible Quotations*. He and his wife, Yusandra, live in Aylesbury, Bucks County, England, and have a son, a daughter and son-in-law, and two grandchildren.

The Book of Revelation for Blockheads

A User-Friendly Look at the Bible's Weirdest Book

Douglas Connelly

Getting a glimpse into the future is always intriguing, especially when that glimpse comes from God's Word. But let's face it, the book of Revelation has some pretty weird stuff in it: seven-headed beasts, locusts with gold crowns, a city coming down from the sky. What does it all mean, and how does it help you in your Christian faith? This lighthearted yet accurate guide to the last book of the Bible will help you overcome the confusion.

Engaging and user-friendly, *The Book of Revelation for Blockheads* helps you:

- Understand the message of this often misunderstood book chapter by chapter
- Discover what Revelation says about how end-time events will unfold
- Make sense of all the symbolism
- See how Revelation relates to other parts of the Bible
- Learn how others interpret controversial parts
- Worship God with a new vision of his glory and ultimate triumph and of what that means for you

Softcover: 978-0-310-24909-2

Pick up a copy today at your favorite bookstore!

The Bible for Blockheads—Revised Edition

A User-Friendly Look at the Good Book

Douglas Connelly

If you have a hard time making sense of the Bible, *The Bible for Blockheads* is for you. It will transform what might seem like gobbledygook into incredible significance—enough to change your life. It can do so because the Bible is more amazing than you've ever dreamed and packed with riches. Making sense of it is no mystery. You'll even have fun as you learn!

The Bible for Blockheads—newly revised and updated—helps you:

- Discover how the Bible's message unfolds from start to finish
- Learn how the Bible developed over many centuries
- Familiarize yourself with the main divisions of the Bible and its 66 individual books
- Find out proven principles for accurately interpreting what you read
- Acquaint yourself with important people, places, and events of the Bible
- Learn key biblical terms and discover the different types of literature represented in the Scriptures
- Get a handle on the Bible's historical and cultural background
- Discover why the Bible among all books is called "God's Word"

Softcover: 978-0-310-27388-2

Pick up a copy today at your favorite bookstore!

ZONDERVAN®
.com

Share Your Thoughts

With the Author: Your comments will be forwarded to
the author when you send them to *zauthor@zondervan.com*.

With Zondervan: Submit your review of this book
by writing to *zreview@zondervan.com*.

Free Online Resources at

www.zondervan.com

Zondervan AuthorTracker: Be notified whenever your
favorite authors publish new books, go on tour, or post
an update about what's happening in their lives.

Daily Bible Verses and Devotions: Enrich your life
with daily Bible verses or devotions that help you start
every morning focused on God.

Free Email Publications: Sign up for newsletters on
fiction, Christian living, church ministry, parenting, and
more.

Zondervan Bible Search: Find and compare
Bible passages in a variety of translations at
www.zondervanbiblesearch.com.

Other Benefits: Register yourself to receive online
benefits like coupons and special offers, or to participate
in research.